Springer Series on _____
ADULTHOOD and AGING

John J. Herr took his Ph.D. in psychology through the Ethyl Percy Andrus Gerontology Center at the University of Southern California. Subsequent to completing a clinical psychology internship at the Palo Alto Veterans Administration Hospital, Dr. Herr was awarded the Hancock Research Fellowship at the Mental Research Institute in Palo Alto. He is currently in private practice in Campbell, California. He also serves as a Research/Clinical Associate at the Mental Research Institute and a consultant to the Family Study Unit at the Palo Alto Veterans Administration Hospital.

John H. Weakland, a clinical anthropologist and licensed marriage, family, and child counselor, was originally educated in science and engineering at Cornell University, but after six years of engineering practice returned to Columbia University for graduate study in anthropology and sociology. Research work on human communication with Gregory Bateson led him to participate in the formulation of the "double-bind theory" of schizophrenia, and in the founding and development of family therapy. He has published two books and over forty professional papers on a variety of anthropological and psychological topics. A Fellow of the American Anthropological Association and an Advisory Editor of *Family Process,* he is currently a Research Associate at the Mental Research Institute, and Associate Director of its Brief Therapy Center.

COUNSELING ELDERS AND THEIR FAMILIES

Practical Techniques for Applied Gerontology

John J. Herr
John H. Weakland

Foreword by James E. Birren

SPRINGER PUBLISHING COMPANY
New York

*To The Luke B. Hancock Foundation
and Barbara McLachlan,
without whose support and encouragement
this book would never have been possible.*

Springer Publishing Company, Inc.
200 Park Avenue South
New York, N.Y. 10003

81 82 83 / 10 9 8 7 6 5 4 3

Library of Congress Cataloging in Publication Data

Herr, John J
  Counseling elders and their families.

  (Springer series on adulthood and aging; v. 2)
  Includes bibliographies and index.
  1. Aged—Psychology. 2. Aged—Family relationships. 3. Counseling.
4. Gerontology. I. Weakland, John H., joint author. II. Title. III. Series.
[DNLM: 1. Aging. 2. Counseling. 3. Family. WT104.3 H564c]
BF724.8.H46   362.6   78-26365
ISBN 0-8261-2510-7
ISBN 0-8261-2511-5 pbk.

Contents

Foreword

Herr and Weakland have shown us that the field of gerontology is growing up and some professionals are willing to be pioneers in addressing important problems. We are becoming sophisticated enough to know that growing old is not always a problem. Many older adults are indeed having the time of their lives, enjoying life and its opportunities much more than they had in the earlier years when they were in school or meeting problems of career and family. Unfortunately some older adults have problems of health, physical and/or mental, may not have enough income, and may be lonely and alienated. This book addresses itself directly to many of these problems in the context of the family.

It is still the family, despite all of the social changes that have surrounded it, that offers the older adult emotional and physical support. While it is often the middle-aged child who is concerned with problem/solution and communication with the older adult, sometimes the elder can still have an older parent. The increased life expectancy can easily result in a family organization of four generations, which can magnify problems of communication. One of the issues that families often face in relation to older members is the dynamics of guilt. Guilt as a response not only can result in unexpressed problems, but also places limitations on the kinds of solutions that are worked out. The dynamics of guilt in a family may indeed encourage psychological dependency of the oldest members in the later years. Perhaps the older person's role in the family is the last frontier awaiting open communication. How do we handle with our own families the legal and financial issues surrounding us? What are the kinds of services that our older parents may need? How well do we really know the needs of our parents, and in our desire to be helpful do we really find out what they are interested in?

Obviously the effectiveness of families in dealing with the issues of aging is a function of their communication style. While families are crucial support systems for older adults, they can limit themselves and tie themselves in knots of ineffectiveness, as *Counseling Elders and Their Families* shows. How to untie the knots or find a path out of the communication jungle is the topic of this book.

Herr and Weakland give us a format for approaching the problems of the older adult in the family context. Presumably if we follow their professional opinions and suggestions, family life will not only be better for the older adult, but for younger adults as well. The way adults have communicated over a lifetime may seem to make family life insurmountably rigid, and yet this book gives us hope that the family, which is a self-governed unit with rules, can be changed. Even families with long-standing patterns of behavior apparently can be brought to change. While it is commonly recognized that families have often used their young children as scapegoats, older members of the family are also used as scapegoats for the uncertainties of other generations facing their own realities. Family members of different generations may also pair off, so that the older adult can be caught in the cross-fire of others.

Relationships between human beings, beginning with the essential dyad of the man and the woman, involve negotiation. Rigidity of family rules creates problems if there is no basis for negotiation. If there is no basis or opportunity for a negotiation to meet personal needs, the older adult may indeed employ his symptoms as an aggressive way of maintaining control and power.

One of the startling statistics coming out of surveys in Great Britain was the fact that six out of seven individuals diagnosable as having organic brain syndrome were living in their own homes. This suggests that demonstrable organic brain deterioration is not in itself a reason for institutionalization, and it shows the adequacy of the family in providing support and a favorable psychological equilibrium.

It used to be that when we thought of a family we had an image of a young couple with small children living in suburbia. But families grow up, and they must deal with the changing needs of the family members of all ages. This book helps us perceive how we can be more effective as families in meeting the needs of individual members even though they may embrace a wide range of needs and ages.

Counseling Elders and Their Families is a provocative and useful book and one which will go a long way to professionalize the future of gerontology so that more of us will have a zest for life as we negotiate the daily needs of family members. In addition to the professionals (e.g., social workers, psychiatrists, psychologists, and family counselors) who will read this book out of necessity, it is also likely that educated family members will use it as a source of new insight and information on old but neglected problems. We begin our lives as members of a family, and most of us will spend our later years as family members, for better or worse. This book will make it for better.

June, 1978   JAMES E. BIRREN
                                                  Andrus Gerontology Center
                                                  University of Southern California

Preface

Though often neglected, the importance of including families in the search for solutions to many of the problems of aging could not be more clear. Unfortunately the relationship between elders and their families is like the weather, easy to talk about but difficult to do something about. Hard is the lot of a helper who encounters a family in distress, who knows something should be done, but has no idea of where or how to start. The question is not whether to work with families on the problems of the aged, but how. More likely than not, the helper resorts to providing external supports that have little lasting effect. The purpose of this book is to provide the student or practitioner with a way to start helping families to help themselves: a theory-based, yet succinct and practical approach to dealing helpfully with some of the problems of the aging and their families.

This book is directed to applied gerontologists. The term *applied gerontologist* can include anyone providing service to elders: administrators, social workers, physicians, nurses, psychologists, occupational therapists, physical therapists, recreation leaders, senior center coordinators, ministers, attorneys, and paralegal aides. The term certainly describes students or graduates of applied gerontology degree or certification programs—from the community college to the professional school level. This book is not intended as a shortcut to becoming a family psychotherapist. Needless to say, psychotherapy should be left to trained professionals concerned with specific psychopathologies. Instead, this book is a practical guide to solving problems related to daily living regardless of the fact that at times these problems may include odd or difficult behavior on the part of one family member or another.

Our work divides, informally, into three sections. First, we discuss some broad issues of approach and practice fundamental to applied gerontology.

Second, we discuss family-oriented problem solving in general: the development of this approach and its connection with gerontology, the evolution of the related practical process, and the sequence of stages comprising this process: (1) approaching the family system; (2) determining the problem; (3) determining attempted solutions; (4) determining goals; (5) comprehending the family sys-

ix

tem; (6) mobilizing the family system; and (7) winding up, giving credit, and terminating a counseling relationship.

Third, we present case examples for several major types of aging problems that could have family solutions. These problem areas include independence and loneliness; intergenerational struggles; alternative living arrangements; confusion; hypochondriasis; and death, grief, and grave disabilities. We close with a few encouraging and cautionary words.

In the end matter, in addition to references and the index, we have included two appendixes listing relevant further reading in Family Counseling and Family Therapy and in Mental Health and Aging. More specifically, to those planning to use this work as an initial or early text on counseling elders, especially in classes composed of those who are helping professionals but not professional gerontologists, we suggest supplementing our work with Butler and Lewis's *Aging and Mental Health: Positive Psychosocial Approaches.* Instructors for classes composed of applied gerontology students may also find Butler and Lewis to be complementary.

The idea for this book came specifically from the authors' shared experiences while working for the Family Interaction Center (FIC) of the Mental Research Institute (MRI) in Palo Alto, California. The Family Interaction Center was originated within MRI on the initiative of Dr. John E. Bell and was later directed by Dr. Elaine Sorensen. The purpose of the FIC was to explore and provide family counseling for families in which some problem involving an elder member existed. Its work was aided by grants from the Luke B. Hancock Foundation, the Lucie Stern Foundation, and the Administration on Aging, U.S. Department of Health, Education and Welfare (Demonstration Grant #93-P-5735519), whose support we gratefully acknowledge. In addition, many private individuals made generous and appreciated contributions to the FIC or to its predecessor, the Family Futures Center.

In turn, the FIC and therefore this book owe much to prior family work at MRI since its founding by Dr. Don D. Jackson in 1959. In addition to those already named, Virginia Satir and Jay Haley were especially significant in the development of the Institute's work in its early years. In 1966 Dr. Richard Fisch initiated the Brief Therapy Center at MRI, whose members included Dr. Paul Watzlawick and Dr. Arthur Bodin; the Center's work has contributed much to our own thinking and practice. Finally, though he was never directly associated with the Institute, the imaginative and creative approach to problems of Dr. Milton H. Erickson has affected us greatly through his writings and personal contact. If this work proves useful in dealing with the problems of elders and their families, credit is due largely to these people; if not, the fault is ours.

We would also like to thank a number of people who contributed to the preparation of our manuscript. First, Claire Bloom, whose typing and comments were most valuable during this book's embryonic stages. Peggy Smith and Judy Tombrink helped carry on the typing at later—and increasingly harried—stages, despite many other demands on their time and energy. It may be confidently presumed that any work such as this can arise only from an organizational base of support, both material and personal, but we wish to state explicitly our indebtedness to the Mental Research Institute— most specifically its Board of Directors, with special thanks to those members and their friends who volunteered to help proofread our manuscript, to Dr. Jules Riskin, Director of the Institute, and Dr. Luis Fernandez, its Deputy Director.

Finally, we would like to thank Dr. Sandy Osborne for her remarkably versatile and dedicated services. Few authors are so fortunate as to have their final manuscript prepared by a combination of skilled typist and trained clinical psychologist. We did, and we deeply appreciate her work and her advice, and her grace under great pressures of time.

JOHN J. HERR
JOHN H. WEAKLAND
Palo Alto, California

Part I

Counseling Elders:
General Considerations

1

The Applied Gerontologist:
Responsibilities and Restrictions

Suppose for a moment that you are working in the field of aging. You
might be an information and referral worker, the administrator of an
Area Agency on Aging office, a psychologist, a nurse, a social worker,
or a college instructor teaching a course in gerontology—not necessarily a counselor exclusively, or even primarily. Yet because your
interest in elders is known, more than likely you will repeatedly be
faced with questions from relatives, friends, and clients about problems associated with aging. Imagine, then, that an elder walks into
your office and asks for help in these terms:

> ELDER: I understand that you are an authority on aging. Well, I have
> a problem for you. I am 80 years old, a widower for 30 years. Two years
> ago, my only son divorced his wife, deserted his family, and took up with
> another woman. I lent him $5,000 at the time because of the rough spot
> he was in. Now, here it is two years later and he hasn't even got the
> decency to remember me on my birthday. What kind of son is that? I
> may be old and alone, but I still have my pride and I don't have to put
> up with being treated like that. I want the name of a good lawyer who
> will understand my position and help me change my will. Imagine, not
> even a card on my birthday.

First, what is the situation? A problem obviously exists. A stranger is asking you for help about a very personal matter: his relationship with his son. He asks you to give him the name of a lawyer who
will understand him. Is he really asking you for a lawyer or for
understanding? Does he really want to cut his son out of his will or

is he really longing to have more contact with his son? Why, after two years, is he suddenly so intent on doing something? Could the elder's health be failing; might he be facing some other crisis that has focused his attention so sharply on the relationship between him and his son? Perhaps, in his indecision, the elder is looking to you to signal whether or not he should go to the lawyer: if you give him a lawyer's name, he will follow through on changing his will, while if you suggest some positive alternative, he might follow through on your suggestion.

Second, what should you do? There are, of course, many choices. For example, by ignoring part of the situation, you could maintain that there is no personal problem. Rather than address the elder's loneliness and need for love and contact, you could simply dismiss him by saying, "I'm sorry, the law really isn't my specialty. I don't think I can help you." By ignoring the other possible reasons this man has appeared in your office, you could "safely" refer him down the line, to be someone else's problem.

Another choice you might exercise would be to admit to yourself that the elder may have a personal problem requiring more than just talking to a lawyer, but to tell yourself: "This problem is not my responsibility." If you use this excuse, you might then find yourself plagued with a nagging doubt: "If I don't help, who will?" However, a dutiful look over your desk full of obligations might be enough to drive even the most persistent nagging doubt from your mind.

Still a third choice might be to employ some self-defensive indecision: "I'd like to help; I recognize the importance of the problem and I realize that if I don't take some action there may be no one else to help, but I don't even know where to start. This is just too big a problem for me."

For many applied gerontologists, none of these courses seems satisfactory. Most people who are involved in the field of aging want to be personally useful to elders. This applies not only to individuals in service delivery fields such as social workers; nurses; physicians; attorneys; psychologists; occupational, physical, speech, and recreational therapists; information and referral workers; legal aides; retirement counselors; the clergy and police; but also to administrators of aging programs at all organizational levels. Those whose work is primarily administrative supervision and referral necessarily meet the same kinds of questions and judgments about situations concerning elders that our example illustrated. The purpose of this book is to serve as a guide to help the sincerely interested become more effective in helping elders and their families.

Restrictions

Counseling, of course, is very much a process of being "personally useful." Most people have an image of how counseling takes place: The counselors are expressively yet neatly attired; counseling sessions take place in wood-paneled rooms with deep carpets, behind solid hardwood doors. Clients and counselors sit in soft leather chairs, contemplating magnificent views through large windows. The mood is peaceful. There are no outside interruptions. The counselors exude confidence. The clients are cooperative, intelligent, appreciative—and adequately affluent. They leave their sessions feeling much better for having been exposed to the wisdom of their counselors.

Such conditions are only an ideal, a fantasy. In actual counseling you will find yourself exposed to difficult or chaotic situations. The need for help may be clear to you without its nature being clear. Specific advice may be urgently solicited during the height of a crisis. Like most professional people, you will find yourself very busy. Thus, the first problem that will come between you and your prospective clients will be *lack of time.* Where will it come from? What other duties will you have to set aside (professional or personal) to make the time? Will you come in early or leave late? How will your spouse or children be influenced if you take time from them to devote it to serving elders and their families?

Suppose you are lucky enough (or resourceful enough) to have the time; next, you will have to find *a feasible place to talk.* Many counselors do not have a private office; even if they did, many elders or their family members might find it impossible to get there (stairs, transportation, etc.). Quite possibly, you will find that you will be doing counseling in corners of cafeterias, public lounges, borrowed office space, hospital rooms, and in clients' homes. Finding a space where you and your clients can be reasonably comfortable may be a problem in itself, even before you get down to talking.

Another problem that you will have to face is that for many of the people with whom you will work, *economic limitations* will be a constant strain. One frustration that you will have to face is that a fairly simple solution to an individual's or family's problem might be quite available, if they had the money for it. Many of your clients will not have the money. What then? Here, as in the other areas mentioned above, you will be handicapped even before "counseling" begins.

Restriction of your *referral options* may also relate to the limits imposed by your clients' economic resources, as well as this lack of money being a problem of its own. You may frequently feel that you have encountered a problem in which your client or clients could benefit considerably from a long-term experience with a psychotherapist. Hopefully, the psychotherapist might help them to understand themselves better so that a fundamental change in personality could take place such that they would be able to better cope with the future. This path may not be feasible financially. More to the point, many people feel insulted when referred to a psychotherapist. This is a difficulty, not only in the general population, but particularly in the older cohort (a group of people of approximately the same age —similar to a "generation"), to whom psychotherapy seems less acceptable, as implying "mental illness."

While all these restrictions pose problems that must somehow be dealt with if a counselor is to be really helpful, these last two restrictions—clients' limited economic resources and the stigma attached to a referral to a psychotherapist—probably appear most limiting and most difficult for aspiring counselors. That is, as a gerontologist and a human being, you see a problem that you know something about; you realize that if you, personally, do not become involved with that problem, no one else will. Referral may not be feasible, yet your own training in helping elders deal with their problems is necessarily limited. A major purpose of this work is to address the question implicit in these circumstances: Given these realistic limitations, what can you ethically and usefully do?

Bridging the Gap: Ethical Options

To bridge the gap ethically between the ideal and the realities of counseling elders or their families, you must first be willing to limit your goals appropriately, so that whatever counseling you choose to do can be effective and helpful.

Realistic Goals: Revising the Situation
Instead of Reforming the Person

Rather than looking toward long-term personality change, your efforts will need to be directed at helping elders and their families solve their situational problems. That is, rather than trying to change your clients basically, it will be your responsibility to be useful to them as they are. Fortunately, most of your clients will simply be trying to cope with the problems that often, and naturally, arise with advancing age, rather than suffering from any psychopathology. But even where occasionally some neurosis or character disorder seems present, your counseling aim is not to treat this disorder. Rather, in either case it is limited to helping clients deal more effectively with the situational problems that confront them; and doing so may make the consequences of any pathology that may exist considerably less troublesome. From time to time you will find yourself tempted to try to change a client's personality or values, instead of helping the client change the situation. Such temptations are understandable, but should be resisted.

Being willing to counsel clients on situational problems is predicated on the belief that some relief from problems is better than no relief at all. While almost everyone would agree that it is ideally best to solve problems at the root cause, gerontological counselors ordinarily are unlikely to have the resources, time, and expertise required for long-term psychotherapy aimed at fundamental personality change. However, it is a frequent observation among highly trained psychotherapists that when dealing with situational problems, success often breeds success. Consequently, although you are not approaching the problems of your clients from a psychodynamic point of view, you may often note that clients who find their lives changing for the better are able to break vicious circles of defeatism, so they can continue on an upward spiral toward making their lives better in other respects.

Just as there are situational problems which have solutions, there are other situations in human existence which could be classified as having no really satisfactory solution—yet how they are faced and handled makes a great difference. This class of events might be called *life's difficulties*. Some examples of such life's difficulties are death, divorce, pain, disease, existential loneliness, and irreversible material and social loss. Since the experiencing of loss runs through these examples much as it does through the process of aging, it should not be surprising that life's difficulties and the intrapersonal pain that almost inevitably accompanies these situations are prominent in the experience of elders. Your work as a counselor will therefore also be involved in helping elders and their families deal with life's difficulties. Your responsibility will largely be preventive; that is, working with elders and their families with the limited goal of helping the family avoid making an unhappy, painful situation worse than it necessarily must be.

Doing Well What You Do

Even—perhaps especially—with limited goals, it is essential that you do well what you do. The aim of this book is to identify appropriate, limited goals in working with elders and their families, and to specify methods of implementing them. But of course it should not be your only learning resource. Other written sources, observation of counseling, recorded materials, supervision, and self-supervision can all be valuable.

Additional reading. Unfortunately, for historically complex reasons, the field of gerontological counseling has been more or less neglected compared to the fields of child, marriage, or young adult counseling. There are, however, several books on the subject as well as many professional journal articles. While most of these works are theoretical in nature, they should be of value to your work, particularly after you have had some field experience. A partial bibliography is included in Appendix A.

There are a seemingly unlimited number of books and papers written on the topic of individual and family counseling. While these rarely include discussion of the problems of elders and their families, they frequently discuss specific counseling techniques that might usefully be modified for work with elders. Again, as a starting place, the partial bibliography in Appendix B provides you with an opportunity to begin looking for titles of possible interest and value.

Observation. While reading about counseling is important, the best way to prepare yourself to begin counseling is to observe someone. If there are counselors who are working with elders and their families where you work, where you attend school, or at your field placement, you might ask if they would allow you to observe them working with some of their elder clients. If no one is available who works with elders, it might be possible to find someone who is working with adults or families so that you could at least get some realistic view of what actually goes on when people get together to talk about their problems, feelings, and relationships. If you are fortunate, you may have facilities with a one-way window where you can observe a session without actually being in the room. However, such facilities are not absolutely necessary since it is quite possible for clients, counselors, and trainees to become adjusted to sharing the same room.

Where there are several counselors seeing different clients, you will want to sit in with more than one. After all, counseling is a very personal business; frequently one counselor's style is quite different from—yet just as effective as—another's. For example, it is useful for the trainee to realize that for some counselors meeting with some clients, sharing their good sense of humor seems to fit, whereas other counselors and clients may share a greater sense of seriousness. Some counselors take a leading role more directly, while others are more reactive. After watching counseling sessions, it is always a good idea to spend a few minutes with the counselor to check out the direction that was taken and the counselor's ideas in taking it.

Especially if you are not in a position to observe firsthand how counseling is done, you will want to take advantage of the films and videotapes that are available on the subject. Unfortunately, the rental fees for visual materials are often so high as to discourage individuals from using them. Audio tapes, however, are in rather copious supply, usually at a very reasonable cost, and can be quite informative. For films, videotapes, and audio tape selections in the field of counseling, you should check with a librarian who deals in audiovisual aids. Most college and university libraries have such a resource person (frequently an entire AV division). For rural areas, universities and colleges can arrange for interinstitutional loans. In short, a sympathetic AV librarian who is aware of your limited finances and understands your interests can be invaluable to your early and continued training.

Getting adequate supervision.   When you begin using some of the techniques in this book (along with other techniques or approaches you might have seen or read about), it will be helpful if you can get some type of supervision. Getting supervision requires finding a supervisor. Look first for instructors or colleagues who are involved in working with elders and their families. If none is available (as is often the case) look to people who are counseling younger adults, couples, or families. These potential supervisors might be clinical psychologists, clinical social workers, psychiatrists, marriage, family, and child counselors, psychiatric nurses, or other professionals who have had formal training and experience in helping people to cope with problems.

It is desirable to have your supervisor observe your work directly, if possible. Having your supervisor sit behind a one-way window is usually the least distracting method for being supervised, although some trainees experience some stage fright during the initial session. Surprisingly, most clients are complimented by the increased attention represented by the one-way window rather than threatened by it. For most counselor trainees, the best way to broach the topic is to introduce whoever will be sitting behind the window to the clients, before the formal session begins. Such an introduction might take the form: "I'd like to introduce you to Dr. Jones. I've asked Dr. Jones to sit behind the one-way window today to watch our meeting because I've found that her comments help me to be more effective in my counseling. I'm wondering if that will be all right with you?" If the clients agree, it is often anxiety-reducing to all to show the observation room (the room behind the window) to the clients so that they feel more a part of the process.

Usually, however, you will not have a one-way observation facility available. Hopefully, you will be able to have your supervisor observe your work by sitting with you in the interview room as you talk with your clients. If even this form of direct observation is impossible, we suggest that you make audio tape recordings of your sessions (with your client's knowledge and approval) so that your supervisor can at least hear firsthand how you interact with your clients.

Supervising yourself with your colleagues. The most important supervision you get, however, will come from yourself. You must maintain the ultimate quality control of your work. This kind of supervision never really ends throughout your career. One way to ensure that you will supervise yourself is to meet regularly with a group of your colleagues who share your interest and efforts in working with elders and their families. These meetings can be used to plan, review, and discuss current cases. Audio or videotapes (if facilities are available) can be used in this process. If you are willing to ask, you will find that your colleagues can shed new light on problems you may be having in doing your counseling. Even if they are at your own level of training and experience, their position of relative detachment from your cases can provide the benefits of greater objectivity. By and large, your growth as a counselor will depend on how readily you are able to admit to yourself when you are having a problem with your clients and how quickly you seek advice from your colleagues on alternative ways to deal with the problems you are experiencing.

Knowing when you are in too deep (over your head). There are two signs that indicate that you have an ethical obligation to seek help from a qualified colleague or a supervisor: when your client gets worse; and when nothing continues to happen. IF IN DOUBT, ASK FOR HELP. To comment further would only negate our central message: he importance of asking for help when doubt arises.

Beginning Here

In counseling, as in any skilled craft, the novice needs to begin some-where. This chapter has attempted to delimit some of the most basic ground rules to help in that beginning. The next two chapters are devoted to elaborating some of the general principles of counseling to aid in that same end, painting in broad strokes the dos and don'ts of counseling elders and their families. The beginning is here.

2

Practice: What to Avoid

Frequently the most difficult skills counselors must learn involve their own self-discipline. Indeed, skilled counselors are differentiated from well-intended lay persons largely by what counselors *do not* do. Put another way, counselors learn from their training that there are certain interactional traps that must be avoided in order for counselors to be useful to their clients. Inexperienced counselors often fall headlong into these traps and, with the family systems they serve, end up feeling angry and frustrated. Accordingly, the purpose of this chapter is to examine some of the behaviors skilled counselors try to avoid, while remembering that there are exceptions to every rule.

Avoid Arguments

For the purpose of this discussion, we will define an "argument" as any situation in which one person attempts to induce another person (or persons) to make a change in behavior or in state of mind (attitudes, values, or affect) by repeated, persistent explanation. A counselor may of course offer a point of view differing from that of a client. But if the client does not accept this first offering, repeated presentation of the counselor's view, no matter how much it is based on reality or logic, or labeled as just a discussion or clarification, constitutes arguing with the client.

The reason counselors generally should avoid arguing with their clients is that arguments rarely prove useful. Most often, arguments are destructive to the client–counselor relationship, because the client, who is seeking understanding and help, usually ends up feeling that the counselor is not understanding, but is insensitive, deaf, or stubborn and righteous in his or her views. To appreciate fully the importance of the counselor–client argument, it is important to explore at greater length how arguments begin; the consequences of such arguments for clients; and how to recognize when you are in an argument with a client, and how then to usefully get out of it.

Understanding How Arguments Begin:
Appreciating the Illogic of Being Logical

Most of us pride ourselves on being reasonable and logical. Most of us believe that if we act in good faith, we will be able to solve our problems with one another by being reasonable and logical. Most of the time, this approach works. In the field of law, for example, such a resolution of problems takes place every day when people work out their business misunderstandings without need to resort to calling their lawyers to threaten law suits against their adversaries.

Yet there are situations in which being reasonable and logical, even in good faith, is of no value in the resolution of problems. These situations occur when what is reasonable and logical to one person is not reasonable and logical to another. At this point, the lawyers are called to obtain through the courts a decision on who is reasonable and logical.

While the courts do the best they can with what they have, the fact that the United States Supreme Court (the ultimate court of appeals) has nine justices suggests that questions of "what is reasonable and logical" must be dealt with consensually, not absolutely. After all, there are no stone tablets available to clarify, once and for all, the ultimate Truth of the Universe.

Realistically, then, what we believe to be logical and reasonable is a function of our values. Values are very difficult to change under even the most extreme circumstances. It is probably this fact that explains why, after close decisions by the Supreme Court, losers are far more likely to say to their adversaries, "The smart justices voted for me," than to say, "I'm sorry for putting you through all of this, you must have been right all along."

In law, as in the root of human behavior, the worst disagreements invariably come during situations in which, according to their own value systems, opponents are behaving in what they see to be a reasonable, logical way. In a sense, such opponents would rather be "right" than compromise to solve the problem. Similarly, counselors are most apt to argue with their clients when they insist that their clients adopt the same view of the world as their own, rather than to empathically change their position to be useful to their clients. Generally, if you find yourself arguing with your clients, you should be aware that you may be allowing your need to defend your values to get in the way of providing the help your clients seek from you.

Getting down to specifics, suppose you are working as a paralegal aide. In the course of your helping to prepare her budget, an 80-year-old widow complains that she is barely getting by on her small social security payment. She asks you if anything can be done. You suggest to her that she might qualify for SSI (a federal program administered through the states via the counties to supplement social security pensioners at the low end of the income spectrum). Before you can make a full explanation, she states emphatically, "I refuse to take welfare."

At this point, your client is giving you the message that she feels very strongly about welfare. Her presence in your office demonstrates that she is willing to accept some kind of assistance, but her statement leaves little question as to the fact that if the assistance is "welfare," it will be unacceptable. The experienced counselor, wishing to be useful to the client, would explore in a nonthreatening, accepting way exactly what about welfare was unacceptable to the client so that whatever programs of assistance might eventually be held out would not be described by the counselor in terms that might be interpreted by the client as "welfare." On the other hand, the inexperienced counselor would argue. Since the purpose of this section is to demonstrate how arguments come about, let us observe how such an argument might go:

> **COUNSELOR:** Wait a minute, you're not being logical. You just told me that by the last week of each month you have to eat cat food. Why eat cat food when with SSI you can eat good food?
>
> **CLIENT:** I would rather starve with dignity than to accept public charity.
>
> **COUNSELOR:** That doesn't make sense. Why would there even be welfare if it weren't meant to be used?
>
> **CLIENT:** How could I hold my head up in my church if people knew I was on welfare?
>
> **COUNSELOR:** You've earned the right to the benefits from all the years of taxes you've paid.
>
> **CLIENT:** My children would just use this as an excuse to tell me I'm too old to take care of myself.
>
> **COUNSELOR:** You can't eat your pride.
>
> **CLIENT:** I would rather starve to death.

Unfortunately, both client and counselor are "right," *according to their own sets of values*. At the point when value systems clash between counselors and clients (invariably disguised as discussions about what is "logical" or "reasonable"), many counselors are content to label their clients negatively. Such labels take such forms as "the client is unable to deal with reality" or "too unreasonable to work with." It takes a considerable amount of professionalism to realize that your clients are as entitled to their value systems as you are to your own and to realize that it is your responsibility to be useful, not judgmental.

Consequences to the Clients

Respecting your clients: maintaining rapport. Failure to disengage from a developing argument usually has more profound results than simply keeping the client from harvesting the immediate fruits of your wisdom. More likely, by arguing with a client you will lose rapport.

For example, probably the most common rapport-destroying, argumentative statement in the behavioral repertoire of unsophisticated counselors is "You shouldn't feel that way." This statement is usually delivered in a sympathetic voice, thereby making it very confusing for the client since "You shouldn't feel that way" is really an argumentative statement challenging the validity of the client's feelings. After all, the client's feelings are facts. Maybe the counselor does not want the client to feel that way, but that is the way the client feels.

Consider the situation in the previous example of the paralegal aide and the 80-year-old widow. Suppose the counselor had answered the elder's statement that she would rather starve by saying, "You shouldn't feel that way." Such a response would probably be taken as a sign by the elder that the counselor did not really understand how strongly she felt about being on "welfare." Further, she might assume that the counselor did not care enough about her to find out how and why she felt as deeply as she did. In short, any move to argue her out of her feelings will be far more destructive than constructive to the relationship between the counselor and the client.

If you are lucky, when you get into arguments with your clients you will lose, or at least argue to a draw. Occasionally, however, you may find that you win an argument—only to discover that the cost was to lose your rapport. The reason for this phenomenon is simple: no one likes to lose face. Therefore, whenever you find yourself working hard to convince an individual or family that you are "right" (about anything), you must ask yourself if proving yourself "right" is worth the risk of distancing yourself from your clients.

Coexisting with ambivalence: appreciating how arguments "backfire." While arguing wastes time and offends the feelings of your clients, probably the greatest threat it poses to the welfare of the individuals and families you serve is that your argument might "force" them into taking a position, in opposition to your argument, that is not in their best interest. Worse yet, this is apt to be a position they might not have taken, except for the argument with you. This usually occurs when people have ambivalent or mixed feelings. As an example of ambivalence, let us return to the elder who appears asking for help but refuses "welfare." On the one hand, she has come to your office seeking help, which can only be interpreted as an expression of her dissatisfaction with her current level of existence. On the other hand, she clearly has very strong feelings about charity, welfare, and independence.

In a sense, she is in the midst of an inner struggle: her feelings of deprivation and dependence battling her feelings of pride and independence. In other words, she has ambivalent feelings. If you were to argue one side, it is very probable she might argue the other. For example, when you say, "You must take welfare," she replies, "I won't take a dime of charity"; but if you were to insist, "Welfare is available, but maybe you shouldn't take it," she might well reply, "I'm entitled to everything I can get, I paid taxes for 64 years."

Arguing with clients is especially likely to backfire since we know from social psychological studies that people are more likely to come to believe (internalize) something they have actually said, than to believe what has been told to them. Therefore, putting clients in a position where they must argue one side of their ambivalent feelings leads toward their convincing themselves that your view is simply wrong. In the example, the harder you argue with the elder to take "welfare," the harder she will argue why she should not. If the argument persists, she will eventually convince herself the side she has been arguing is absolutely correct. Ironically, she will go back to eating cat food because of what you said and how you said it.

In automobile sales the phenomenon of the "backfiring argument" has been known for years. In fact, automobile salespersons use it to their advantage to make a sale. For example, a good car salesperson who knows that a customer cannot decide between a Ford and a Chrysler will never criticize the competition. After all, he understands the customer's ambivalence and therefore knows that no matter what he says, the customer will argue with him. If he is a Ford salesman, he therefore will probably say something along the lines of, "I must admit, Chrysler makes an awfully good car," and let the customer respond, "Yes, but they charge an arm and a leg for it. Dollar for dollar, I think Ford does better." Good salespersons can always "help" ambivalent customers to sell themselves.

What do car salespersons and counselors have in common? They all share the ability to push decisions contrary to that which might ordinarily be in their clients' best interest. In the case of a car, it is not so important. In the case of providing essential human services that may affect both the quality and quantity of clients' lives, the luxury of "pushing" arguments is not one that can be afforded. Inexperienced counselors often believe that the worst that can come of arguments is that the clients will not take the counselor's useful advice. Actually, the situation is far more grave, because arguments can provide the impetus for clients to reject useful positions they might have taken had it not been for the counselor.

In sum, when people come to you holding ambivalent feelings, as a counselor you are in a very powerful position. You can use your power to explore options or to eliminate them. It may make you uncomfortable to realize how much influence (for the better or the worse) you can have on your clients. But denying the power of your position will not annul your impact. It will only result in a lessening of your self-restraint and discipline in situations that call for professionalism.

Recognizing When You Are in an Argument

In arguments, both clients and counselors feel as if they are not being "heard." Recognizing when you are arguing, then, is recognizing when you are not being heard. One sure sign that you are not being heard by your clients is the "Yes, but . . ." sign. Usually, this interaction takes the form:

> **COUNSELOR** [after a fine logical, brilliant argument]: I am sure that now you can see just how it is.
>
> **CLIENT:** *Yes, but* the point you are missing is . . .

Whenever you hear individuals or their families saying "Yes, but . . .," it is a warning that you are not being heard. Since to be useful and effective you must present yourself in a way your clients can hear you, the "Yes, but . . ." is a signal that you need to stop arguing and quietly, in the privacy of your own mind, reevaluate what you are trying to do.

The situation is basically the same—though more subtle and requiring more attention to detect—when clients do not say "Yes, but . . ." overtly, but either apparently agree or are silent, yet fail to actively get with your message and its implications for thought and, especially, for new actions.

Getting Out of an Argument Usefully

What should you do when you find yourself hopelessly entrapped in an argument? Resuming the example of the paralegal aide in the midst of the argument with the antiwelfare elder, rather than continue to press your case you might say, "You know, I realize that I have been trying to change your mind on something that you have some definite feelings about. Could you excuse me for coming on so strong, and explain the situation to me once more?" Another approach might be, "Although I didn't mean to, I think I've been arguing with you instead of listening to you. Could you help me out by spelling it out to me again, while I pay better attention?"

Avoid Overinvolvement

Any good counselor necessarily is humanly concerned about the problems of clients and their family members, becomes involved with them by discussing important and emotional issues, and must establish rapport to work effectively. Yet these important necessities must not be allowed to to lead one into overinvolvement. Overinvolvement, with its accompanying loss of balanced perspective, easily leads toward several problems, any of which may seriously interfere with the effectiveness of counseling. These problems include taking sides in the family, falling into accusations or threats, getting caught in the middle, and letting the family's problem become your problem.

Making Accusations

When people behave in overtly unpleasant ways, even experienced counselors may find it difficult to avoid making accusations or threats in return. This can be particularly difficult when a relative appears attacking or highly critical toward an elder, whom the counselor sees as the primary client and probably as the person most in need of help and understanding.

For example, suppose you are a physical therapist who is working with an 82-year-old man who has recently lost his wife of 58 years. As your patient, he is presenting a clinical picture related to a stroke. His progress has been quite satisfactory, but you are reluctant to discontinue his physical therapy because toward the end of each appointment he tells you how depressed he is at the prospect of returning to his son's home to face his "cold, spiteful daughter-in-law." When you follow by asking for specifics, he gives you detailed accounts of how she has called him "senile" in front of several of her friends. When you make an appointment to see them together (ostensibly to discuss how she can help with some of his physical therapy at home), she begins to discuss his case as if he were just a piece of meat. At this point, you might want to defend your elder patient by saying something like, "For goodness sake, have you no sense of decency? Your father-in-law may have some physical problems, but he certainly is a human being with feelings. Yet you discuss him as if he weren't even here. I will not allow that in my office!"

While such an accusing statement certainly expresses moral indignation, it would probably be of little value to the family or even to the elder client himself. Usually, such a statement (or any other accusation) merely decreases the chance for honesty and self-disclosure by increasing defensiveness and the solidification of opposing positions. In the case under discussion, the elder might be quite gratified that you took his side, but the daughter-in-law will probably feel attacked and abused. Remember, the elder will be going home with her, not you: she has a chance to settle her score with you at his expense.

Even worse than such short-term retribution is the probability that you have missed a chance to improve the family situation by indulging yourself in righteous indignation. Usually, when family members begin to treat an elder in a depersonalizing way, it is a sign that the family members are feeling weary, frightened, and uncertain. Your information is too limited to take any such strong stand. Perhaps the daughter-in-law has just lost her own father after a long downhill battle with debilitating strokes, or her own physical health is impaired (for example, she may have recently been diagnosed as having cancer). At the very least, it is probable that she has been trying to be helpful to her father-in-law as best she knows how, but is tired and discouraged. By accusing her of being crass and insensitive, you have only made her feel more misunderstood, uncertain, and threatened. You have hindered rather than helped, since your client's welfare depends in part on her cooperation.

A *threat* is an escalation of an accusation. The problem with threats, aside from the aforementioned, is that even if you can make good on your threat ("Do what I say or I'll report you to the authorities . . ."), this only ensures that the individual or family will comply to the minimal letter of your demand, not to the spirit. Threats turn people off—can you ever remember wanting to be honest and open with anyone after they threatened to sue you?

Most individuals who are accused or threatened by a counselor have an inner response that is understandable, but difficult to say: "If you knew how I am feeling, you would never say such a thing to me." Therefore, when you find yourself making accusations or threats, you yourself should take this as a sign that you probably do not fully understand how everyone in the family system is feeling their circumstances. (If you did, you would be able to think of a different, more acceptable way to get the message "action needs to be taken" across).

It is very rare to find a genuinely horrible, despicable human being. Yet it is not rare at all to find human beings acting horribly and despicably to members of their family, particularly elders, because of conditions in their own life. A counselor can help to alter the conditions that make people act horribly and despicably, but not by threats and accusations.

Taking Sides

Making threats and accusations with family members is really just one form of taking sides. In order to justify taking sides, you must believe that one party is "right" and another "wrong"; put another way, that one party is the "victim," another is the "perpetrator." Unfortunately, family systems are not so simple as this, largely because they are systems of *inter*action. In most families, right and wrong are replaced by *quid pro quo* ("this for that"). In other words, members trade off in the roles of apparent perpetrator and victim. The daughter-in-law seems the perpetrator when she calls her father-in-law "senile" in front of her friends; the father-in-law may seem the perpetrator when he criticizes his daughter-in-law for being disrespectful in front of his son. None of their needs will be met by declaring one of them "right" and the other "wrong."

It is especially easy to make the error of taking sides in a family situation when you hear one side or observe only a few isolated events (such as two or three counseling sessions). If it were possible for you to see the entire constellation of family behavior simultaneously, it would be clearer that everyone is right and everyone is wrong.

When as a counselor you take sides, you perpetuate the myth that some one person is at fault. Even worse, your participation in taking sides solidifies the position of the alleged perpetrator by lending credence to the view that you are incapable of being fair and understanding. If anything, taking sides within a family tends to tear it further apart rather than to help it to heal.

Getting Out of the Accusing Position

When you find yourself taking sides, it should be a sign to you that you have joined the family too much. Sharing such an observation can often be helpful to the family and an excellent way to extricate yourself from taking sides within the system. For example, if as the physical therapist in the example you realize you have criticized the daughter-in-law because of your sympathy with the father, you might then say, "You know, right now I feel like I'm taking sides and accusing you [looking at the daughter]. I know that I get so close to families sometimes that I act like another family member. I'm wondering if either of you ever feel ganged up on at home by other members of the family?" Such a statement serves to get "the accused" member out of the hot seat, validates any feelings that they were being "ganged up on," and gives all members of the family an equal opportunity to volunteer some new information on how their family system works, without having to confess wrongdoing.

Other Ways of Recognizing When You Are Overinvolved

At this point you may be wondering why it would not be useful to become involved as a "member" of the family system. After all, wouldn't being a family member place the counselor in a particularly empathic state of mind? The best answer is that there is such a thing as being "too close" to be useful. The family is going to you to gain and use your larger perspective, not to add you to their family. The finest service you can render is to get close enough to their system to be able to see it clearly and offer useful comments, but not so close as to become enmeshed in their difficulties.

Since most people in the helping professions who are learning counseling techniques are compassionate, feeling individuals, they frequently find it very difficult to discriminate being empathically and constructively close from becoming overinvolved with a family. Since optimum "closeness" is intimately related to optimum outcome of counseling, it is imperative for the new counselor to learn how to make this discrimination. As an aid to this process there are at least three clues that you can use: First, the family's problems become your problems; second, you are more worried for your clients than they are for themselves; and third, your "helping" doesn't seem to be helping.

The family's problems become your problems. When you begin to take a family's problems home with you at night, you are probably doing a disservice to the family you are trying to help. It is important that as a counselor you be able to experience your feelings within a counseling session; however, to allow yourself to be so consumed by an individual's or family system's problems that your personal life is affected is to discard the professional perspective—a small but measured distance from the problem—which makes your services useful. Often, inexperienced counselors or well-intended lay persons believe that how personally troubled they are over their clients' problems is a good measure of how compassionate and effective they are as counselors. Unfortunately, the opposite is true: the degree to which your clients' problems become your problems is usually directly proportional to how ineffective you are becoming in the counseling sessions.

While there is no certain way out of this dilemma for the counselor, you might want to try sharing your experience with the family (or individual): "Last night I noticed myself really worrying about what we talked about last session. One of the things I was aware of was how much pressure I am feeling to *do something.* I'm wondering if you are feeling that same pressure?"

You are more worried about the situation than your clients. Another sign that you may be getting too close, and trying too hard, is when you discover yourself finding problems for a family (or for an individual) that are not problems to them. In a way, this position is the "If I were you, I'd be worried" posture. Since you are not your clients, it is usually just as fruitless to try to talk them into accepting the problem you see for them as trying to talk them out of feeling the way they feel. On the one hand, people differ in their values, and therefore what is a "problem" for you may not be a serious matter for them. On the other hand, denial of a truly serious life-threatening situation on the part of a client indicates a need for professional psychotherapy for the client, a service you are not trained to perform. In any event, worrying more about a situation than your clients do will not make you more effective either in your own counseling or in making a skilled referral.

Most frequently, when you are feeling more concerned about a situation than your clients or their families, it is because you don't have enough information. Often you can get yourself off your own hook simply by saying, "I have the experience of being really worried about this problem that doesn't even seem to be a major concern for any of you. I'm wondering if you have some information about the subject that I don't, which would put it in a different perspective."

Occasionally you will find yourself experiencing concern for the family or one of its members which is shared by your clients, but not explicitly expressed. In other words, the people in the family who are worried will not admit it. This situation occurs most frequently when family members attempt to "protect" each other from "worrisome" details. Under these circumstances, the best you can do is to leave the door open for discussion.

Returning to the case of the father and his daughter-in-law for an example, suppose that at the end of the session an agreement is reached to get together a couple more times. The daughter-in-law tells you she can come next week but not the week after because she has to go to the hospital to have breast surgery. Her matter-of-fact tone of voice denotes no more fear, anxiety, or depression than if her scheduled surgery were just a trip to the market. You worry and obsess over her pain and apparent denial for a week. At the next session, after it is clear that she is not going to bring up the topic, you might want to venture forth with, "I have been worried all week about your breast surgery. Do I need to be?" Such a statement leaves the door open. Who knows, the surgery could be anything from radical mastectomy to an elective breast reduction for cosmetic reasons. On the other hand, it could have represented a very threatening topic that both the daughter-in-law and the father felt reluctant to broach (each "protecting" the other) until sanctioned by you.

In any event, if after being asked your clients tell you that you worry too much, respect their views.

When "helping" is not helping.   Whenever a family's problem becomes your problem or you are more worried than the family members themselves, you are probably in a position of helping too much. In this book, an effort has been made to describe the services of a counselor as being "useful" to a family as opposed to "helpful." The reason for these semantic gymnastics lies in our firm belief that one of the greatest traps into which any counselor can fall is trying to *help* someone else. The harder you try to help, the more your pride and ego get invested in the cure. Clients rarely need a counselor whose pride and ego are tied up in their cure. As stated above, what clients do need is a counselor who can patiently provide a more objective perspective on what seems to be happening in their lives and allow them to determine for themselves what needs to be done, what they themselves must do to bring this about, and on what kind of a schedule.

Returning to the above example, it is not your responsibility to "help" the daughter-in-law get along better with her father-in-law. How she and her father-in-law choose to relate is their shared responsibility. On the other hand, it may well be that because of their present circumstances, it is very difficult for the two of them to see the nature of their conflict in any overall perspective. You can be useful to both father and daughter-in-law by providing an opportunity for the two of them to get together outside of their normal circumstances and by giving them the opportunity to examine the changes that each must make for peace to prevail. In this case, if after a few sessions the daughter-in-law and father-in-law are still unwilling or unable to change their behavior toward one another, rather than getting wrapped up in further fruitless "helping," you might want to consider the possibility that you are helping so much (probably by uncritical sympathy with their difficulties) that your clients are not feeling the need to help themselves.

Avoid Speaking for Another

For the inexperienced counselor, one of the most disconcerting moments in a session occurs when an individual or family falls silent. The silence is terrifying. The terror inexperienced counselors feel when they encounter seemingly interminable silence is quite understandable. After all, you are there to be useful. If the family or client wants to be quiet, they could be quiet at home. After only a minute of silence, a sense of urgency to perform a miracle (help too much) usually sweeps over the inexperienced counselor. The more the counselor feels the need to do something, the more useless he or she becomes. Rather than being harmful, silences are often very useful in counseling for the following reasons: First, you will probably be usefully surprised at the information you gain when someone other than you finally decides to speak; second, by being appropriately silent, you get out of the way so that the family can conceive their own solutions.

Being Usefully Surprised

Suppose that you are a police officer in a community with a public housing project for elders. Because you took a continuing education course in applied gerontology, you have been assigned responsibility for responding to all nonemergency complaints from the project. You answer a "disturbing the peace" complaint filed by Mrs. Baker, an 81-year-old widow living alone in her apartment. Mrs. Baker tells you that the problem is with her neighbor, Mrs. Zilk: "She must be getting deaf and senile to leave her radio on so loud. You can hear it now!" Since Mrs. Zilk lives next door and since you can barely hear her radio, you begin to suspect there is something more involved in Mrs. Baker's complaint than just too much noise. When you go next door to tell Mrs. Zilk of the complaint, she looks down at the ground and begins to cry. You get them together in the courtyard outside their apartments by telling them you need more information for your report. Both comply with your request, but refuse to answer any question with more than a "yes" or a "no." You feel stuck. Rather than pursue a course that is not working (continuing to ask open-ended questions), you decide to simply sit silently with the two women.

After ten minutes, Mrs. Zilk says to Mrs. Baker, "How could you call the police on me? You used to be my best friend." In this case, by waiting patiently, you have gained considerable information: instead of dealing with two people who have been antagonists for years, you know now that the opposite once was true. In addition, your silence has shifted responsibility for solving the problem between the two women from you—and the police force—back to where it belongs: on the two elders themselves.

The temptation to speak for your clients in a session is probably never stronger than when there appears to be a verbal mismatch. Suppose that instead of ten minutes of silence, Mrs. Baker had presented you with ten minutes of verbal insults thrown at Mrs. Zilk. Mrs. Zilk, in turn, wept prodigiously, inviting you with eye contact to rescue her. It would take a considerable amount of self-restraint to prevent yourself from verbally jumping in to rescue the weeping Mrs. Zilk. Yet by rescuing her prematurely, you might never determine what is really going on between them. Many individuals use their silence as a method to get others to speak for them. But "rescuers" never know exactly what is on the mind of "silent victims," and by speaking for them the rescuers ensure that they will never find out. Such a "rescue" is not really a service.

Out of Their Way: Allowing Clients to Conceive Their Own Solutions

Another good reason for allowing clients to speak for themselves is that the solutions clients conceive for themselves are apt to be the solutions they will most readily pursue. There is a real temptation for inexperienced counselors to forget that their relationship with their clients is one of guide, not prophet. A guide is responsible only for pointing out possible alternatives, while a prophet points out the "correct" alternative. Very frequently, clients will try to place you in the position of prophet by asking so many questions that you do most of the talking. While it may be gratifying at some level to be thought of as "the person with the answers," it is usually not as useful to the family as being an effective guide.

To be an effective guide you must work to make your services no longer needed; that is, to teach your clients how to find their own alternatives. Often this tack is best pursued by leading an individual or family to a place where their alternatives are clear without explicit help from you.

As you grow as a counselor, you will find yourself using silence effectively, so as to leave the thrill of discovering the solution to a problem to your clients.

In avoiding speaking for another, it is probably most helpful to keep in mind two simple rules: First, never say something for clients that they can say for themselves; second, when in doubt, remain silent. Adhering to the first rule requires that you be willing to allow your clients to find out how smart they are instead of how smart you are. Adhering to the second rule requires great composure since the silence of the counselor is often challenged by clients.

These challenges take of the form, "Why don't you say something?" or "How long are we going to sit like this?" Rather than being confrontive or blaming in return, you might say, "I hear your frustration with the silence, I'm frustrated too. I'm wondering what makes it difficult to talk just now?" Or, "It doesn't seem like I can find any of the right questions to ask. I can't even figure out how to get the information I need to ask better questions. I wonder if any of you will help me out?"

3

Practice: What to Pursue

In the previous chapter, some major pitfalls for the novice counselor were introduced. This chapter presents some positive personal characteristics and communication skills that serious counselors try to develop. The issues raised in this chapter are not intended to be comprehensive, but do represent rather widespread judgments regarding the characteristics of a good counselor (Rogers, 1957).

Being Genuine and Empathic

Being Genuine

Being genuine means being yourself. Putting on a "professional mask" or trying to impersonate the stereotype of a perfect counselor usually just puts your clients off. Since trying to "be yourself " is a bit similar to trying to "be spontaneous," it is important to examine what it really means when you try to be genuine with both yourself and your clients.

For example, suppose you are an administrator for a retirement job placement service that employs a man in his early 80s who continues to work part time despite his advanced case of diabetes. Because of his eyesight, his wife drives him the 30 miles to your office twice a week. She is in her late 70s. You chat with her from time to time and it seems to you that she is holding up rather well despite the strain. It is apparent to both you and his wife that the elder gets a great deal of pleasure from his days in the office; this seems to add meaning and variety to his life. Without previous warning, both his wife and his oldest daughter (who lives in the area) accompany him to his next scheduled workday. His daughter announces to you in front of everyone in the office, "Mother can't stand the strain of these drives. This will be Daddy's last day." When her mother begins to protest mildly, the daughter slaps her on the face and hisses through gritted teeth: "Mother, shut up! I've made the decision and it's final."

In relation to such a difficult situation, what does being genuine really mean? First and foremost, being genuine means allowing yourself to experience your feelings without feeling the need to apologize for or act on them. In the above example, before saying anything it may be best to experience all levels of your feeling: First, you would probably be experiencing anger at the daughter for emotionally and physically assaulting her mother; for not considering your opinion as to what would be best for her father; and for trying to butt in where —in your opinion—she did not belong. While these feelings of anger might seem unacceptable to you—after all, you are supposed to be "understanding"—it is essential that you admit to yourself that you are experiencing them. You do not want to get into the position of denying how you feel to yourself.

The next step, after recognizing your anger about the situation, would be to try to get in touch with what is behind your anger. Generally, counselors and clients alike experience anger when they are feeling threatened, overwhelmed, and helpless. Rather than fostering the myth that you "shouldn't feel that way," it is important to recognize how you are feeling and why.

When you are aware of what you are feeling, then you are in a position to decide how best to make that information available to your clients. Being genuine in your communications with your clients is the process of sharing information about your feelings. Sharing your feelings about yourself is very different from sharing your thoughts with your clients. Often, inexperienced counselors confuse making brutally direct evaluative statements about their clients with sharing their own experience of the situation.

For example, a direct but destructive response to the daughter might take the form: "Stop acting like such a child," or "You sure do come on strong." You might, in fact, be thinking such thoughts, but they are thoughts about the client, not about yourself. A comment on your own feelings might take the form: "I'm feeling overwhelmed and helpless. I'd like to be useful, but I don't even know where to start."

Developing Empathy

If being genuine is the process of understanding and sharing what it is like for you to be in your shoes, then empathy is the process of understanding and sharing how it must feel to be in your client's shoes. Generally, when you have developed empathic feelings for your clients, you will be able to understand how they may have felt compelled to commit even the most outrageous behaviors.

The challenge in developing empathy for the elders and families with whom you work is to be able to know how it feels to be each person in the family system. For the family portrayed in the example, it would be important for you to understand how the daughter was feeling when she acted as if she had no choice but to invade her parents' life abrasively; how the mother was feeling that made her unable to stand up to her daughter's assaultive public behavior; and how the father was feeling that left him seemingly powerless to control his own destiny. In other words, in developing empathy, the counselor seeks to understand the circumstances and feelings that lead to the behavior of each individual in the family system.

It must be stressed that profound understanding (empathy) and approval (judgment) are independent of one another. That is, it is possible to understand why someone did something as seemingly capricious and hostile as publicly slapping an aged parent without necessarily having to approve of such behavior. In fact, it would be difficult to find a counselor working with the aged who would condone such behavior on the part of the daughter. It would not be difficult, however, to find many experienced counselors who might understand such behavior on the part of a middle-aged child.

Becoming an effective counselor requires the ability to put your value judgments second to your concern for your clients at times. Sometimes, when your values have been severely challenged, you may find yourself thinking about a client: "I can't understand how anyone could do a thing like that." At these times, you need to reflect on your own value system to clear the way for a greater understanding of your clients.

Expressing Unconditional Positive Regard

Unconditional positive regard is the process of projecting to your clients a sense of acceptance without conditions. In other words, it is demonstrating to your clients that no matter what they may have done—or are continuing to do—you accept them as valuable human beings. In a sense, unconditional positive regard is valuing people without reference to their specific behavior.

It is through the expression of unconditional positive regard that you remove yourself from the position of judge: As human beings, all your clients can be "right."

Often, when individuals do something that in retrospect is difficult for them to support or explain, they may become quite defensive about their actions. This defensiveness is heightened by any feeling of being judged. From the point of view of developing rapport with individuals and their families, the role of counselor is far more apt to create a safe, trusting atmosphere if such defensiveness is lessened by offering such clients acceptance for what they are.

It must be emphasized that accepting clients for what they are is very different from accepting them for what they promise to be, particularly for clients who feel they are presently unacceptable.

A word needs to be devoted to clients who apparently go out of their way to get you to hate and reject them. Usually, these are people who go out of their way to get everyone else to hate and reject them. For these clients, it is especially important that you give them the message: "No matter what you do, you will not be able to get me to hate you. I may get angry with you, I may be hurt by you, but I will not reject you." As with understanding any other clients, the best way to understand and deal with someone who is trying to get you to hate them is to ask yourself, "What would my life have to be like so that the only way I would have to relate to other people would be to try to get them to reject me?"

When you are able to honestly say to your clients that you understand their situation so well that under circumstances similar to theirs you would probably feel and act very similarly, you probably have mastered the art of being genuine and empathic, and of showing unconditional positive regard.

Improving Communication Skills

In the course of interacting with your clients, it is important that clear communication take place. Clear communication on your part not only eliminates many misunderstandings, but it also provides a model for your clients to follow when they leave your office. The principles listed below are generally recognized (Watzlawick, et al., 1967) in the fields of family and individual counseling as useful in establishing and maintaining clear communication.

"You Cannot Not Communicate"

You, along with everyone around you, are always communicating. Even silence often is a form of communication. For example, suppose you are an Area Agency on Aging director. You have been asked by two of your elder assistants to settle a disagreement between them. Both are volunteers who help publish a monthly newsletter. Each threatens to quit if the other is not fired. When they are both seated in your office, you invite them to tell you about the problem. The first elder, looking self-assured, loquaciously defends his position as the other elder sits silently. Even under your prompting, the second elder limits his contributions to grunts or nodding his head. Is the second man not communicating? Actually, he is giving many messages: The first message he is giving is that he cares enough about what is happening to come to your office. If he did not care about working for you, he would simply have quit and avoided an uncomfortable meeting. The second message his silence is giving you is that he doesn't feel safe enough to say anything. If he wants to keep his position yet is not feeling safe enough even to defend himself, you can deduce that he is probably feeling discouraged. Further, he is likely to be experiencing his discouragement as hurt or anger.

Just as your clients are always communicating to you, you are always communicating to them. Restricting your questions to factual information gathering and your comments to unemotional "uh-huh's" may convey disapproval (lack of unconditional positive regard) to your clients. It is not helpful to delude yourself into thinking that you can impose an opaque mask of professional reticence. Instead, it is important for you to be as aware as you can of the communications you are sending and your clients' responses to them. For instance, three "innocent mannerisms" on the part of the counselor are often read by clients as messages that the counselor wants to keep distance: first, looking frequently at the clock, gazing disinterestedly at objects around the room, or looking out the window; second, placing a large amount of office furniture between you and the client; third, crossing your legs and arms tightly across your body as you listen to your clients.

Messages Have More Than
One Level: Be Congruent

The reason that you cannot not communicate is that messages have more than one level. Complicating matters even more, any given message (verbal or nonverbal) may have, not only different meanings, but conflicting meanings. As a counselor you will frequently be faced with the challenge of deciphering what your clients really mean. For example, suppose you are a nursing home administrator visited by a couple in their mid 60s who have come to discuss the placement of the wife's mother. The wife tells you that her mother wandered into the couple's bedroom the night before without her clothes. When her husband asked the mother to leave, the elder cursed at him. According to the wife, the husband then issued the ultimatum that either the mother had to "be placed" or he was moving out. At this point in the conversation, the wife turns to her husband. With her nostrils flaring and her teeth gritting she says, "The reason we're here is that I always do everything my husband asks me to; isn't that right, dear?"

At the first level, the level of content (the words taken by themselves without the context of the situation) the wife is telling you that she always dutifully obeys her husband. After all, she had said, "I always do everything my husband asks me to do." At a second level, however, her sarcastic tone of voice and the annoyed look on her face give the conflicting message: "I am angry. I won't be pushed around this easily. This matter is not settled."

At still a third level, you have her nonverbal behavior, that is, she is physically sitting in your office. Confusing? To say the least! When people send messages to one another at different levels which are incongruent with one another, it is very difficult to know what they mean. For example, does her presence in your office and the content of what she has said mean she will cooperate with the staff to make the placement work? Or by the tone of her voice and her facial and postural mannerisms is she signaling to both you and her husband that she will do everything within her ability to make the placement such a disaster that her husband will have to back down and apologize?

When the different levels of communication are incongruent, you may experience yourself wanting to say, "What do you mean by that?" Since "What do you mean by that?" can be considered as a challenge to many people (they hear, "Do you want to argue?"), there are other ways of dealing with this issue. In the example, you might want to say to the wife, "I'm sorry, but I'm not exactly clear on what you just said. On the one hand, I hear you saying that you are willing to cooperate in a placement, but by the look on your face and the tone of your voice it doesn't sound as if you've really convinced yourself that would be the best course. I wonder if you could tell me how you'd feel about bringing your mother here if your husband hadn't said what he said last night?"

While your clients have you to help them be more congruent in their messages to you and to one another, they will rarely ask you to clarify confusing, incongruent messages which you send to them. Probably the most difficult messages to keep congruent are those which you send when you are experiencing anger or disapproval of a client (or a whole family).

As mentioned above, being silent does not always work in trying to prevent your true feelings from showing. The best way of dealing with a situation in which you are feeling uncomfortable about your clients is to simply verbalize how you are feeling, and ask the individual or family you are working with to help you to explain your feelings. For example, suppose you are a recreation director who leads a group of community elders in an "autobiographical group (a group in which all are in the process of writing or reciting their autobiographies)." At each meeting, there is one man who always seems to "top" the story of the previous speaker. Finally, as one woman finishes telling her story of being in the Alaska Gold Rush, the one-upsman stands up to boast, "That's nothing compared to my trip to China in 1935." At one level you are angry with him for discounting the story of the woman (who is also lonely and needs recognition) who just presented her story. Even though your anger and your identification of "victim" and "perpetrator" is a signal to you that you have not allowed yourself to understand all the elder's feelings, you are still feeling angry. While ultimately you will want to gather more information about him until you can understand why he feels the need to do what he does, for the present, such an "empathy course" is not practical because you are not feeling empathic: you are feeling angry. Rather than attempt to hide the anger, it might be more useful to acknowledge it (be congruent) without being cruel: "Excuse me, Mr. Jones, but when you said what you said just then, I felt myself getting a tight feeling in my jaw and felt a flash of anger. I'm not sure I know what that's all about. I wonder if you [looking at Mr. Jones] have any idea what those feelings in me are about."

The Message Sent Is Not Always the Message Received:
A Basis for Simple "Misunderstandings"

Taking radio as an example, we can see several reasons why the message sent is not always the one received. For example, the transmitter can be broken, working at low power, or so powerful that it overloads the circuits of the receiver. Likewise, the receiver can be off, broken, or the circuits so sensitive that any message at all creates an overload. Sometimes the transmitter and receiver are both working perfectly, but there is so much electromagnetic disturbance (static) in the air that the message just does not get through.

Radio communication is simple compared to human communication. Aside from the physical problems involved with speech, people have the additional problems of attention and perceptual set. Both these problems are so important in helping people—including yourself—to communicate more effectively that we will explore them in greater detail.

Attention. Attention is a key element in understanding what someone else has to say. Lack of attention can lead to misunderstandings. In the case of misunderstandings, the problem is frequently made worse by the fact that the parties involved are not aware of a misunderstanding taking place. That is, they believe they understand the other person (or persons) perfectly, even though they do not. Much has been made thus far about how counselors are to avoid the conscious traps of getting into arguments with their clients. The purpose of this section is to illustrate problems your clients will have avoiding misunderstandings (which generate arguments) among themselves and to give you some tools to help them extricate themselves from those misunderstandings.

It needs to be emphasized that often misunderstandings simply mask deeper conflicts of interest. Therefore, the novice counselor should not expect miracles from clearing up misunderstandings alone. The conflicts will still need to be dealt with. Given this warning, let us turn our attention to how misunderstandings between family members can come about through inattention and what as a counselor you can do about them.

Often, if you are working with two individuals in a family, you will observe that during disagreements, while one member is speaking, the other is rehearsing a response. Frequently such rehearsals interfere with listening (attending) to what the other family member was actually saying. For example, suppose you are an attorney: a 35-year-old man (Mr. Ax, Jr.) and 68-year-old father (Sr.) come to your office to discuss a conservatorship for the mother—who has remained at home. Before you can say anything, the father begins arguing bitterly that his wishes are not being considered. The son interrupts to vehemently deny any wrongdoing. He insists that he is doing "exactly" what his father has asked him to do. As the argument bounces from one side back to the other with mounting intensity, it grows clear to you that the principals are so busy arguing that they are not even listening to one another. While you have been thinking about what is happening, the argument has escalated to the point where the son charges: "In 35 years you have never respected my judgment. I suppose it's hopeless to think you would start now." *A bit off the topic of a conservatorship.*

The problem is to get both parties to listen to one another instead of using the time when they should be listening to prepare their own defense—or to chart the course of a grand counterattack such as, "In 35 years you've never respected my judgment." The best technique to slow down the argument is to ask the clients to tell you what they just heard the other person say. In this case, as the attorney, you might say, "I'm a bit confused with the problem that is confronting you both right now. I wonder if we could go back to the beginning? Mr. Ax, will you tell your son in as precise a manner as possible what exactly you want him to do. [Looking at Mr. Ax, Jr.]: I would like you to listen carefully so that you will be able to paraphrase what you hear your father say. You don't have to agree with what he says, but it would be helpful to me to be sure you understand what he is saying."

Cognitive sets.   Another problem that interferes with making sure the message sent is the message received has to do with how human beings store information. Most of us have a tendency to respond to what someone else says based on our experience of the person speaking and the circumstances in which they speak. For example, the question, "What do you mean by that?" has a very different meaning if it is spoken defiantly on a street corner in Brooklyn than it does in the office of an expensive Beverly Hills psychotherapist. Not infrequently, a word or a phrase has a neutral or positive meaning to one person and a negative meaning to another. The difference in meanings associated with words or phrases is often great between generations.

For example, suppose you are a minister leading an evening Bible study group. After you make a rather controversial statement about a particular interpretation of a biblical passage, one of your eldest parishioners stands up to challenge you. Most of this group sit docilely back and accept uncritically whatever you tell them; consequently you are pleased that this elder can feel comfortable in intellectually sparring with you. Attempting to share your good feelings about this, you say, "Mrs. Franklin, I really admire your aggressive tenacity. This group wouldn't be the same without you." Rather than looking pleased, she draws back looking crestfallen. She does not consider that she may have misunderstood you, because in her own mind she would label anyone of her sex "aggressive" only if she wanted to be critical. You would probably have little luck convincing her that she misunderstood you. After all, in her mind (cognitive sets established by her experience in growing up—which, incidentally, consists of far more years of experience than your own) there was nothing to misunderstand: you were clearly and obviously making an insult. You might have more success in trying to straighten matters out if you were to apologize and say that you "mis-spoke"—which actually you did, since the compliment you were trying to pay turned out to be taken as an insult.

While cognitive set misunderstandings can be rather easily cleared up when you recognize them and take responsibility for them, they are not always easy to recognize. Occasionally asking your clients to tell you what they heard you say not only serves to encourage them to give you their attention, but also seems to clarify points of misunderstanding between what you thought you told them and what they understood you to mean. Again, the counselor's assuming responsibility for having "mis-spoken" usually helps to set the record straight in the least amount of time.

When cognitive set misunderstandings occur between members of the family, the situation is a bit more difficult. If you spot what appears to be a rather unexpected response on the part of one family member (usually hurt or anger) in response to a word or a phrase by another, you might ask the "offended" party to tell you what they heard the "offender" say. Such action provides an opportunity to clarify what the possibly misunderstood family member really meant.

Other disruptions.   Some other disruptions in communication can take place that are worth mentioning. For example, tired people do not make good listeners or clear speakers. Obviously, this applies equally to clients and counselors. Do not think you are doing your clients a favor by working yourself to exhaustion. You will only be setting them up to pay a price for your inaccuracy.

Another disruption to communication occurs when counseling takes place in a location with many distractions in the background. Frequent misunderstandings may be a clue to a counselor that a more private, less distracting environment will be necessary for

more progress to be made. This possibility may be especially important to consider when working with elders demonstrating some hearing impairment.

Ask, Do Not Assume

It is not uncommon for family members (or counselors) to make
unwarranted assumptions about what other family members are
thinking. For example, suppose you are a public health nurse working for the county. Two middle-aged sisters make an appointment to
see you. They are planning a trip across the country to visit their
parents (mother, 67, and father, 75). Their father has been in a convalescent hospital for several years suffering from a progressive brain
disease. They tell you that their mother, a retired professional singer,
has become severely depressed over the last year, requiring "shock
treatments." The oldest sister seeks your advice: "Is there a hospital
or retirement home where Mom and Dad could live together?" Her
question appears to indicate a shared decision on a specific course of
action.

Rather than assume that they have made a decision agreeable to
both, it is best to check out the matter. Therefore, you ask each sister
individually, "If this choice were up to you alone, what course of
action would you favor?" Each gives a similar response, the essence
of which is that both would prefer attempting to establish some kind
of social support network for their mother (meals on wheels, telephone reassurance, outpatient psychotherapy) before going as far as
institutionalization. As each sister tells you what she would prefer,
the other looks startled.

Suppose you were to say, "Now I'm confused. We started talking
rather specifically about institutions, but I think I'm hearing that,
individually, you would both place institutionalization of your
mother rather far down your list of options." You should not be
surprised to hear one sister say, "Well, I just assumed that you [look-
ing at her sister] wouldn't be able to live with yourself unless Momma
was completely safe in a hospital," and to hear the other reply, "The
only reason I talked about a hospital was because I assumed that was
the only way you could be satisfied with."

Between clients and counselors, the greatest opportunity for
misunderstanding comes when clients are being politely vague. Under these circumstances it is tempting for the counselor to "assume
the best," or take a doubtful statement at face value. Frequently, to
"assume the best" means to leave unasked a question that may "pain-

fully complicate," but clarify, the problem. Such a situation might exist if a recently widowed elder asks for your help to find money for her children, who "can't afford to have me live with them." It might be very tempting to assume that money really is the issue; if you could help her and her children find some more money, the problem could be solved. On the other hand, it may well be that money is just an excuse and even if the children were wealthy, they still would have no room in their home for your widowed client.

If you "assume the best" (that it is simply a matter of dollars and cents), then you might be pursuing a solution that is not a solution at all. If you ask, rather than assume, you risk an answer that might seem a tremendous blow to the elder's pride and dignity ("We don't want mother to live with us"). It is certain, though, that you will not be of use to the family nor will the family be able to find a solution to their problem until the real cards are on the table. Consequently, to do your job well, you must ask the difficult questions. "Assuming the best" will be of more harm than help in the long run.

Agreeing to Disagree

In some families, members seem to argue with one another until there is a clear winner or loser. This communicative style puts a severe strain on relationships since generally, whenever there is a winner and a loser, the loser retreats emotionally to await (or set up) another argument in which the tables can be turned.

From time to time you may find families in which the stakes seem so high that no one is willing to end a quarrel by losing or giving in. A useful technique to help the family detour around such a disagreement so that progress can be made in some other area is to say, "Well, the one thing you two can agree on is that you definitely disagree. As long as we have some agreement on that, maybe we could turn our attention to . . ."

Just as families find themselves drawn into arguments, so do counselors find themselves drawn into arguments with their clients. Arguments should be avoided if possible, as discussed in the preceding chapter. Yet sometimes you may find yourself in so deep that there does not seem any way out without someone losing face. In such a case, you can apply the same technique of agreeing to disagree, to free yourself and your clients from the impasse and get on to other more important issues: "It feels to me like neither one of us is likely to convince the other that he is wrong. I feel stuck. I wonder if we could at least agree that we disagree, so we might turn our attention to something else."

Making Direct, Personal Statements

Another problem exists in communication when people do not speak for themselves. Imagine the situation of a couple in their mid 70s sitting with their middle-aged daughter. The father wants the daughter to understand: "When you don't call me, I feel unimportant." There is a great deal of simple eloquence in such a direct, personal statement. First, it is irrefutable. The elder's daughter might not want her father to feel that way, but that is the way he feels; his feelings, after all, are facts. Second, such a statement is neither an accusation—he is not saying his daughter has done anything wrong —nor is it a request—he is not asking his daughter to do anything differently. All the elder is doing is to share his feelings. If anything, such phrasing reinforces relationship. In other words, the father is communicating, "What you do affects me." Even when the effect is "feeling unimportant," there is no *intent* implied; that is, the father is *not saying,* "You are *trying* to make me feel unimportant."

Given the simplicity and power of such direct, personal statements, it is a wonder that they are not used more frequently. Unfortunately, indirect impersonal statements seem to abound. Because indirect impersonal statements are confusing, much of your work as a counselor will be to help people rephrase vague, impersonal statements into those that are direct and personal.

Working backwards, let us examine how "When you don't call me, I feel unimportant" would be more confusing and accusatory if changed to be less personal and more indirect: "It's not proper for a daughter to ignore her parents," or "Why don't you call more often?" or "All of my friends have the same problem of being ignored by their children." In all of these "bad examples," what is missing is the information that when the daughter does not call, the father feels unimportant. Misunderstandings easily arise when family members begin to argue over the information available, without realizing that they do not have the whole picture. For example, this family could get into an argument over what is the "proper" relationship between a middle-aged daughter and her parents; or the daughter could provide several good reasons why she does not call more often; or they could develop a discussion of the problems of all of the father's friends. What would not be discussed *because it was not mentioned* would be that the father feels unimportant when he does not get a call from his daughter.

Individuals may interpret even direct, personal statements as demands or requests for change. More often, though, such statements are useful simply to share how you are feeling with someone whose life affects your own. In a sense, this information about yourself is a gift. If you really did not care about the other person, instead of exposing your own vulnerabilities, you would probably just withdraw. Direct, personal statements are certainly not ultimatums, but are information that people need about one another to develop more satisfactory solutions to their common problems.

Helping clients to use direct, personal statements can be particularly useful with family members who tend to create misunderstandings by being impersonal and vague. Remaining with the elder couple with the middle-aged daughter, the family could get into a long, unproductive argument over the father's statement, "All of my friends have the same problem of being ignored by their children." Misunderstanding her father's real message, the daughter could challenge him at several points: "That's because all of your friends just humor you along," or "That's because all of your friends don't have anything better to talk about," or "Oh, Dad, you know I'm not ignoring you," or "I don't see how you can say I'm ignoring you when I talk with you on the phone whenever you call."

Suppose, as the counselor, you were injected into this discussion. What might you do? For a start, you might want to turn to the father and say:

COUNSELOR: Bob, I know that we have gotten off onto talking about your friends, but I wonder if you would be willing to share with us what it is like for you when you don't hear from Janet [the daughter]?

BOB: Well . . . I feel ignored.

COUNSELOR: How do you feel when you feel ignored?

BOB: Hurt, unimportant.

COUNSELOR: So when you don't hear from Janet, you feel worried, hurt, and unimportant?

BOB: Yeah, that's fair enough.

COUNSELOR: Janet, did you know that this is how your Dad is feeling when you don't call him?

JANET: No.

COUNSELOR: Is that the way you want him to feel?

JANET: No.

COUNSELOR: Bob, what did you just hear Janet say?

BOB: I heard her say that she didn't know that I was feeling worried, hurt, and unimportant when she didn't call.

At this point the family can go on to talk about the real problem, which is how to take care of the father's needs without suffocating the daughter. This is an entirely different approach from talking about the problem when it is framed as "the daughter's problem" of being improper or intentionally inconsiderate of her father. The daughter will far more likely be cooperative in helping her father with his problem of feelings of worry, hurt, and unimportance than if she is first forced to admit that she is behaving badly.

Part II

The Process of Family Problem Solving

4

Family Systems Theory and Aging

The Origins of Family Systems Theory and Practice

The family systems view of problems and their helpful handling is both old and new. The importance of the family in both the accomplishments and difficulties in life has been commonly recognized in all times and places. More particularly, people have always been somewhat aware of the two basic factors that underlie this importance. First, direct relationships between people—what they say and do with each other—influence the lives and behavior of the individuals concerned widely and profoundly: how they think, act, and feel. Second, the family is the most ubiquitous, enduring, and close-knit locus of direct relationships. Almost everyone belongs to a family or at least a quasi-family group, and in every family particular styles of interaction develop and persist over long periods of time.

On the other hand, the significance of family members to one another has been so much a matter of common experience as to remain largely unstudied and unanalyzed. The impact of family interactions has been especially ignored in many sorts of situations or difficulties that were seen as exceptional or abnormal. Aging and its attendant problems have, for instance, in the past been viewed largely in either a medical-physiological or a broad socioeconomic framework rather than from a family-interaction point of view.

Since we believe that it is essential to include considerations of family interaction in dealing with the problems of elders, this chapter will examine how the family viewpoint first developed in relation to the problems of children and young adults, and then how it generalizes to the problems of elders also.

In general, the family has been an object of formal scientific interest, especially in sociology and anthropology, for a hundred years or so. Such study, however, has largely been a matter of detached theorizing or factual survey rather than close involvement. The family systems theory (how family members influence and are influenced by one another) that is relevant here has arisen only in the past 25 years, largely in connection with the clinical movement known as *family therapy*. Ideas about the family developed in the family therapy movement were born from practical context and purpose: they were problem and action oriented, closely related to the concrete data of close observation of actual family interaction. For these reasons, the origins and development of the family therapy movement will be central in this review. On the other hand, it is important to recognize that what follows is not a complete review, or even summary, of the complicated development of family therapy and related family systems theory. To attempt such a review would result only in listing many names and ideas that, while significant in their own place, would be irrelevant and even confusing for our present purpose.

Family therapy and its associated theoretical ideas about family systems and family interaction developed in a complex way, arising out of highly dispersed and quite varied work. Moreover, the sort of contribution made by different workers, as will be evident later, varied greatly; some contributed observations, some theoretical ideas, and some technical approaches, while others, no less important, were in the best sense primarily promoters, calling attention to the importance of the family and encouraging others to venture into this relatively unknown and perhaps dangerous terrain. For all this variety and range, though, two chief seedbeds of family therapy and theory can be identified: 1. child guidance work with neurotic or delinquent youngsters and 2. treatment of schizophrenic patients, largely but not exclusively adolescents or young adults. These two areas seem very different, and both seem far removed, in type of problem and in age of persons involved, from problems of aging. Yet one theme common to these differing origins of family therapy is potentially very relevant for aging problems: recognition that some problematic behavior was refractory to existing methods of understanding and treatment that focused on the "deficits" of the individual exhibiting the problem, along with attempts to do better by broadening one's view of the problem situation by including the family as the primary context of any individual's experience and behavior. These early attempts at family therapy understandably involved slow, groping, step-by-step progress away from ideas and practices focused on the individual patient and toward a wider view, rather than any instant and overall recognition of the nature and significance of family systems and patterns of interaction.

In work with problems of children, for instance, the importance of the child patient's mother had been recognized for years. Ordinarily, this understanding led at most to individual, psychodynamically oriented treatment of the mother and the child separately; there seemed little concern about the father. Against this background, it was a major step when Nathan Ackerman, an orthodoxly trained psychiatrist and psychoanalyst, began about the late 1940s or early 1950s to work in New York with whole families *conjointly* (together), even going so far as to send his colleagues to make house visits. It seems probable that, in making this important and controversial step, he was much influenced by his earlier experience with impoverished mine-workers' families in the late 1930s, during which time he observed firsthand the severe effects on a family when the father was unemployed over a long period (Guerin, 1976). Ackerman went on to found the Family Institute in New York to promote the family view by extensive speaking, writing, and teaching of younger colleagues. Ackerman remained, however, primarily a dynamic clinician rather than a researcher or theorist, and his views of the family continued to be more concerned with psychodynamics than with structure and interaction patterns.

Another pioneer who moved into work with families in search of better means of treating problems of children, especially adolescents, was John E. Bell. In a preface to his monograph on "Family Group Therapy," Bell wrote:

> To find an adequate treatment method for the disturbed adolescent is one of the major problems in psychotherapy. Conducting therapy with this age group has been so difficult that many have said we should not try to treat adolescents . . . we should modify his situation but postpone the attempt to do psychotherapy with him until he becomes an adult.

Bell continued that he was,

> troubled by this defeatist attitude toward psychotherapy with the adolescent, partly because at his developmental stage the need for help is so patently demonstrable and acutely felt, and partly because the difficulties in treatment may have arisen from our inadequate under-

standing of him, and thus from our using unsuitable approaches such as individual psychoanalysis and therapy with groups of adolescents. It was against this background of some urgency that the method of treatment I have called "family group therapy" was developed [Bell, 1961].

Specifically, in 1951 Bell heard that John Bowlby of the Tavistock Clinic was experimenting in cases of problem children and adolescents by having whole families come in for therapy. As it turned out, this was a misapprehension: Bowlby was only having occasional family conferences as an adjunct to conventional separate treatment of child and mother. Fortunately, by the time Bell learned of this error his imagination had been fired, and he was already involved in a series of 20 family treatment cases. This work was soon (1955) followed up and extended cross-culturally by work with another set of families, of different cultural and socioeconomic background, in Scotland.

In the early 1960s Salvador Minuchin, Edgar Auerswald, Braulio Montalvo, and their associates

began to be interested in the families of the delinquent children at the Wiltwyck School [a residential school, mainly for minority slum children, north of New York City] because we were confronted repeatedly with situations which yielded perplexities unanalyzable by the usually individualized approaches. We were faced with the irony and hopelessness of dramatic failures despite intensive, individualized treatment of these children and agonizing concern for their welfare (Minuchin et al., 1967).

In other words, Minuchin's group recognized that attention was being focused on the individuals and on wider social systems, but not on the basic social system of the family—a situation that has also been true of most efforts to deal with aging problems.

Minuchin and his co-workers secured research funds to study disadvantaged families with more than one identified problem child, to generate hypotheses and develop techniques to treat these families as families, rather than as simply individuals suffering from internal deficits that required individual psychotherapy for each family member.

It has been alleged that support of this work was largely an act of desperation, since traditional treatment had failed and the patient population was seen as hopeless (Guerin, 1976). Despite the "hopeless" patient population, broadening understanding and treatment of problematic behavior to include the family paid off. It was found that the very "chaos" of these "disorganized" families occurred in patterns, which, on close observation, could be recognized and related to the behavior problems, and that interventions could be devised that were helpful in altering these patterns and the associated delinquent behavior.

From Wiltwyck, Auerswald went on to work in New York City and to begin considering problems in the interaction between family systems and the wider system of social agencies (Auerswald, 1968), while Minuchin moved on to head the Philadelphia Child Guidance Clinic, to work on psychosomatic problems from a family perspective, and to develop his concepts of structural family therapy (Minuchin, 1974).

Meanwhile, roughly contemporaneously, a family systems view and related treatment approaches were growing out of work with schizophrenics. In terms of difficulty and discouragement, working with this patient group resembled working with disturbed children and adolescents but was even worse. It was then widely believed that psychotherapy with schizophrenics was a useless endeavor. Schizophrenics were considered so out of contact that no therapeutic relationship could be established. Further, rather like aging, the "disease" involved a progressive, irreversible downward course. Nevertheless, again motivated by a mixture of humane curiosity, dissatisfaction with individualistic approaches, and hope for something conceptually and practically better, a number of people began to study treating schizophrenics together with their family members.

In 1951 Murray Bowen started joint work with schizophrenics and their mothers at the Menninger Clinic; by the mid Fifties he had moved to the National Institute of Mental Health (NIMH), where he began hospitalizing whole families of schizophrenics for research and treatment. In this work, over time, Bowen moved progressively from a focus on specific points, such as the existence and means of handling emotional distance among the parents of schizophrenics (Bowen et al., 1959), to a general theory of family system functioning and its relationship to emotional illness (Bowen, 1966, 1976).

Lyman Wynne took over at NIMH after Bowen's departure to continue family studies and treatment of schizophrenia. Wynne later moved on to the Department of Psychiatry at the University of Rochester. At the beginning, Wynne and his co-workers examined families of schizophrenics in terms of role behavior and overall family role structure (Wynne et al., 1958). They did much to develop descriptive concepts (such as "pseudo-mutuality") facilitating the observation and identification of patterns characteristic of such families. This work represented an important and difficult task since these families' interactions were often complex and subtle and since there was almost no existing language for describing family interaction, only individually based terms. Wynne in particular has been a major continuing proponent of basic and careful family research.

Although both their approach and terminology differed from that of Wynne, Theodore Lidz, Stephen Fleck, and their co-workers at Yale were similarly concerned with identifying and defining characteristic patterns in families of schizophrenics. In particular, they identified "marital schism" and "marital skew" as two alternative patterns for the parents in these families (Lidz et al., 1957) and explored relationships between family environments and symptomatology (Lidz et al., 1958; Fleck et al., 1957).

Even amid all this diversity of family workers, Carl Whitaker, first in practice in Atlanta and later at the University of Wisconsin, has been a unique and important figure. Primarily a skilled and dedicated therapist willing to work with "impossible" cases like schizophrenics, he has strongly emphasized the importance of the family, while taking an overtly atheoretical or even antitheoretical position (Whitaker, 1976).

Finally, there is what has loosely been called the Palo Alto Group, an evolving conglomerate of quite different people, who have worked together at different times united by a common concern to describe, understand, and treat problematic behavior among family members. This group is the primary source of our own orientation.

In Palo Alto, family study and treatment arose out of the juncture of two streams of interest. On the one side, there was the research project founded in 1952 by anthropologist Gregory Bateson to investigate the nature of communication. For complex reasons, the study came to include a specific interest in the communication of schizophrenic patients. Since the project had from its outset viewed communication as interactional (involving more than one person), the interest of the investigators (Bateson, Haley, Fry, and Weakland) naturally led on from the study of interactions between patients and interviewers to the study of schizophrenics communicating in their natural environment—that is, with the members of their families (Bateson et al., 1956). From such study, it was a short and logical step to attempts at treating schizophrenic family systems.

Recognizing their lack of specific clinical familiarity with schizophrenics, Bateson's academic group enlisted the help of Don Jackson, a clinically skilled psychiatrist. Jackson was familiar with hospitalized schizophrenics as consultant in the Palo Alto Veterans Administration Hospital, where he, like others, had wondered about their common pattern:

1. improvement in hospital,
2. return to the family, and
3. relapse back to hospitalization.

In addition, as a psychiatrist in private practice in a relatively small community, he had come into considerable contact with family members of the patients he treated, including ambulatory schizophrenics. Even before joining the Bateson group, he had begun to wonder about family influences on his clients, even going so far as to have some joint meetings with a patient and a parent or spouse.

While this collaborative effort of people from several academic and clinical disciplines was initially focused on family interaction and family therapy in schizophrenia, in Palo Alto as elsewhere it led rather quickly toward concerns with family interaction in general. The family approach was found to be useful in treating a wide range of human problems beyond schizophrenia or juvenile delinquency (Jackson and Weakland, 1961).

One primary outcome of all this diverse exploratory study, practice, and thinking about family interaction in relation to various human problems was the development of a set of basic ideas that became shared, then spread to newer workers and wider areas of application. There is no single and final statement of these related concepts. Different family workers have differed in their terminologies, emphases, and explicitness. Nevertheless, the family therapy movement does involve some basic consensus, and those ideas most significant for our present purpose may be summarized as follows:

1. Communication and interaction between people powerfully affects the behavior of every individual involved: their *thoughts*, *feelings*, and *actions*.

2. Correspondingly, regardless of past events, characterological and physical traits, or social circumstances, how people interact with each other in the *here-and-now* very significantly influences how they function, for better or worse.

3. In any durable relationship, patterns of interaction develop, more or less rapidly, and then persist not because any particular behavior is fixed or inherent in itself, but largely because of reciprocal reinforcements. It should be noted that, at a more abstract and general level, this implies a primary concern with cybernetic or

circular causation (how elements within a system interact to maintain the status quo, or lead to change); rather than the older, linear, historical model of causation (Maruyama, 1963; Wender, 1968; Watzlawick et al., 1974).

4. Although such interaction may occur, and be important, in any social organization (a school, a work group, etc.), it is *particularly important in the family,* since this group is ubiquitous and its relationships are long-lasting and of great emotional and practical import for the individual members.

5. There is "a problem" when some behavior arises and *persists* that is seriously distressing either to the individual himself or to others concerned about his behavior. From a systems view, plainly, *other behavior must be occurring within the system of interaction that provokes and maintains the problem behavior inadvertently and in spite of efforts to resolve it.*

6. The resolution of a problem requires either some appropriate change of behavior or behaviors within the system of interaction or a change by the participants in their evaluation of the behavior ("Really, that is not such a serious matter after all").

7. Accordingly, the primary task of a counselor or therapist is to help people make such changes in behavior or interpretation, which they have been unable to identify and make on their own.

This interactional view of the nature of problems and their handling basically involves only a few rather simple ideas. The implications of this view, and the potential advantages associated with its application, though, are profound. In the first place this view focuses squarely on the here-and-now situation, which is directly accessible to observation, inquiry, and influence. This approach differs from those that focus on the past, which is accessible only via recall, often inaccurate, and which cannot, in any case, be changed. Second, the focus of this approach is not on the concrete difficulties or limitations involved in any problem situation. Rather, it addresses their *handling* by the parties involved as most significant. While the concrete difficulties and limitations of problems may be fixed, how those difficulties and limitations are being handled is always potentially open to useful and beneficial change. Third, because of this focus and because of its emphasis on circular causation, this approach can help counselors and their clients faced with large problems avoid the discouraging belief that either global change must somehow be achieved or extensive and continuing support will be necessary. Instead, the possibility is raised of accomplishing small but strategic changes whose effects will be reinforced by interaction within the system; the vicious circles involved in persistence of a problem can thus be replaced by beneficent ones.

All of the above of course is not to say that this particular view of problems is comprehensive or "the answer to everything." All views are partial approaches to reality; none is a complete and final answer, either in theory or in practice. But it does offer a useful and positive starting point for approaching many kinds of problems. Additionally, should this relatively direct, simple, and immediate approach fail in any particular situation, it does not bar the door to more complex and "deeper" approaches, such as the exploration of the unconscious or the distant past.

Applying the Family Systems Approach to Problems Associated with Aging

Application of the family systems approach to the problems of elders went more slowly than in the fields associated with problems with children and young adults. In general, geropsychology has been much later in developing than other areas of clinical psychology or psychiatry. Part of this retardation in development can no doubt be attributed to the influence of Freud himself. Freud held that psychoanalysis was of limited use to older patients. He considered it was inappropriate for two reasons: First, he believed there exists an increased rigidity with age. Second, he believed that for psychoanalysis to deal successfully with the mass of historical material which elders would present would require extensive, if not infinite time. Consequently, without Freud to "light the way," geropsychology was more or less ignored.

Had there been more activity in the field, the family systems approach would have probably been seen earlier to be applicable to elders. For example, there are many similarities between the problems associated with advanced age and adolescence. Both adolescence and senescence are characterized by periods of rapid physical change: the adolescent waxing in vigor and strength, the elder waning. From a social and economic point of view, adolescence and senescence are also characterized by major changes. As they move toward adulthood, adolescents are expected to leave childhood, take on employment, and begin their own family life. Elders, on the other hand, find their situation the reverse, losing their employment to forced retirement and their children to families of their own. For families with adolescents and elders, these changes frequently result in a redistribution of family power: The adolescents seizing power from the middle generation, the elders yielding power to the middle generation. Power is rarely yielded without struggle; power struggles frequently result in family problems.

Just as elders are stressed by developmental demands like adolescents, they bear labeling similarities to schizophrenics. For example, problems associated with age have traditionally been viewed as presenting a progressive, irreversible downward course. As stated above, this view reflects an attitude similar to that held by mental health professionals toward schizophrenics in the early Fifties. As with the schizophrenics, old-age problems have been attributed to deficits within the aging individuals—usually organic (biological) deficits.

The similarities in how elders, schizophrenics, and troubled adolescents were viewed led to similarities in how mental health professionals came to handle their problems. Since the "problems" were conceived as existing within the individual, the individuals were removed from ordinary society to an institution where special help could compensate for their deficits. For the adolescent, this approach usually meant placement in a foster home, special school, or reformatory. For the schizophrenic, such a solution led to a mental hospital. For the elder, the placement was usually into a substitute "home"—sometimes a nursing home but often a mental hospital.

In a sense then, elders were living in the worst of all possible worlds regarding mental health: they had all of the developmental challenges that create problems for adolescents with all of the labeling liabilities that create and sustain problems for schizophrenics. Not surprisingly, the mental hopsitals were stuffed with elders. By the mid Sixties it was becoming apparent that mental hospitals were doing more housing than helping. Where was mental health in aging to go? The stage was set to consider the family systems approach.

By 1966 several preconditions to applying a family systems approach to the problems of aging were met. First, the family systems approach had been around long enough to begin to prove itself useful. Mental hospitals were being replaced by community mental health centers. In a sense, the existence of the community mental health center validates the concept that mental health cannot be defined in the absence of a social system. Therefore, an alternative model to viewing behavioral problems now existed for practitioners who were working primarily with elders.

Second, Shanas and Streib (1965) published a landmark collection of papers reaffirming the significance of the family system to elders. In a sense, Shanas and Streib raised the consciousness of the growing gerontological community, pointing out that elders need to be viewed in the social context of their families.

Third, a broader definition of "family" had been discussed by Sussman and Burchinal (1962). Sussman and Burchinal held that an *extended kin network* of both blood relatives and friends was more important in consideration of the social systems of elders than simply blood relatives alone.

The first paper in the gerontological literature proposing family interaction as a potentially primary etiological factor in problems associated with aging appeared in 1966 (Brody, 1966). The same year, in the family therapy journal *Family Process,* Brody and Spark (1966) suggested that the family, rather than only the aged family member, should be considered the client in dealing with problems associated with aging. In that paper, they modestly concluded, ". . . family therapy may offer opportunities for new perspective." Finally, the family system approach and the problems of aging were wed.

General Types of Problematic Interactions in Families with Aging Members

Earlier in this chapter we discussed the development of the family systems approach as including the observation and treatment of particular family interactions that seemed related to the existence of problems. In family work and aging, similar progress has been made in exploring the areas of family interaction associated with the problems of aging. Spark and Brody (1970) discuss several family interactions that are problem-generating in younger families and that can also appear in families with older members. For example, teenagers are often *scapegoated* by their parents as "causing all the trouble in the family." Similarly, elders are often the objects of the same type of scapegoating. By way of example, in both family situations, an unhappily married middle-generation husband and wife can avoid dealing with the realities of their dissatisfactions with one another by shifting the blame for their misery onto their children, or onto their parents. In the scapegoating situation, "If only our teenager were more respectful to me" and "If only mother were not becoming senile" can be equivalent statements.

Another type of problematic interaction that occurs in younger families is the setting up of a *parental child.* That is, a child is induced to act more in the role of the parent (responsible) than the actual parent. A similar condition can develop in families with older members when unrealistic support demands are made (or believed to be made) by the elders on their middle-aged children. Also, young families sometimes reject or *extrude* children. Families with older members may do the same thing, although generally it is the elder, rather than the child, who is extruded.

In families having members of all ages, two family members may "team up" against another in so-called *dyadic alliances*. For example, a mother and daughter vs. father alliance that begins in childhood may continue into the daughter's middle age. While such an alliance might not be too serious in earlier years, its continued existence gets in the way of solving problems when the stresses of aging occur.

Another problematic family interaction is the *symbiotic relationship*. Child mental health workers have long recognized that some parents become so involved in the lives of their children that the psychological boundaries where parent ends and child begins become blurred. This pattern of interaction may persist throughout the lifespan. In families with older members then, in the persisting symbiotic relationship, elder parents may not be able to "let go" of their middle-aged children. Likewise, middle-aged children may not be able to separate their own lives and being from those of their parents. In the latter case, middle-aged children may suffer severe disturbances in their own functioning when their aged parents begin to decline.

Gottesman, Quarterman, and Cohn (1973) describe the importance for mental health of congruence between the elders' physical capacities, societal demands, their own expectations, and the expectations of their significant others. By definition, significant others are drawn from the family/extended kin network. Consequently, *incongruencies between younger and older* family members can be seen as potentially problematic interactional phenomena.

Peterson (1973, 1974) describes a problematic interaction of advanced years as *role inversion*. Role inversions may occur between husband and wife (for example, if the husband becomes disabled, the wife may take over his former duties) or parent and child. Kahana and Levin (1971) describe still another problematic interaction associated with age in which a family facing a crisis with an elder finds itself in a vicious cycle of *fearful withdrawal* in which each distancing maneuver on the part of the elder precipitates a self-defensive withdrawal on the part of younger relatives.

Specific Tasks Associated with
Particular Problematic Interactions

While there are certain interactions (i.e., scapegoating) that seem to be troublesome in any challenge the family faces, there are certain tasks or challenges that seem to strain the best of family interactions or create especially problematic interactions for elders. For example, Soloman (1973) and Brody (1974) have described developmental tasks or stages through which aging families must pass in the normal course of development. They see the failure to master these tasks or stages as similar in consequences to the failure of younger families to master the tasks and stages appropriate to them. Other authors have identified certain specific situations beyond life's usual tasks that can yield difficult interactions:

Physical rehabilitation.   Davies and Hansen (1974) have suggested that in the physical rehabilitation of elders, the quality of interaction with the family is essential. Peck (1974) suggests that ". . . if the rehabilitation of one family member goes sour, it most frequently is a sign that other family members are involved in some uncooperative strategy" (p. 478).

Institutionalization.   The institutionalization of an elder family member is a particularly stressful time for the family as well as for the elder. Cath (1972) has suggested that just before the elder is institutionalized, the family goes through the process of *electing the "do something" child.* That is, one family member (usually a middle-aged child) is elected to "do something." The process of this interaction is particularly important when institutionalization appears to be an inappropriate solution to the elder's—and thus family's—problem.

Berezin (1970) describes another type of family interaction associated with institutionalization which he labels *partial grief.* This is the period in which the family seems to know the gravity of their elder's illness before they have been told. Berezin feels that the family members' reaction to partial grief can result in guilt: "When guilt becomes the steam motivating the family members, the reactions can be quite extreme, irrational, and unmanageable" (p. 60).

Miller and Harris (1967) reported an interesting finding that in almost half of the institutionalized elders they were studying, improvement in the patient was offset by a deterioration of the quality of family interaction. Miller and Harris explained this paradoxical finding as an example of *family homeostasis.* That is, most families attempt to maintain the family system as it is, even when times are difficult. Thus, changes in the status quo resulting from the behavior of one member (improvement in the elder) will frequently result in a homeostatic behavior in another (deterioration in younger family member). This term was first used to describe younger families (Jackson, 1957) in which improvement by one child (e.g., a teenage troublemaker suddenly begins to do well in school) is offset by deteriorating behavior in a sibling (the child that was previously making straight A's gets pregnant).

In a later paper, Miller, Bernstein, and Sharkey (1975) elaborate on the theme of family homeostasis. They propose that frequently families extrude an elder family member through institutionalization when the institutionalization is not necessary. Rather than changes in the elder patient's medical condition, some other event in the family system has upset the family equilibrium, leading the family to request an inappropriate institutionalization.

In the same paper the authors also describe how the staff of an institution often become extended family members and are apt to be drawn into interactions as part of the family system.

Asking for help.   Because old age is a period of physical change, when families feel overwhelmed by problems associated with aging they generally approach their family physician. In other words, the first opinion families usually seek for behavioral and interactional problems with their elders is a medical opinion (Gurian, 1975). Consequently, the modern generation of geriatricians (Gurian, 1975; Miller et al., 1975) stress the importance of assessing the family interactions as an important part of any clinical assessment of an elder. Gurian suggests considering the following questions whenever there is a report of "mental illness" symptoms for an elder:

1. Who is asking for help?
2. Who has established that the behavior is a symptom?
3. What are the intra- vs. the interpersonal issues?

Concluding Remarks on Family Interaction and Problems Associated with Aging

To this point, possibly the strongest proponents of the importance of the interactional view when considering the problems of aging are Savitsky and Sharkey (1972):

> Family interaction constitutes a significant form of personal relationships in the aged. This applies not only to the individual in his active participation in family life but also to an assessment of *fluctuations in*

chronic, medical, and neuropsychiatric disorders and of factors involved in the *precipitation of acute disturbances.* Exploration of the
"family" context, utilization of family interviews, and work with individual family members are essential factors in the diagnosis and management of disturbed behavior. Exploration and interpretation of
family . . . patterns constitutes significant components of staff orientation in institutional and extramural practice [p. 19, italics added].

It is not the goal of this book to make you an expert in the
assessment or treatment of "fluctuations in chronic, medical, and
neuropsychiatric disorders in aging," nor is this necessary. Further,
it is certainly not essential that you understand the complexities of
each and every pathogenic family interaction to be able to begin to
apply counseling techniques based on family systems theory to many
of the everyday problems of elders and their families. It is our goal
to illustrate that conceptualizing even the most severe problems of
aging in a family systems framework is neither a new nor a radical
departure from accepted techniques in the helping professions, and
to describe counseling techniques based on this conceptualization. In
short, the question is not *whether to use* the family systems approach
to understand and deal with problems commonly associated with
aging, but *how to use* this approach effectively. The balance of this
work therefore will focus, first generally and then more and more
specifically, on the process of counseling, based on MRI's extensive
experience in working with families of all kinds and more particularly on the two-and-a-half years' experience of the Family Interaction Center with over 170 family systems that involved some
problem concerning an elder.

5

Evolution of the Process

An Overview of Family Intervention Issues

In an earlier chapter we examined the rise of family systems theory, primarily out of the work of the early family therapists, and summarized a general interactional view that developed from their observation and study of a variety of problems, seen in relation to family contexts. These general concepts about the nature of systems and interaction and about problems and their resolution, however, do not yet reach the matter fundamental to counselors in practice: What should one *do* to help people faced with problems?

As embryonic family therapists, all of the pioneer family systems theorists were of course also concerned with this question. They pursued it in two different but related ways. First, since the general concepts they developed about family systems have significant implications for practice, they made efforts to think these implications through and state them explicitly. Second, they tried out family treatment approaches related to these implications, observed the consequences, and fed these observations back for further refinement or alteration in theory and practice.

What these early workers did and learned constitutes an essential base for subsequent developments in family work, more specifically for the practical application of this general viewpoint to aging problems. It would, however, be a lengthy, complex, and difficult task even to summarize their contributions to practice. Quite a few of the central figures in this field (though of course not only here; the same has been true for most approaches to counseling) had more to say about general orientations than about specifics of technique and taught more by demonstration than by explication. And, as noted, there were involved many people of different backgrounds, working with different problems and populations, and often struggling forward in semidarkness, learning from missteps as much as from positive steps. Moreover, while over time many questions of technique have shaken out, settled down, and become clarified, quite significant differences still exist among various individuals and groups practicing family therapy. Thus, any overall survey of family therapy techniques would, in the present context, be more confusing than enlightening.

Despite their many specific differences, those who laid the foundations for family work also had much in common—and the common ground was apt to be more fundamental. Therefore, rather than attempting to describe the practical methods of various people separately, we will begin by laying out some of the most basic and general aspects of approach and methods and then proceed toward more specific questions of technique. With this progression, the existence of divergent approaches becomes more evident and significant. To deal with this problem, we will mention major alternative stances in family treatment, but then concentrate primarily on the line of conceptual and technical development that led to the particular approach to the family and aging problems that we will be describing in this work.

In the beginning, there was unity. Essentially all of the early family workers placed a major emphasis simply on deliberately attending to the family and the interaction of its members—bringing them together and listening and observing carefully. This practice still persists, although by now it may seem simple and obvious. Yet there were good reasons for stressing it, which largely still hold today. First, this orientation involved a marked change from an established focus on the individual, his inner states, and the past, and change seldom comes easily. Second, the focus of an observer's attention is always of great importance. If one does not look in a certain direction, even what may be evident there is not perceived. Third, family interaction was a new area of observation, so seeing clearly was bound to be difficult; perception depends not just on "what is" but also on prior experience and whether or not concepts for classification and organization of perceptions already exist. "You can't believe what you don't see: rather, you can't see what you don't believe . . . this bears out what Coleridge said as to the necessity of having the idea before the facts could be of any service to one" (Machen, 1966) —or before the facts could even be perceived.

It was clear, then, that a systems or interactional view always implies that any particular behavior or person must not be viewed in isolation from the behavior of other members of the system. That is, one must gather information on the family context of any problem. It was also rather clear and generally accepted that since problems by definition involve ongoing or recurrent behavior, one should correspondingly look toward ongoing or recurrent features of the family context—such as family structure or persistent patterns of interaction—rather than unique events or transactions in the family.

The originators of family therapy were also in general agreement that the primary task is to alter interaction among family members positively, despite the fact that resistance to such change is a natural feature of any system and even though the members' resistance may be unintended and unwitting. Accordingly, the counselor working with families was from the beginning seen as necessarily an active agent in promoting change in family interaction.

All these points were and are basic in the family therapy viewpoint, and taken together they went far toward defining an approach to practice that was very different from that of conventional psychodynamic therapy, with its individual focus, orientation to past events and deeply buried meanings, and passive, long-term therapeutic stance. Yet much remained undefined. For instance, even the original agreement that close attention must be paid to family interaction soon required further specification. Is this to be done by active, directed inquiries or more by observation and reaction—a difference in stance that tends to pervade and shape a therapist's whole treatment approach (Beels and Ferber, n.d.)? Also, since so much goes on among family members that it is quite impossible to attend to everything, just where should exploration of the family system be more particularly directed? Similar problems soon arose and became insistent for other aspects of practice also. In short, the basic principles of the family approach left unresolved important practical issues about the three major facets of practice: 1. What information should be gained about any given family? 2. What and how much change need be attempted (the question of treatment goals)? 3. What sort of action should the therapist take to promote such change effectively?

On all these points, the pioneering family therapists differed considerably, and their followers still differ. The current state of these differences in orientation and practice has recently been reviewed and outlined by Madanes and Haley (1977). It is not necessary to recapitulate their work here, but a brief outline of some of the major differences among family therapists about basic information, goals, and therapist activity is useful as a basis for understanding the focus and rationale of our own orientation to practice.

In regard to information, while complete knowledge of any family is impossible, as stated, many family therapists have sought to expand this area of inquiry beyond here-and-now family interaction. Satir (1964), for instance, thought it important to inquire about the getting together of the parents in the present family, while Bowen (1976) and his followers focused also on *their* parents, or even further back into family history. Some family workers, not content with what family members say explicitly, have laid great stress on nonverbal communication and unintended messages (Scheflen, 1965). Others view overt behavior not as primary in itself but as indicative of underlying and more important feelings and attitudes. There have also been related differences regarding the depth and completeness of view needed; that is, beyond the problem at hand, how far did a counselor need to inquire in order to develop some global or overall view of family structure and functioning?

Quite naturally, all these differences have been accompanied by differences in judgment as to who needs to be seen in the treatment sessions. Many family therapists have had a flat rule that all members of the patient's immediate family must be present at each session. Some took a more flexible position, seeing less than the entire family at least sometimes. Still others have gone further in the opposite direction, bringing in grandparents, officials, and close neighbors for "network therapy" (Speck and Attneave, 1971).

Regarding goals of treatment, the most common position has been that a revamping of basic family organization or interaction is required. This in itself, however, is no simple standard. In the first place, some saw this as the original and prime target of treatment, while others saw relief of symptoms of the presenting problem as the first aim, but one that must then be followed up by further work directed to alteration of more basic dysfunctional interaction, lest the problem return or another take its place. In the second place, while all these approaches involved some concept of a "good" or "ideal" family system as the target of treatment, this ideal was usually implicit—often referred to only in terms of personal and family "growth"—and was therefore difficult to define or evaluate, and probably varied considerably among different family therapists.

The question of how a therapist should intervene to promote the envisioned goal is no less complex, and usually no more explicit. One major orientation, apparently a reaction to observing the pathogenic effects of vague and contradictory messages, has been toward the furthering of "good communication"—open, clear, and direct. In some instances, as in the work of Ackerman (1966) for example, this presumably was to follow naturally from "opening up" the family so that ordinary restraints on communication would be lessened, family members would speak their minds more freely, and positive adjustments would ultimately follow. Other workers, in what appears to be a family variant to "insight" therapy, took a rather didactic, clarifying approach: if the therapist can get a clear view of family communication, then change should follow some combination of explanation of present patterns to the family and direct instruction on how to communicate differently and better. On another front, Minuchin's (1974) "structural family therapy" emphasized altering family organization and alliances, but was not very specific as to what the therapist must do to bring about this desired end. Bowen (1976) stressed that the therapist should promote greater individuation among family members—more separation from the "undifferentiated family ego mass" —and less unhealthy involvement in "triangulation," often furthered by having patients revisit their families of origin to revise relationships that had remained fixed in the parent–child mold of years past.

Evolution of the Present Techniques

Our own orientation, to be discussed and exemplified in the following chapters, may include elements from all of the positions mentioned above, yet it differs considerably from all of them in basic outlook. While it involves a more extensive and explicit integration of theory and technique than other approaches to family counseling, its primary aims are more modest. It is oriented toward the resolution of specific problems presented by clients. It may therefore appear superficial in comparison to approches that aim at general family reorganization or, in some sense, "growth." Certainly its aims are limited practical ones, concerned with easing difficulties in the daily life of individuals and their families rather than global family change or cure of basic psychopathologies, which we believe are best left to other, long-term treatments. Yet this orientation may have some advantages of simplicity and feasibility, especially in situations that are difficult and call for change, yet are limited by realistic constraints. Such situations appear frequently in dealing with elders and their families.

This approach is based on three sources. First, there was extensive and varied experience at MRI and its predecessor research projects in applying the family systems viewpoint and related ideas concerning the nature and importance of communication built on the work of Gregory Bateson (Watzlawick, Beavin, and Jackson, 1967) to treatment practice. Early statements on this were produced by Jackson and Weakland (1961) and by Haley (1963). Also during this early period, much was being learned from intensive behavioral study—conducted by direct observation and tape recording, followed by inquiry and discussion—of what prominent therapists actually said and did in their interviews (Haley and Hoffman, 1967).

These early prescriptions or suggestions for practice, however, now seem too general in some respects and too rigid in others. They recommended seeing the entire family as a rather fixed standard, sought to discover overall patterns of family organization and interaction as presumably corresponding to identifiable classes of problems, and construed the concept of family homeostasis as implying that, unless family reorganization was thoroughgoing, a new problem was very apt to arise if the presenting one was treated successfully. For instance, resolution of a problem of child behavior would bring to the surface parental conflict previously masked by the difficulties with the child. Haley's work in particular also stressed the payoffs subtly associated with symptomatic behavior, viewing both family difficulties and therapy largely in terms of covert power struggles among the individuals involved. Although Haley has contributed greatly to the advancement of skills in family work, including our own, and has become more specifically problem-oriented (1976), many of these emphases still characterize his later work while our own orientation has changed considerably.

Second, such change occurred largely in connection with work at MRI's Brief Therapy Center, started by Dr. Richard Fisch in 1966. Formed partly in reaction to growing tendencies of family therapy toward greater length and complexity, the Center began as a cooperative effort to explore whether a variety of problems could be resolved more effectively and efficiently by 1. sharpening the treatment focus on the main presenting problem, and 2. utilizing maximally any available means of therapist influence that appeared to offer promise of rapid change in significant problem related behaviors, whether or not these means appeared customary, direct, or even logical. This concern with effective means of intervention actually represents a continuing and increased interest in one old but basic technical problem: how can a therapist most readily and usefully promote necessary change in a rigid system of family interaction? Even in MRI's early work it is clear that, beyond such simple and head-on means as didactic clarification of family interactions, we were seeking ways to utilize the complexity and power of communication—the power so amply evident in promoting family conflict and pathology—in more positive and therapeutic ways to promote family healing. Our search for effective therapeutic influence had also been aided, from very early days, by study of the hypnotic and therapeutic techniques of Milton H. Erikson (Haley, 1967, 1973). The Center's stronger focus on the presenting complaint and immediately related behaviors, while a simplifying departure from inquiry directed at the whole family system, can also be seen as quite consistent with the basics of the family systems view, and indeed as pursuing an element of this more rigorously: the Center aimed to concentrate maximally on the here-and-now problem situation, that is, exclusively on the current problem behavior and such other current behavior as appeared most overtly and directly related to it.

Except for these two initial guiding principles and a background of prior experience in working with families, the Center apparently was working on an empirical, trial-and-error basis. Yet after several years of such work, with most of a varied lot of problems being resolved or much improved within the Center's limit of ten sessions, the staff members began to realize that they were in fact working in similar and repetitive ways; an organized and consistent—but implicit—approach had to be present. Accordingly, time was taken to analyze the basic principles and related rules of practice involved, which proved to be few in number (Weakland et al., 1974; Watzlawick et al., 1974).

Most fundamentally, in concentrating on the presenting problem, its immediate context, and means of intervention, the Center had definitely moved away from the questions that had traditionally preoccupied both therapists and clients—"Why do we have this problem? Where did it come from?"—to a focus on the questions of persistence and change—"What behavior is occurring that perpetuates the problem behavior? What changes in behavior would be needed to alter this cycle?" Once formulated, it became evident that this approach was consistent with the basic principles of the family systems view and in fact represented a more thorough and serious adherence to them. In particular, the systems model involves a cybernetic view of causation rather than the older linear view. That is, from a cybernetic point of view, the behavior of any part of a system of interaction is to be explained by relating it to other features of the system as it currently exists (but not necessarily to all of the system equally; the important possibility is open that some behavior or some actors in a system may be highly relevant to a problem, but others only minimally so), and not by seeking its roots in the history of the part or even the whole system. In this view, to put it most simply, *the problem* fundamentally involves a vicious circle: between the problem behavior as such and other behaviors that provoke a repetition or an escalation of this problem behavior. Accordingly, the counselor's task lies in 1. clarifying the problem behavior, 2. identifying what other behaviors in the system are maintaining the problem behavior, and 3. altering these maintaining behaviors so as to interrupt the vicious circle.

Theoretically, in the case of family problems, such reinforcing behavior might involve any other aspect of the family system. In practice, work at the Brief Therapy Center repeatedly and typically found such reinforcement to lie in some aspect of the efforts the patient and/or family members were making to resolve *the problem.* Ironically, in a very important sense the "solution" was the most basic problem. It should be made very clear that this conclusion does not imply any malevolent intent. On the contrary, the situation typically is one of people trying to help solve *the problem,* sincerely and with determination, but in inappropriate ways. Typically, also, these errors are human and understandable to anyone—especially a counselor—who has adequate information and perspective on the family systems involved.

This view of problems has two further general implications. On one hand, such a vicious-circle view suggests that through spiraling escalation even a minor initial difficulty can develop into a very serious problem—a course of events that does indeed correspond with common life experience. On the other hand, fortunately, it suggests that if a vicious circle can be interrupted, a beneficent circle might be established and therefore that a small but strategic positive change could set further and progressive improvement in motion.

These basic ideas also lead rather simply and directly to a systematic approach to practice. In general outline, this consists of the following related steps:

1. Establishing initial contact with the client(s).

2. Inquiry and definition of the problem. In terms of concrete behavior, what is the main problem, currently; how is this behavior a problem, and to whom—the Identified Patient (I.P.), others, or both?

3. Inquiring into handling of the problem. Again in terms of concrete behavior, what is each significantly concerned person doing in attempting to contain, handle, or resolve the problem?

4. Inquiry as to minimal goals. What, in terms of clearly observable behavior if possible, would be judged as indicating not what is ideally or ultimately hoped for, but a small yet significant improvement in the problem?

5. Observation of the positions of the I.P. and others. What is the view of the problem and of counseling that each involved person initially holds? Changing attitudes or behavior requires first a knowledge and understanding of where people are starting from.

6. Review and strategic planning. A review and summary of the above points are needed, usually after the first session, as well as a check for completeness of information. The therapist should make an initial estimation as to appropriate goals, persons most involved in the problem, persons most open to change. What appears to be crucial in maintaining the problem, and how can the therapist, especially, avoid similar behavior?

7. Further interviews, specific interventions, and evaluation of their effects.

8. Termination.

Finally, the framework just described has been adapted, added to, modified, and further specified in various ways in the course of MRI research and counseling work aimed specifically at problems of elders and their families. As a significant part of these changes, the therapeutic techniques above were specifically modified to be available to a more diverse group of helping professionals, including applied gerontologists, by changing their focus from psychotherapeutic work encompassing a wide range of major problems to goal-oriented counseling in more limited situational problems and with correspondingly limited aims.

The following chapters describe the resulting approach at some length. In considering this approach, however, it should always be kept in mind that it is offered only as one potentially useful point of view and related procedure. While naturally we think this approach has value, we do not suggest that it—or any other approach—represents universal and final truth. The last word will, in our opinion, never be spoken.

6

Approaching the Family System

Consider the System

The purpose of this book is to help applied gerontologists solve the problems associated with aging by viewing them in relation to the elder's social-support (interactional) system. The primary social-support system for most people, including elders, is the family or extended kin network. These points should be obvious, but it is important to reemphasize them because people do not usually "present" in terms of a social systems problem. It is up to the gerontologist to recognize and reconceptualize individual client's plights in family system terms, rather than to expect the clients themselves always to recognize and describe this underlying context of their difficulties.

For example, if you are a social worker, an elderly client is unlikely to tell you, "The only reason I'm asking for welfare is that I don't know where else to turn for help in solving the problem in my social-support system posed by the recent marriage of my oldest daughter." More likely, the client will "present" along such lines as, "My disloyal daughter and her no-good husband have thrown me out of their home," or "I'm so lonely that life isn't worth living," or "I have no place to live." In the first, ideal example, it is clear that a family systems problem is involved and, correspondingly, a family systems approach is needed. But in the more realistic examples, it would be easy to fall into the trap of simply thinking, "This person is an abandoned isolate," or "This person is depressed," or "This person has nowhere to spend the night," and accordingly focus too narrowly—for instance, on a search for low-cost housing.

To be on the safe side, then, one should deliberately consider a problem in the full context of the client's social system. Look, and inquire, beyond the individual with *the problem* to the social group (generally family, but possibly a system of nonrelated persons) with interrelated problems. Ultimately, the reason for recognizing the family system is that you will not be able to solve the problem without changing the system.

Making the Approach

Being Available

If you want to be of use to elders and their families, then obviously you must make contact with them. From an organizational point of view, the first step in approaching families with problems is to let it be known within your agency that you are available to see such clients. In fact, not only are you available to see elders and their families, you are eager to see such clients. Such information may at first be spread informally, until you have gained enough confidence in what you are doing to go more public.

For example, suppose you are a senior center coordinator. You have an hour or so a day that you would like to make available to some of the elders in your center. You might, informally, over coffee, tell the information and referral (I & R) worker that you would be interested in becoming involved with one or two cases that involve elders who are having problems with their families. You might go down to sit with the I & R workers next time they visit your center to select a case yourself. If you work in a small center, you could call fellow coordinators at other centers and simply mention your interest. Since family problems are often quite entangled, you might be surprised at the response you receive.

Such administrative visibility is unnecessary if you are working in a position where you meet many elders face to face. Most people working directly with elders find an abundance of problems waiting for attention. For example, suppose you work for a Congressman as a liaison person for elders. A 75-year-old man and his son come to your office because of problems they are having with the Veterans Administration. During your conversation you observe that the son is doing almost all of the talking and referring to his father as if the father were not even present. At one point, while telling his father's medical history, the son points casually at his father and announces, "Since his cancer surgery he's been acting senile; I don't even think he knows where he is."

After you hear the son out, you turn to the father and ask, "I think I know what your son wants, but what do you yourself want?" The old man begins to weep and says, "What difference does it make?" What could you do?

Depending upon how available you want to be, there are several options. If you want to be unavailable, you can look at your watch, exclaim about the lateness of the hour, and close the interview by explaining that you have to move on to your next appointment. Or you can give an understanding nod to the son and tell him you will do all you can with the Veterans Administration and excuse yourself from the interview. On the other hand, if you want to and can make the commitment to be available, there are several different approaches that you might want to consider.

The first and most obvious way to be available is to maintain eye contact and remain silent. Give the father an opportunity to come out. Perhaps all you really need to do is to be in the room, attentively. Alternatively, you might maintain eye contact with the old man and simply say, "I wonder if it might help to talk about it." Another approach might be to turn to the son and ask, "Did you know that your dad was feeling that way?" Still another approach might be simply to comment, "I'm glad you brought your feelings out, Mr. Jones. I could almost feel your pain across the table."

In situations that are not traditional "counseling" environments, it is not uncommon for one or more members of the family to attempt to change the subject. Family members often may feel that it would be inappropriate to "air their dirty linen" in front of you. In the example above, the son might say, "Dad, I've explained to you a hundred times why I'm doing what I'm doing. Let's get back to the problem with the VA."

To be available, the counselor needs to give permission to the family to talk about feelings and personal problems. To extend this kind of permission, the counselor might want to say, "It would be all right with me if we were to spend some time talking about how both of you are feeling and how you might be stuck in trying to work this problem out. In fact, many of the people who come to this office find it rather useful to talk things out with a third person in the room. Sometimes another viewpoint can be useful." Yet another way of giving permission might be: "Sometimes it's easier to solve problems with the government when everybody is sure of what they want. I wonder if it might not be a good idea to spend a few minutes talking about what both of you really want in this situation. In some ways, I guess, I'm sensing that both of you are feeling a bit misunderstood. I'd like to check that out with you."

The fact that you are going to talk about feelings instead of the exact specifics of the problem situation does not mean that you have to label your meeting (or the part of your meeting devoted to talking about feelings) as something "out of the ordinary." It would be very inappropriate for you to comment to the father and son, "I can see that you folks have made a mountain out of a molehill. Obviously you need counseling. Luckily for you, I'm also a trained counselor." Usually laying any kind of label ("You need counseling") on a family or its members costs the clients more than it benefits them. Usually it is much better to *reframe* any kind of inquiry about how people are "feeling" into terms of the information necessary for you to do your job correctly. In this way, you make yourself available to the family at "no cost"—that is, without the family having to accept the label of "needing counseling."

Still another way to remain available is to gently acknowledge that many people have hidden agendas when they seek your advice. For example, you might be a visiting nurse approached by your patient's worried daughter-in-law, who begins to ask you questions about the "mental state" of your patient. Folk wisdom has it that people generally have two reasons for doing anything: the reason that sounds good and the real reason. After you listen patiently to the daughter-in-law's questions, followed by her observations of how the old woman is becoming "senile," you say, "You know, what you have been telling me makes sense to me, but somehow, I get the feeling that there is something else on your mind. If you wouldn't feel that I was being too intrusive, I wonder if you'd be willing to share it with me?"

Of all the different methods of being available, probably the most powerful is encouraging the hidden agenda to emerge. In almost every aspect of working with elders, an opportunity presents itself to learn both reasons the elder or family member has come to you. Many applied gerontologists often leave the hidden agenda hidden, intentionally or by default. After all, if you are working on an I & R telephone line, it is much easier simply to answer the overt question "Where do I catch the bus?" than to dig further and discover that the elder caller's hidden agenda is to discuss the terror she is feeling over having just had a stroke and the friction that her disability—of which being unable to drive is only one manifestation —is causing in her relationship with her daughter. In the end, what limits the level of problem disclosure by your clients is your availability, not theirs.

When Being Available Is Not Enough

Many times, no matter how much effort you have made to be available, family members may be extraordinarily reluctant to share any of their feelings with you or with each other. While such a reluctance is anyone's right, it is also often related to how the family problems have developed. It seems safer to some counselors simply to label such a family as "resistant," "unappreciative," "uptight," or "hopeless" than to try to be helpful and risk failure. Such labeling may be good for the counselor but is rarely useful to the client. If you are willing to go further after simply being available has not worked, here are some techniques you might find useful.

Stepping down: sharing the pleasure of helping. Imagine you are a speech therapist working with an elder who has suffered a mild stroke. It is clear to you by her posture and facial expression that she is feeling quite low and that this depression of mood is serving as an obstacle to what should be a rather straightforward recovery. Your attempts to be more available to her have been ignored. In fact, she has told you that she does not even want to come for speech therapy, but her daughter has not given her any choice. The message she is really sending you is "I don't want help for myself." This response is not uncommon from elders, who may be feeling at a low ebb for any number of reasons. On the other hand, most elders respond quite positively when they can trade the role of "being helped" for "being the helper." That is, many elders may refuse help for themselves, but are willing to do almost anything within their power to help another. Therefore, if the speech therapist is willing and able to be available as a counselor, he needs to reframe the relationship between himself and his patient as one that will benefit him more than the elder. Such a reframing allows the elder to share the satisfaction of helping. While at one level there is a certain ego gratification for any helping professional in appearing to be an unquestioned authority figure, such an approach is apt to lack, not only humanistic value, but effectiveness as well. Being able to step down from the unquestioned authority role usually gives the practitioner more latitude in being useful.

In the case of the speech therapist, he might try saying, "I really feel awkward asking you this question, but if I don't, I'll get into trouble with my supervisor." Another statement might be, "I wouldn't blame you for not wanting to answer my questions, but I hope you will. I usually find I learn a lot more about life from working with my older patients than they do about speech from me." In each case, the request for information is made in such a way that the elder has the sense of doing a favor for the speech therapist instead of the speech therapist doing a favor for the elder. Being able to share with the elder the pleasure of helping is an act of genuine human compassion. Sadly, not all "helpers" are willing to help this much.

If you are in the role of student, you are in an even better position to share the pleasure of helping. After all, how will you learn unless you have some patients with whom to practice? Consequently, asking for cooperation from elders would go something like this: "I really wish you could help me by answering these questions. I'm just a student and I really need your help to learn how to do this. You probably won't get very much out of this procedure, but talking with you about your situation really is important to me."

Steps to encourage hesitant family members. In working with families, situations are defined in terms of family problems, rather than in terms of one individual having or being *the problem.* Consequently, in family counseling, it is usually desirable to have as many family members present as possible when holding a session, especially early in the process. Having such family representation is useful for several reasons. First, by mere physical presence, each family member is demonstrating some concern with the situation. Second, having more than one person admitting to a problem suggests to all assembled that the matter is more complex than just one person with something wrong.

For example, suppose you are a member of the clergy and are called by a distraught 45-year-old female parishioner who tells you that her father has just been picked up by the police for the third time because of his drinking. She asks you to talk to him about it. You know enough about the family situation to realize that the old man is lonely and has been drunk only three times in his life, each time resulting in arrest. You also know that the only time anyone in his three-generation household ever takes notice of him is when he has been arrested for drunkenness. Therefore, you see the family as not only suffering from the effects of his behavior, but also contributing to maintenance of the cycle. Since you got the call from the daughter, you assume that she must be involved in the family situation to a considerable degree. At this point you would like to see as many of the people who are living in the home with Grandfather as possible when you see him in order to, first, demonstrate to Grandfather that everyone is concerned; and second, take the pressure off Grandfather by showing him that his drinking is only part of a larger problem of the family system.

There are several approaches you might take. For example, you might say to the daughter, "It would help me in working with your father if I could get together with your entire family to talk this matter over." You are not agreeing or disagreeing that Grandfather has a problem. You are simply asking to meet with the entire family to gain a clearer perspective of the situation. Remember, it is neither useful nor desirable to label a family as having a problem. While ultimately Grandfather needs to be relieved of the burden of his label, his need for relief is not acute: he has been carrying the label for some time. While approaching the system, little is to be gained by forcing a label on or off the family or its members. Much more is to be gained by involving the family in such a way that they can work together.

Suppose that at the first session you find that the daughter's husband will not come to counseling. You might consider calling him yourself to say something along the lines of, "I'm really working at a disadvantage here because I'm sure that you have some important information to offer and it's very difficult for me to make sense of what's going on without it. I guess what I'm really saying is that I would like to hear your side of things to give me a better perspective on what's going on." Just because his wife has said that he will not come does not mean he will not. Maybe she is not sure she wants him to be there!

Another twist that can occur is the situation in which one or more family members agree to come to a meeting but then fail to appear. To emphasize the importance of each family member to the problem under discussion, the counselor can go ahead and leave an empty chair for each missing family member. While this technique cannot make up for the different perspective that each family member can provide, it does allow for making the point symbolically that family problems are more complex than just one family member with *the problem*.

Even if you cannot get full family participation—and you usually will not—do not despair. The most important part of working with families is not attendance at sessions but instead the counselor's conception of problems in terms of family systems rather than in individual terms.

Challenges to your competence.   One of the inevitabilities in trying to be useful to other people is the challenge to your competence. The challenge can be phrased as delicately as a simple inquiry about your training and education or as harshly as an assault on your integrity as a human being. While the questions, "How old are you, dear?" and "How dare you be so impertinent as to think that you could possibly help me?" may not be the same in content, they are the same in meaning: can we trust you? How you as a counselor handle challenges to your competence will indirectly answer the question of trustworthiness.

When given a bit of nondefensive thought, the question, "How do we know we can trust you?" makes a lot of sense. Would you, for example, be willing to share your hopes and fears with someone you did not trust? Would you be willing to open up what you considered to be your difficult or fragile family relationships to inspection by someone you had no faith in? Of course not. In a way, when an individual or family challenges your competence, they are communicating, "We care enough about ourselves to insist that we work with someone we can trust." Such sense of self-worth is really a good prognostic sign. While a challenge to your competence may be painful to you personally, you can at least take heart that it is a good sign for your clients.

In general, then, when confronted by a challenge to your competence, remember to answer the question, "How do we know we can trust you?" Generally, the best way to demonstrate you are *not* trustworthy is to become defensive and recite your degrees and training. As an experiment, you might even want to try reciting your degrees and background to a couple of families just to prove this point to yourself. Watch their faces carefully to see how negatively they will react to your defensive display. The fact is that almost everyone acknowledges the folk wisdom: "Smart people don't have to prove to you how smart they are." To repeat, you are not being challenged on how smart you are; you are really being challenged on how trustworthy you are. If you cannot even hear your clients' real question, how can you expect them ever to trust you?

If the general form of the challenge to your competence is "What are your credentials?" then the general reply might be, "I'd be happy to tell you about my qualifications, but I have a sense that what you are really asking me is whether or not you folks can trust me. It's a good question and it shows me that you care enough about yourselves to want the best help you can get. I only wish I had a good answer. I guess the most I can say is that I try my best but at times I make stupid mistakes. If I didn't think I could be useful, I wouldn't be doing this kind of work, but I'd understand if you'd like to hold back a bit until you have a better sense of how well I do my job."

There are, of course, specific questions that bring fear to the heart of any beginner. The most infamous of these questions is *"Are you just a student?"* Suppose you are a recreation student doing a field placement with a senior center. A dispute arises over the fee you have charged a 91-year-old man. He appears with his 60-year-old son and daughter-in-law at your office door to discuss the matter. Since the entire matter entails less than $2.00, you suspect that the family has appeared with a double agenda and is using the activities fee as a "ticket" to talk. After you clear up the issue of the $2.00, you decide you have the time to commit to a counseling relationship, so you wonder aloud if there might be anything else on their minds. The 60-year-old son casually mentions the problems he and his wife are having living with both their father and their 35-year-old retarded son. Before he goes any further, he looks you in the eye and says, "Are you just a student?" You might want to reply: "In some ways, I'm glad you asked; a lot of people don't even care enough about themselves to find out who is working with them. I am just a student; I can see why you feel the way you do. Just because I've had a lot of courses doesn't really prove I know as much as I could or should. I do know that if I'm going to be useful to you and your family, I'm really going to need a lot of your help. In a way, that puts more burden on all of you. Do you think my being a student will stop you from talking more?" By taking this approach you have demonstrated to the family that you are honest and not defensive. You have left the decision on trust where it belongs, back with the family.

Another twist on "What are your credentials (how do I know I can trust you)?" is the not-so-innocent question, *"How could anyone your age hope to understand my situation?"* Suppose, for example, you are working in a managerial position for a labor union pension fund. An 80 year old man, in obvious ill health and considerable pain, makes an appointment to see you. By the nature of his questions about the pension fund, it looks suspiciously as if he is terminally ill and considering suicide. Trying to be available, you remark, "I have a sense from the kinds of questions you've been asking me that you are thinking about something more. I wonder if it wouldn't be a good idea to take a few moments to talk directly about how you're feeling." Fire blazes in the proud old man's eyes, and he almost spits at you, "How could anyone your age possibly understand my situation?"

Since he is right, it would be of little reassurance to the elder to argue this point. Instead, you might say, "I'm afraid you're right: my age is a real handicap. I like to think sometimes I can be useful to my clients, but basically, I learn a lot more about life from my older clients than they do from me. When it comes down to it, because of my age and lack of experience, you'd be doing most of the work and I'd be getting the most gain. It would make sense to me if you were reluctant to share anything about yourself with me." Using this approach, you are free from having to assure the elder of your competence and you allow him room to reassure you that you do have some degree of competence. In addition, you are acknowledging the wisdom of the elder's years and admitting that you have something to learn from him. You are also giving him the important signal that in counseling most of the work is done by the client, not the counselor. In the end, you have reframed the situation so that his unwillingness to be counseled has become a reluctance to share his life experiences with you. For most people, it is easier to turn down counseling than an opportunity to share life experiences with a young person.

The final challenge to your competence to be examined here takes the form of the statement: *"The situation is hopeless; no one could possibly help."* Suppose that you are a coordinator for a group of elder volunteers. You get word that one of your volunteers has failed to show up for her assigned duties. When you finally reach her home, you are informed by her niece that she has broken her ankle and is in the hospital. From the tone of voice the niece uses, it sounds as if your volunteer had broken her neck rather than her ankle. When you visit your volunteer in the hospital, she seems her normal, capable self. When you speak to the niece about when your volunteer can return home, she alludes to the possibility that the family will not allow her to return home. Being available, you offer, "I wonder if it would be useful to talk about the problems of making a home for her." The niece looks at the ground and mutters, "The situation is just terrible; I don't think there is anything anyone can do."

It is, of course, impossible to know if the situation is really hopeless. It is obvious, however, that the niece is feeling hopeless. Therefore, the niece is really asking you, "Can you recognize how hopeless I feel?" If you can show her you understand how she is feeling, she will probably trust you; if not, she will be even more insistent, and hopelessness will prevail. Being aware of what she is seeking, you might want to say, "You're probably right. I guess I just let my hopes get in the way of my judgment. Your aunt has this broken ankle, which I'm sure is eating up her savings; she probably has lots of other debts and may even be behind on her taxes. She's certainly not a young woman anymore, so there's no telling how long it might take for her ankle to heal, and the whole time that it is healing she will be an extra burden to her family, which probably already has plenty of difficulties to begin with. I guess I just wanted to see if I could help in any way, but under the circumstances I'd probably feel the same way as you." Alternatively, you might say, "I can understand why you're feeling at the bottom. Sometimes my being a professional do-gooder gets in the way of my noticing that things really can be impossible; my meddling might make things even worse. I can see the advantages of leaving things where they are."

Approaching the problem from this direction gives the family member room to tell you, "Things may be bad, but they're not as bad as you say." That is, you give the pessimistic family member an opportunity to take the other side of her ambivalent feelings. The key is to leave space for the family member of the elder to be positive, and then to reinforce your statement with your silent physical presence. Remember, you're not selling a used car by high-pressure tactics. As long as people know that you understand what they are feeling, and that you accept their feelings, they know that you are available. They do not have to take advantage of your availability at that particular moment—although you might wish they would.

Probably the best reason never to appear to take matters more lightly than the most concerned relative is that they may have information about the situation which you do not. It could, in fact, have been that your volunteer was about to be evicted from her home by the marshal for back taxes, was suffering from a terminal illness, and had broken her ankle on the way to the medicine cabinet, where she was going to take an overdose of sleeping pills. Imagine how patently foolish you would have sounded to her niece if you had said, "Cheer up, it's *only* a broken ankle."

Restraining Your Optimism Positively

In attempting to make yourself available, the most likely trap into which you may fall is the incorrect use of optimism. An optimistic spirit is of great value to any counselor. Optimism of spirit, however, should not be confused with direct expression of optimism to the client. The two are quite different. An optimistic spirit on the part of the counselor provides the energy and the impetus to become involved and to stay involved. Careless optimistic statements, however, are likely to invalidate the feelings of the clients, set the stage for failure, and serve only as a crutch to all involved.

Part of the confusion over therapeutic optimism comes from one's own personal experience. A sense of optimism is a sense of relief. It is a positive feeling. When you encounter a family that is having difficulties that you perceive as readily solvable, you will have a natural inclination to want them to share your feeling of optimism. That is, you want to share with them the good feeling that "Things aren't really as bad as they seem; there is hope." Regretfully, people who are feeling pessimistic are not buoyed up by counselors who tell them that their pessimism is unfounded. Telling someone to be more optimistic is like telling someone to be more in love. You simply cannot direct someone into feeling something he or she does not feel. In fact, the harder you try, the more likely you are to add to your client's pessimism. Recall from Chapter 2 that attempting to "talk" clients out of one side of their ambivalence is likely to have a reverse effect. If you choose to be overtly optimistic with a family, you must be prepared to assume the responsibility for any negative effects your overt expression has on progress of the family later.

Risk of invalidating feelings. One of the unkindest cuts of expressing too much optimism is that it often has the effect of invalidating the client's feelings. For example, you are a nursing home administrator who has been tipped off by a charge nurse that a 74-year-old female patient has not had a visitor in two weeks. Since the family usually visits daily, you assume some outside help might be useful and go to her room to make yourself available. As you sit down next to her bed, you are met with a tirade of her complaints, beginning with her teeth, moving down her body to her feet and away from her body onto her family for daring to take a vacation while she is in the hospital. You know that your goal of making contact and developing trust will be subverted by an abundance of optimism. After all, you might not want the patient to be feeling pessimistic and depressed, but that is the way she is feeling.

It is bad enough that your patient is actually feeling hopeless. It is worse still if she is to be denied making contact with you because you refuse to acknowledge her feelings. To be available, you might want to say to your patient: "I can really hear that you are feeling right down at the bottom of the barrel, physically and psychologically. Here you are with all these physical problems that may even get worse before they get better, if they get better at all. On top of all this, your family seems to have practically deserted you. You know, as bad as you're feeling, I don't understand why you aren't feeling even worse."

Even if a family member or entire family is feeling at "the end of the rope," you can understand their pessimism; then at least they are not at "the end" by themselves. By understanding their pessimism, you can communicate at a deeper level to your clients, "I hear you; I understand. I accept you and the pain you are in. I am not labeling you crazy, neurotic, complaining, or nasty for how you are feeling. I am with you."

Setting the stage for failure.   Another problem associated with uncontrolled optimism stems from its attempted use as a lure to get families into counseling. Counselors present themselves in such a way that they communicate, "I can help, I can help! Counseling will be worth it." For example, suppose you are a retirement counselor. Acting on a suggestion from an interested third party, you contact the family of a recently retired physician. According to your information, the elder physician's son believes that his father needs to be doing some kind of meaningful work. The son is involved because the elder is living with his family, seemingly causing problems with the son's wife. To get the family to enter counseling, you assure the son, "No problem. We can take the pressure off you and your wife in a snap. I'm a dynamite counselor when it comes to motivation. Physicians are in such enormous demand that placement should be no trouble. Just bring in your wife and your dad tomorrow. You all will be feeling happy as a clam by the end of the week." What happens when everyone is not happy as a clam by the end of the week?

By being overly optimistic, you have set the stage for failure. When happiness does not suddenly abound, it will seem as if either the family has failed or the counselor has failed. In reality no one has failed, though the counselor has made an initial error. It takes time for a family to develop problems; it only makes sense that it will take time to resolve them. The problem is that unrestrained optimism sets up unrealistic goals and expectations, virtually ensuring failure. Early in your relationship with a family, you can ill afford to make claims that you cannot back up. Each time you fail to deliver, family members are apt to lose confidence in you. The only worse outcome is if, instead of blaming you, the family members blame themselves or each other for failing to live up to your unrealistic expectations. In this case, you have increased the level of dissension and scapegoating in the family rather than reduced it. You have done the family more harm than good with your optimism. In a sense, your use of optimism as a lure in your telephone call has set up the family for an indeterminant period of misery when your—and now their—false expectations fail to be met.

Reexamining the case of the family of the retired physician, you might have contacted the son and said, "Bob Robertson told me that your family is experiencing some discomfort with your father's new role as a retired person. As a retirement counselor I have had some experience in working through situations that seem to have some similarities to yours. Sometimes I find I can be useful; sometimes not. The only time I'm certain I cannot be useful is when people haven't even heard about me. At any rate, I just wanted to check in with you folks to let you know that I am not only around, but also interested."

A crutch for the counselor. For many individuals who aspire to be counselors, there seems to be a pervasive notion that if you cannot give a client or a family anything else in the way of counseling, you can at least give them "hope." As this chapter has tried to point out, nothing could be further from the truth. In fact, if all you have to offer a family by way of counseling is optimism that things will get better ("It's always darkest before the dawn," or "When you've hit bottom the only way to go is up," or "Things always turn out for the best") then you are apt to be doing as much harm as good. There is no question that optimism has a role in counseling; to reiterate, to be useful, optimism needs to flow *from* the clients *to* the counselor. Using optimism in the interest of your clients calls for a great deal of restraint. If you are about to burst with optimism but your professional judgment tells you to keep your feelings to yourself, you can say, "I'd really like to be optimistic and reassuring and tell you that everything is going to turn out fine tomorrow. But my professional judgment just won't let me do that. We must wait and see how things develop."

A crutch for the family. The final problem with optimism occurs when the family or some of its members have too much optimism, particularly when that optimism is presented as faith in your power as a counselor. To be specific, suppose that you are a dietician at a nutrition site. You are approached by an elder who tells you that she is bringing her brother, also an elder, to your site because she is unable to make him eat "what he needs" at home. She confides to you, "I just know you'll be able to pound some sense into his head and make him eat. All of us [she, her nieces and nephews, and her own children] are so desperate. We just know that you can help."

While such an approach by a family is certainly gratifying to the ego of the counselor, it is usually a sign that the family is setting the counselor up to "take over" family or individual responsibility. Usually this responsibility (self-maintenance) has been taken from one individual (in this case, the elder brother) by another (the elder sister) who, quite expectably, then could not manage it ("he won't eat"). Sometimes the responsibility is passed directly from the client to you ("I just know you can make me want to eat," or "You just have to make me want to eat"). Obviously, if you are going to be effective, each member of the family system will have to assume responsibility for him- or herself.

To turn around such seductive optimism, you might try saying, "I certainly do appreciate the confidence you have in me. But, while I feel pretty good about what I do, I think it's important that you also understand that sometimes I fail miserably and am no help at all. What hope there is lies mainly in your ability to help me." After making such a statement, you must be prepared to listen to the most dire predictions of what will occur as the result of any failure you might have. At that point, you might want to add, "I'm afraid that I would be doing you a disservice to guarantee I can be useful, when it's really uncertain. I'll try my best and expect the same from you. In any event, we must all be prepared for the possibility that nothing will change, or that things might even get worse."

Needless to say, when making such a statement your insides will tighten up. Nothing is more difficult than to make eye contact with desperate people and tell them that their optimism and faith in you is not totally well-founded. It will pain you and it will pain them, for the short term. But taking the opposite course and allowing yourself to be seduced into accepting unrealistic responsibility for solving the problems instead of leaving the responsibility where it must belong (with the people who have the problems) will only serve to ensure that pessimistic predictions will come true.

In conclusion, useful restraint of optimism may be the most difficult skill to master. It is one of the major skills that separates skilled counselors from lay persons with "good intentions." Because usefully restraining optimism runs contrary to the popular notion that good counselors mobilize people in pain by carefully applying heavy doses of optimism, there is an enormous amount of resistance to trying the technique of restrained optimism for the first time. If one never tries it, of course, one will never see how effective most counselors (and ultimately families) find it. Hence, the vicious circle continues and the erroneous folk wisdom is perpetuated. We prefer to leave the matter with you: if you choose not to restrain your optimism and bank solely on your good intentions, that is your right. However, you will be assuming responsibility for any negative effects your unrestrained optimistic expressions will have on the progress of families with which you work. Your good intentions may ease your conscience, but they will be of little use to members of family systems who may have to live with the consequences of ineffectiveness.

7

Determining the Problem

After you have made yourself available to an individual or family, you next must get down to determining the problems that they are hoping you will help them solve. In other words, after getting acquainted, it is time to get down to specifics. The purpose of this chapter is to explicate the importance of specificity and to illustrate certain techniques counselors can employ to aid their clients in the process of problem determination.

The Virtues of Specificity

No Definition Means No Solution

When people are having problems, it is often very difficult for them to specify exactly what is bothering them. Suppose for example that you are working as an I & R worker who gets a call from an angry-sounding elder who announces, "I'm depressed." He refuses your referral to the county mental health center—"I already tried them, they don't know what they're doing"—but seems willing to talk to you. Hoping to gain more information so you can make a referral he will accept, you make an appointment to see him the following day. When he comes in, he tells you, "I'm just not happy. At my age, no one respects me anymore. Isn't there some way you can help me?"

What information about his problem do you really have? Practically none. Being "happy" has different meanings to different people. For some, being happy means working 50 hours a week repairing automobiles, while to others 50 hours a week working on cars would be pure torture. Similarly, a complaint of "no respect" tells you almost nothing. What constitutes respect? In some families, "being respectful" means calling elder parents daily, inviting them to dinner at least twice a week, and doing all their shopping and laundry. In other families, elders feel they have lost respect from their children if the children will no longer get angry and argue with them—"Now they feel sorry for us," their reasoning might be.

As difficult as it is for you as a counselor to be useful to clients who cannot specify what troubles them, it is even more of a burden to them. Take the elder above; you know he is unhappy and wanting more "respect." Since he has not thought much beyond these vague concepts, his thoughts are limited to how unhappy he is. The more he thinks about his unhappiness, the more unhappy he gets. It is a vicious circle. *As long as his problems have no specific definition, they are by definition without a solution.*

It is unreasonable to think that it is possible to feel less unhappy until you can begin to delineate what it is in your life that is bringing you misery. Unfortunately, it is not at all rare for people who are feeling unhappy to be unable initially to describe what is making them unhappy. In the example, you might ask the elder, "I wonder if you might give me some kind of notion as to what it is specifically that is making you feel so unhappy?" Caught in his vicious circle of attributing his unhappiness to being unhappy, he might well reply, "I don't really know; it just seems like everything I touch turns sour." Again, from such a vague statement, neither you nor your client has any way to see a possible solution to his unhappiness.

What Is Measurable Becomes Manageable

Another difficulty related to such lack of specificity is that until a client actually specifies a particular problem, it is hard for him to have a sense of making progress toward the solution of that problem. If we return to the case of the "unhappy" elder, it will be difficult for him to know if he is slowly becoming less unhappy if he has no way to measure his progress. Clients often get discouraged with counseling and trying to change their lives when they lack a sense that their changed behaviors are having an impact on their lives. It is your responsibility as a counselor to help your clients get down to the specifics of their problems so that not only will they see that some kind of a solution is possible (even if it is only a partial solution) but they will also have some way of measuring even small progress against the obstacles that have been blocking their paths.

The Implicit Becomes Explicit

As difficult as it is to get individuals to relate specifically to their problems, the difficulty is compounded when working with families. One of the reasons for this phenomenon is that family members often are reluctant to disclose family secrets directly for fear of offending other family members. Often the closer the family and the more positive regard they hold for each other, the more this sort of "impolite" disclosure is avoided.

For example, suppose you are working as a physician's assistant screening patients in a hypertension clinic. A man in his early 70s is brought to you by his two sisters in their late 60s. They seem overly concerned about his blood pressure; when you determine that it is within normal limits, they begin to argue with you. You tell them you appreciate their concern for their brother's health and offer to make an appointment with the three of them to provide an opportunity for a private (out of the public clinic), less rushed consultation. At the appointed time, the three siblings arrive. You notice that the brother remains silent while the two women nervously speak in vague terms about the state of their brother's health. You begin to feel that the sisters are hinting that their brother is becoming "senile," although the terms they use and their strained manner make it very difficult to be certain. It is as if the three of them, as well as you, are all "thinking it," but no one is willing to "say it."

In such a situation, the *Identified Patient (I.P.)*—in this case the brother—is very aware of what is going on, but is locked in the posture of "waiting for the ax to fall." Being in such a "protected" position is generally more stressful than actually having the true feelings emerge: what could be worse for anyone's confidence than being in a position in which everyone he loves and trusts is afraid that he is unable to cope with the truth? In the case of the three elder siblings, the brother may be becoming quite depressed, thinking, "They think I'm so fragile they can't even say what's really bothering them."

If you could get down to specifics, one sister might tell you, "I've really been worried about my brother because his checks have been bouncing. I'm concerned he might not be able to handle his own affairs." The other sister might say, "I've been concerned about my brother because he seems to be dressing peculiarly. For example, today he has on different colored stockings." At this point, the brother might then have the opportunity to respond directly to his sisters' special concerns. He might share that he is concerned about

his lapses of memory. Alternatively, he might uncover some problems in the family system that could also account for his sisters'
intense concern for his health: "Since the death of our 94-year-old
mother six months ago, Agnes and Esther have been looking for a
'cause.' I'm afraid they have found me."

For some families, it is the *process* of "walking on eggshells"
around a problem requiring frank, specific discussion that is the
problem. In such circumstances, normal communication and interaction become so stifled and lacking in spontaneity that ordinary problem-solving mechanisms within the family system which would
normally resolve such a problem cease to work effectively. In such
a situation, all the family needs from you by way of counseling is to
help them get down to the specific problem. From that point on, they
will be able to take care of themselves.

Just as ordinarily well-coping family systems get drawn into
avoiding or being indirect about certain issues that generally appear
to have great potential for emotional pain, so will you. You may ask
yourself, "We all know what the problem really is; does this problem
really need to be made explicit?" The answer is *yes!* After all, if
everyone already knows, then nothing will be lost; there will be no
surprises. If, on the other hand, the family is being drained by "walking on eggshells" and the I.P. is feeling anxious and depressed—
imagining that the family members are thinking worse things than
they actually are—then by getting to specifics you have helped the
family immeasurably.

Focusing on the Problem

Early in the Session

Assuming that you have successfully approached the family system
and made yourself available, what next? Imagine your first clients,
sitting in your office waiting for you to do something. What do you
do? Probably the best start is to find out why they think they are
there. There are several approaches you might want to take, depending on your style. For example you might say, "I wonder if each of
you could give me some idea of why you have come today."

Do not be surprised if the responses to such a question include
such statements as, "My mother told me I had to come," or "My
brother-in-law called to ask me if I would come," or "We're here to
help Dad with his problem." Information from all of these responses

can be useful in giving you your first notions of how the family system operates.

Another approach is to say, "I know I've had an opportunity to talk with some of you for a limited time about some personal topics, but I'm wondering what understanding each of you has as to why we are all meeting together now." This approach is particularly useful with a family when you may have talked with members individually, but never together.

Another approach, possibly the most direct, is simply to ask, "What seems to be the problem?" Often this is a difficult question for novice counselors to ask because they are aware of the difficulties that arise when one member of the family is singled out as having *the problem*. Consequently, they avoid using the word *problem*. Whether you use the word *problem* or not, in most of the families you will be counseling, you can expect that someone (usually an elder) will be identified as having *the problem*. Since the I.P. almost always knows who he or she is, the I.P. is rarely protected by your trying to avoid the word *problem*.

It cannot be stressed enough that, at this point in the counseling, it is important to give the family an opportunity to answer your questions without much interruption from you—even if they are interrupting each other; such interruptions give you a clue as to how they communicate with one another and how they deal with a family member who interrupts.

Early in the session or perhaps for the entire first session, as you attempt to stay in the background to listen, the family probably will try to draw you into the discussion by asking you questions. You can use these questions to gain more information. For example, suppose you are counseling a family that consists of a 38-year-old son (the I.P.), his wife, and his 65-year-old father. After describing some peculiar behaviors of his son, the father turns to you and asks, "Do you think he's acting normally?" You might want to respond by saying, "That's a good question and I am willing to answer it. Before I do, though, it would be very helpful to me if you could tell me if *you* think your son is acting normally, and if not, what he would have to do to appear more normal to you?" By responding in this way, you are validating the father's feelings that he has a right, not only to ask you a question, but to get an answer as well. However, by delaying your answer to his question, you—and his son and daughter-in-law—are gaining an opportunity to find out how the father defines "normal" behavior.

Later in the Session

As the first session progresses, or at least by early in the second session, you will want to reorient definition of *the problem* from one affecting only the life of the I.P. to one affecting the lives of each member of the family. In a way, you want the family to shift emphasis from the unproductive position, "He's got a problem," to the more productive, "My life is being affected by his behavior; therefore I have an investment in being here." Your role of guide suggests that you should slowly lead the family members to this insight as opposed to "just laying it out" as a major truth that they must accept if they are to work with you.

As a general example, to help guide a family away from the "he's got a problem" posture, you might want to say, "I'm aware that we have been spending a lot of our time today discussing your grandfather and his behavior. It occurs to me that since all of you love your grandfather and are concerned for his well-being, your lives are being affected too. I'd like to hear from each of you how your grandfather's behavior has been affecting you." When given an opportunity to discuss the difficulties in their own lives, it is not uncommon for family members to discuss issues that are really tangential to their interactions with the I.P. This sort of digression can lead to a greater sense of "connectedness" among family members. Additionally, hearing that other family members have problems is often a great relief to the I.P.

Not all family members seem willing or able to acknowledge that any problems exist beyond those of the Identified Patient. These family members will present to you with the attitude, "It's our grandfather who has *the problem*. If only our grandfather were better, then we'd be happy." These family members genuinely have trouble conceptually connecting their lives with that of the I.P. in their family. In cases like these, it is useful to shift your approach so that the connections between the lives of the I.P. and the non-I.P.'s are made more explicit. For example, suppose you work for the Area Agency on Aging. You coordinate activities with a community advisory board, composed of elders. You get a frantic call from a child of one of the members of the advisory board informing you that her mother has been threatening suicide. As the telephone conversation proceeds, the daughter seems very disturbed. You are surprised because her mother has never given you any evidence to make you suspect her of seriously contemplating suicide. Under ideal conditions, before making any referrals, you decide to gather more adequate information; you arrange for an immediate home visit.

When you arrive, you are greeted by your elder advisory board member (Mrs. Hall), her daughter (Mrs. Norwood), and her teenage grandson, Bill. Mrs. Hall is crying. After 30 minutes of preliminaries, you begin:

> **COUNSELOR:** Up till now we've been talking a lot about Mrs. Hall's depression. Since you seem to be a close family, I'm wondering how dealing with her depression has been affecting the other members of the family.

> **MRS. NORWOOD:** I don't think you understand. It's Mother that has *the problem,* not Bill or I.

> **BILL:** Mom's right. If Grandma were okay, things would be just great.

Rather than argue, you might want to take the tack:

> **COUNSELOR:** Sometimes when one member of the family, like Mrs. Hall, seems to be having a problem, other members of the family find themselves putting a lot of energy into helping her. What would happen in this family if I could wave a magic wand so that Mrs. Hall's problem went away? Where would all of that energy that both of you are putting into Mrs. Hall's problem go? . . . Such a question probably sounds strange, but sometimes when problems are solved, family members find themselves with a lot of extra energy. Sometimes that energy is used for something positive, such as getting involved together as a family, maybe by taking a trip together or talking more. But sometimes that energy gets put to use in a way that is not constructive. For example, Bill, if your grandmother's problems went away, all the energy that is now going into trying to cheer her up might go into worrying about your school grades or social life. I always like to get families to start thinking early about where that "extra" energy might go. Where do you think your energy might go, Bill?

Using this approach, family members are led to an opportunity to tell you the specific things they would like to be doing but are not doing because of *the problem* of the Identified Patient. This technique is really just another approach to help the family get down to the personal specifics of why they are meeting together with you, so that each member of the family has a specific reason for participating.

Being Persistent without Being Offensive

It is frequently very difficult to get clients down to specifics. This problem arises from several sources. First, many clients believe in the notion that if they seek some kind of professional help, the counselor will be responsible for determining the "true" nature of the problem. Many families have the expectation that you will be able to "divine" what is bothering them.

A second, and even better reason for clients to resist getting down to specifics is that for clients who are feeling overwhelmed with their difficulties, there is a strong temptation to look upon one specific problem as if it were one grain of sand on their beach of misery. In fact, clients are often accurate when they perceive that they are going to have to change many things in their lives before they are going to feel much better.

A third reason clients resist getting down to specifics is that they may have to come to you with a very small, vague problem because they are afraid to discuss the specifics of a far greater one. In this case, clients' reasoning seems to be the following: "If we pretend it isn't there, maybe it will go away."

No matter what the source of clients' resistance to getting down to specific problems, it is important that the counselor be aware that no significant progress toward problem resolution will be achieved until a problem is specified. Clients have good reasons in their own minds for resisting the exploration of specifics. Their feelings are legitimate. Equally, counselors need to guide clients to expressing the specifics if the counselors are to be useful to their clients.

The challenge to you is how to be persistent in getting down to specifics without being offensive. In this case, we label as "offensive" any behavior in the counselor that is confrontive and invalidating to the client or clients. Generally, this sort of confrontive and invalidating behavior is expressed verbally in the form: "You're not going to get anywhere until you admit what the problem is," or "Everyone in town knows the real problem; why won't you just admit it?" or "If you don't have any problems, why are you here?"

The best rule to follow when being persistent is to acknowledge that the family members know their own minds best but may have trouble expressing what they are thinking and feeling. Your responsibility, then, is to help them phrase their thoughts and feelings in a way that is sufficiently specific to be useful to them as they seek a resolution to their problem. The best way to achieve this end is to be a reflective listener.

Reflective Listening

Reflective listening refers to the process of listening to your client, integrating all levels of communication (actual words spoken, tone of voice, posture, context of the situation), then carefully paraphrasing back what you understand to be the meaning of the original message. In other words, you clarify that the message sent is the message you received. Reflective listening is not making grand psychological interpretations. Instead, it is simply a process of checking out with the client that you fully understand what is meant. Consequently, it is important to conclude each paraphrasing with a glance at your client or an explicit verbal request to affirm that you "have it accurately," or to correct you if you have it wrong.

For example, suppose you are a labor union representative handling retirement benefits. You get a call from a woman in her mid 30s inquiring about her father's pension benefits. She tells you that he is living with her family (a husband and five children ranging from 10 to 16 years old). In a genuinely concerned voice she tells you that she is afraid her "Daddy's going senile" and wants to make sure he is "taken care of right." You decide that you can commit the time necessary to be maximally useful, and make an appointment to meet with the entire family at their home to consider the situation. You discover from the union records that her father (Mr. Adis) is still employed; has passed a company physical within the last three months; and has an enviable record of positive supervisorial evaluations. His file reveals that only his lack of formal education (third grade) has held him back from promotions. The records also reveal that his wife died three years before and his daughter's address is listed as "temporary."

When you arrive at the home, the family is assembled. The children are nervous and giggling. Everyone tells you that they are there "for Grandpa."

> **COUNSELOR:** When you called me, Mrs. Bell, you seemed to have some concerns about your father's mental health. Mr. Adis, did you know your daughter was worried about you?
>
> **MR. ADIS:** I knew something was wrong, but I didn't know what.
>
> **COUNSELOR:** I wonder what exactly your father has done that gave you enough concern to call me?
>
> **MRS. BELL:** Well, I know this will sound silly, but no matter how many times I ask him, he won't stop drooling tobacco juice or zip his fly.

You asked her to be specific! Sometimes, as in this case, the clients become so specific so soon that the trees are lost for the forest. Accepting her concern for her father's mental health as legitimate, you attempt to integrate what you know from her previous conversation with you, what you know about other people's perceptions of her father (from your files), and your own impression of what it would be like for her to be sitting in her living room surrounded by children, husband, and father, and you try to understand what message she is attempting to send you.

> **COUNSELOR:** What you've said doesn't sound silly to me at all. Let me see if I have it right. Do I hear you saying that when your Dad won't zip his trousers and stop drooling tobacco juice that you feel awkward as a mother because that isn't the sort of example you'd like for the kids?
>
> **MRS. BELL:** That's sort of what I mean [followed by a minute of silence].
>
> **COUNSELOR:** Let me try again. Are you saying that when your Dad won't zip his fly or stop drooling tobacco juice after you asked him to, you're not sure if it's because he's losing his memory or just plain contrary?
>
> **MRS. BELL:** Yeah, that's closer [followed by another minute of silence].
>
> **COUNSELOR:** Well, I want to make sure I get it right. Let me try again. It sounds to me as if when you ask your Dad to do something and he won't do it, you feel pretty stuck because on the one hand he's your father—so you don't feel comfortable giving him orders—but on the other hand he's living in your house and you'd like him to live more by your rules?
>
> **MRS. BELL:** Yeah, that's it.

Now you are on a specific issue broader than "He always drools tobacco juice and never zips his fly" but more narrow than "Daddy's getting senile." The interaction aspect of *the problem* has also been explicated: a problem now exists between father and daughter rather than with the father alone.

It is important to recognize that the process of reflective listening is clarifying in nature. Obviously, each of the counselor's three statements was slightly different in meaning. Hopefully, each subsequent statement can be more clarifying than the one preceding it. In other words, there is an element of trial and error that is ultimately resolved by the client; none of the three statements is correct or incorrect: accuracy is not for you to decide, it is for the client to decide. You may find that you will have to adjust your "statements of understanding" four or five times before the individual with whom you are speaking will give you that "Ah-ha" look or tell you you are accurate. It is essential that you continue to repeat and adjust until you are virtually certain that you understand. Just because you are getting bored—and you will—that is no excuse to settle for less than certainty that your clients feel understood.

Clients will often be reluctant to keep correcting you until you are able to reflect accurately what they perceive as the problem. Usually this reluctance stems from not wanting to embarrass you. It is essential that you convey to them that you will not be embarrassed even if it takes ten sessions to clarify the problem. If you find clients who seem to agree with you just to be agreeable, you might want to encourage them by saying, "I know that this process of helping me to understand what you mean is time-consuming and tedious. But it is very important for me that I know exactly how you are feeling and what you perceive to be the problem that brought you here. Please bear with me. Make sure to tell me if I am reflecting what you mean inaccurately."

Sometimes clients will nod that what you are saying is accurate, but the looks on their faces tell you that it is not. At such points, you might want to say, "I appreciate the fact that you are agreeing with me, but from the look on your face I get the impression that I still haven't picked up all that you mean. Understanding what you mean is my responsibility, not yours, but I'm afraid I'm going to have to ask you to bear with me until I really do have it accurately."

Special Problems with Families

The more people in the room, the more opportunity exists for distracting and/or discounting interaction between family members. Consequently, being persistent is more difficult with families than with family members seen individually. For example, suppose you are a hospital dietician who has been contacted by the son and daughter-in-law of a recently discharged, elder patient. The son tells you he would like an appointment so you could "motivate" his wife to cook more palatable and healthful meals for his widowed mother, who lives in the same neighborhood and is now eating three meals a day in their home. You make the appointment, inviting his mother to attend; you are told that, "It would be better if we could come alone." Rather than risk losing the family before you have even seen them, you agree.

After some initial pleasantries you ask the couple what seems to be the problem. You observe that whatever the husband says is immediately contradicted by his wife—even before you have a chance to check out what you understood him to mean. Typically, a sample of such a conversation might be the following:

> **HUSBAND:** Since her fall, mother has been having quite a bit of difficulty with her digestion, and I just wondered if you might be able to suggest some recipes that would be easier for her than those my wife has been cooking.
>
> **COUNSELOR:** I th—
>
> **WIFE:** There's nothing the matter with my cooking. Your mother has always been a very finicky eater and nothing has changed. I don't know why we're here anyway. It seems to me a waste of time.

Rather than trying to pin down the husband to a specific complaint—thereby ignoring his wife—it makes sense to consider for a moment what is going on between them. You already know that the husband wants you to "motivate" his wife. Generally, when lay persons use the word *motivate,* they mean "manipulate." You also know that the son does not want to discuss the problem with his mother present. Usually, when one member of a middle-aged couple wants his or her partner "motivated" out of earshot of the elder, you can guess that there is an issue of anger and resentment somewhere. It is safe to assume that there is probably an intense unresolved power struggle between the couple over how to deal with the mother. When husbands and wives feel uncomfortable directly addressing issues such as control, they often express their resulting frustration indirectly through overconcern or lack of concern over the well-being of the elder.

Since you are eager not to invent a problem where there is none, but are also eager not to be so shortsighted in your counseling that you cannot see the forest (anger and resentment between spouses) for the trees (mother's diet), you might try saying something like, "It sounds to me as if the two of you have some fairly strong opinions about what's best for your mother. I'm wondering how two people who can be as assertive as both of you seem to be normally make decisions that affect your lives?"

Using such a statement, you reframe "the problem of mother's diet" to a problem of decision making. Husband and wife may not be able to agree on whether or not there is a problem over the mother's diet, but both can agree that there is a problem over deciding if there is a problem. At least now the wife will know why she has come!

If husband and wife agree that they can usually make decisions quite well, then the "problem of mother's diet" can be examined with specific reference to how this situation is somehow different from other situations that were successfully resolved. If, on the other hand, husband and wife agree that they frequently have problems making and keeping the commitments that are associated with major decisions, then the "problem of mother's diet" can be explored in greater depth as an example of the sort of problems they have. In either event, the "problem of mother's diet" has ceased to be exclusively a problem of the wife (husband's view) or of the mother and son (wife's view) and has more appropriately been defined as a problem primarily involving the interaction of husband and wife.

A slightly different approach to take with a family in which there is disagreement among the individuals as to whether or not any problem exists is to acknowledge the problem of there being no problem. For example, staying with "the problem of the diet" couple, another approach might be:

> **COUNSELOR:** It sounds as if you almost have two problems. Mr. Smith, if I'm hearing it right, you are having a problem convincing your wife that more attention needs to be given to the preparation of your mother's food; while, Mrs. Smith, it sounds as if you are having a problem convincing your husband that there is no problem on that score. I wonder what that's like for both of you?

Again, the counselor guides the couple toward discussing their disagreement rather than siding with either husband or wife on the issue of whether or not mother's diet is a problem.

Every now and then, you will encounter a family in which one or more members will pleasantly insist that "everything is perfect." In the "problem of mother's diet" family, the wife might tell you, "Really, there isn't any problem. Everything is perfect between us and in our family. We shouldn't even be taking up your time."

As she speaks her husband looks dejectedly toward the floor, shaking his head. Together with the information he has given you— that he wants you to motivate her out of earshot of his mother—this nonverbal message suggests that there is more wrong than the wife feels safe enough to admit. On the positive side, you know that the wife has some agenda. After all, she is in your office. Even if she is there only to defend herself, at least she is communicating to you that she cares enough about her husband to want to defend herself. To help her to feel safer so she can let down her defenses a bit, you might want to use her ambivalence ("things are so bad, I need to defend myself" vs. "things are bad, I need some help") to her advantage by *backing off* the position that she needs to have a problem if she is in your office. For example, you could say:

> **COUNSELOR:**   I'm surprised you are handling things so well. In most families I work with, the stress involved in opening up a household to let an elder share three meals a day would just be overwhelming. I don't know how you are doing so well. Most of the wives I've come in contact with in your situation are troubled with all sorts of uncertainties about what the future will bring; or they are terribly concerned over the inevitable hassles that occur between generations over the kitchen table; or they resent the fact that they are tied to the kitchen. How do you do it? What's your secret?

There are three advantages to backing off the position "there must be a problem" by asking clients, "How do you do so well, let me in on your secret." First, backing off communicates that you will accept them without conditions. This unconditional acceptance reassures them that they are safe to express their vulnerabilities with you. In other words, if you will accept whatever they say, then it will be safe for them to say what they are really thinking and feeling ("I've always hated my mother-in-law and now that my husband has forced me to feed her night and day, I hate her even more") without fearing confrontation or rejection from you ("What a despicable thing to say about a poor helpless woman. I'll bet the reason you refuse to stop salting the food is that you just want her gone sooner").

Second, it reassures your clients that they can save face if they need to save face. When clients know that they have enough control to save face in a new and frightening situation—such as asking for help—they are often willing to be more honest about what bothers them.

The third advantage to backing off by asking a personally tailored version of "How do you do so well? Let me in on your secret" is that you may find out that some of your clients do have secrets that work for them. Living people are by definition survivors. From time to time, you will be delighted to discover that one family member really is doing something different from the rest of the family that is resulting in a novel solution to a difficult problem. In the "problem of the diet" family, for example, the wife may tell you:

> **WIFE:**   Thank you for asking. I am rather pleased with how I've dealt with this situation. I decided that rather than do all the cooking myself,

I would work part-time so that I could hire a housekeeper for the middle part of the day. This way, I still get to have lunch with my friends, the housekeeper does the breakfast dishes—a job I have hated for 15 years—sees that Mother has a hot meal and some conversation at lunch. Working has been a godsend for me; it's just amazing what a daily three-hour break from the house does for me. I think things are much harder on my husband, who comes home from work exhausted and then feels he has to spend as much time as he can with his mother.

8

Determining Attempted Solutions

After you have drawn from each member of the family what each perceives to be the problem, you must find out what each has been trying to do about the problem. Whether with individuals or entire families, the process is the same. The information you will be seeking includes the solutions the family members have applied to their problems, whether helpful or unhelpful. This chapter will first discuss the practical reasons counselors need to know of all the attempted solutions that clients have already applied to their problems and will then go on to elaborate by example the techniques involved in obtaining this information.

The Significance of Attempted Solutions

There are several reasons why it is important to have a clear understanding of what individuals and families have been trying to do to solve their problems. First, you want to avoid discounting clients by telling them to do what they have already done; second, you may discover that the family has a solution that is working; and, third, the solution may be more of a problem to the family than "the problem" itself.

The Possibility of Discounting Clients

Without first knowing what your clients have tried, you may find yourself in the position of suggesting a course of action to them that they have already found unsuccessful. For example, suppose you are approached by an elder who tells you her husband has just been released from the hospital after an episode of alcoholic hepatitis (a liver disease caused by alcohol abuse). After telling you the problems her husband's drinking has caused over the years, she asks you what you think she should do. Rather than ask her what she has tried to do, you plunge ahead by giving her the "sound advice": "Perhaps it would be useful if your husband would attend a local meeting of Alcoholics Anonymous." Almost before you can finish the sentence she tells you, "Oh, he tried that before he was hospitalized, so you can see how well that works."

By jumping in prematurely with advice, you have at best demonstrated to your client that you don't know all the facts; at worst, that you do not care enough about the client to learn all the facts. Consequently, to avoid discounting your clients, it is imperative to find out what they have been trying to do to solve their problems. The process of hearing them out gives all clients a sense that their actions are important. It emphasizes that they have an effect on what happens. While finding out what clients have been doing with their problems may take time, usually it ultimately saves time in the counseling process.

Not Overlooking a Solution That Appears Helpful

Another reason for finding out what family members have been trying to do about a problem is that someone may have discovered a useful solution. It is not infrequent for clients to discover a potential solution to their problem and then abandon it prematurely. Their reasoning may be, "We tried such and such for a few times and it seemed to work. But then, after a while, we saw it didn't solve everything, so we stopped doing it." This type of information is valuable because it gives you a clue as to what might constitute a starting point that merely needs to be pursued. Since family members know their own family history best, they may be able to give you a clue that you might have otherwise overlooked.

"The Solution" May Be Causing "The Problem"

Still another reason for determining what the family has been trying to do about a problem is that the situation was often not serious until a well-intended family member decided "something needs to be done." A classic example of "the solution" becoming "the problem" is the case of the widowed mother living alone, coping adequately (by her standards), until her middle-aged child, for whatever reasons, decides, "Something has to be done about Mother."

The problem, unfortunately, does not reside with the mother, but instead with the unfounded belief that there is "a problem with Mother." The more the family tries to solve "the problem with Mother"—by such means as moving her into her son's home, where she doesn't want to be—the more problems are created: Mother trips over an unfamiliar piece of furniture in her son's home and breaks her hip; Mother and granddaughter begin to squabble incessantly; Mother complains, "I'd rather be dead than living here," in front of all her children.

Only by finding out what the family has been trying to do will patterns of problem perpetuation become more clear. In the classic example above, the family would be most apt to respond to Mother's threat of suicide by moving her to a different child's home. If pressed for their reasons for choosing another child's home as opposed to "allowing" her to return to her own home, family members would probably take turns explaining to the counselor that it would be out of the question to allow her to live by herself in her depressed condition—which actually is a consequence of enforced living with her children. The family is caught in the vicious circle of creating more and more problems by what they perceive as their solution-oriented behaviors.

Most of the problems you will encounter in your counseling with elders and their families will be problems created and perpetuated by inappropriate solutions. Consequently, in the privacy of your own mind, it is very likely to be the attempted solutions that will ultimately clarify the family's real difficulties for you.

Taking One Problem at a Time

The best way to find out from an individual or a family what they have been trying to do about their problems is to ask. How you ask, of course, will depend not only on the specific situation but on your individual style as well. In general, you might want to say something such as, "Now that I have some sense of how each of you perceives the problems you are facing, I am curious to know what you as a family and each of you as individuals have been doing in trying to help with these problems." Such a statement ties all of the members of the family together, yet gives permission for the expression of individuality within the framework of the family. The problem this approach raises is that if everyone cooperates at once, you will be overwhelmed with information. Therefore, it is best to narrow your discussion of attempted solutions to one problem at a time, and perhaps to request taking turns in responding.

For example, suppose that you are a coordinator for the senior citizen program at the YMCA. A 72-year-old man, Doug, served your group of community elders as a volunteer driver until he fell off a ladder while changing a lightbulb. His fall necessitated surgery to pin his hip. Doug's recovery at his daughter's home has been uneventful except that he refuses to get out of bed. His daughter, Beth, knows of your close relationship with Doug. On her weekly trip to the "Y" to pick up her younger son, Bob, age 13, for trampoline lessons, she stops by your office to ask, with some embarrassment, for "advice on how to handle Dad." She tells you that despite his physician's instructions, her father refuses to get out of bed. According to Beth, Doug has become so demanding that her husband and two teenage sons are pressuring her to "put him in a home." Because of your interest in Doug, you are willing to make time available for counseling. When you ask to meet with the whole family, Beth tells you it "would be impossible. Both my father and husband would be angry if they knew Bob and I were in your office now." From the tone of her voice, you realize she will not negotiate this issue. Since her youngest son is accompanying her, you invite him to participate in the session by asking him how he is being affected. He tells you, "Mom's always either grouchy or crying. She never has any time for me anymore. She doesn't even have time to drive me to school in the morning."

Addressing both of them, you ask, "Now that I've got some idea of what it is that you are facing, I'm wondering what you have been trying to do about it?" It would not be unusual if the mother were to say, "Which problem, the one with Dad, or with my husband and the boys?" Rather than prematurely simplifying the situation by narrowing the discussion from several problems to just the most important—thus denying yourself information about how the family is interacting over a wide variety of problematic issues—it would be best to answer, "At this point, I guess I'd prefer to hear about how each of the problems you've raised here is being dealt with by the family. For me, the easiest way to do it is just to start with one problem at a time. What do you say we start with the problem you are facing getting your dad out of bed, since that seems to be the problem that is affecting the family the most."

What Has Seemed to Be Helpful?

After narrowing down to one specific problem, it is usually quite valuable to ask the clients some variation of the question: "What has seemed to be helpful so far?" Returning to the example, the counselor might say, "It would be easiest for me if we could start with anything either of you have done yourselves—or noticed other members of the family or friends doing—that seems to be helpful getting Doug out of bed."

> **BETH:** Nothing we do ever seems to work.

> **COUNSELOR:** Let me ask you one more time in a slightly different way. I can see that you are discouraged, but maybe there is something that seemed quite unimportant at the time that would be useful to know. . . . Has your father ever gotten out of bed in front of you?

> **BETH:** Well, yes.

> **COUNSELOR:** What happened?

> **BETH:** It was such a horrible episode, I didn't even think it was worth mentioning. I was bringing him his breakfast on a tray, and Dad complained that I forgot the newspaper. I really got angry, I don't know what came over me, and I told him, "I'm not your slave, get your own goddamn newspaper. In fact, get your own goddamn breakfast, you're not getting this one"—I think that was the first time Dad ever heard me swear at him . . . Anyway, after 30 minutes of wailing and complaining he showed up at the breakfast table. I was so embarrassed I almost died.

> **COUNSELOR:** What happened after that?

> **BETH:** He went back to bed. I don't want to go through that every time.

> **COUNSELOR:** I can certainly understand that. Have you ever seen your Dad out of bed on any other occasion?

> **BETH:** Only to go to the bathroom.

> **COUNSELOR:** So he will go to the bathroom. Do you have any idea why he will go the bathroom but not the dinner table?

> **BETH:** He says it's the pain, and by all the moaning and groaning he does, I'm tempted to believe him—I will say, however, that Dad hates the bedpan. For that matter, so do I!

> **COUNSELOR:** But outside of the one episode over the newspaper and his regular use of the toilet instead of the bedpan, he's always stayed in bed?

> **BETH:** Right.

COUNSELOR: Bob, you're being awfully quiet. Have you noticed anything that you or your brother have done that has seemed to be helpful in getting your grandfather out of bed?

BOB: Yeah, well, once Jim got Granddad to come into the living room to watch a ball game when Mom and Dad weren't home. I probably shouldn't be telling you this, 'cause it'll drive Mom up the wall, but Jim told Grandad to "shove it" when he asked Jim to bring the TV set into the bedroom, so Grandad came out, without his walker, and really lit into Jim. Jim was so ashamed he almost died, I thought it was real funny but I didn't say anything about it 'til now.

Rather than point out the significance of what Bob and Beth have said, you might want to let the family have the satisfaction of discovery by saying, "I wonder what sense you make of the incident Bob just described, in the light of Beth's experience when she refused Doug room service?" If both mother and son fail to grasp the connection, nothing is lost; it is just a signal to you that they still are not able to use their own experiences to help them solve this problem. It should be emphasized at this point that family members' failure to grasp such an apparently obvious connection as that between the two similar instances in this example is more the rule than the exception. Families have reasons for doing what they are doing. You must remember: in the case in point, the only time Beth has seen her father move was when he said he was and appeared to be in great pain—which he may very well have been; having a pin put in your hip is hardly a holiday. The only time Bob has seen his grandfather get out of bed was when his older brother violated a strict family rule about politely addressing adults ("It'll drive Mom up the wall"), so that from Bob's frame of reference, his grandfather is still able to get out of bed only under extraordinary conditions. "After all," you might reason along with Bob, "didn't Grandad go back to bed and stay there ever since?"

Clearing Up Solutions That Are Not Solutions

In response to the general question, "What has seemed to be helpful?" you will frequently find family members telling you of activities that seem to you to be *specifically not helpful*. Keeping with the example, suppose the daughter volunteers to you:

BETH: One thing I've tried to do to be useful is to help Dad deal with his fear of falling. I know how afraid Dad must be of falling. So I bought him one of those "walkers." The doctor told me that he must not fall and reinjure his hip. I know how hard it is on a man who was as active as Dad to have to use that horrible thing. So to take the pressure off him,

> I told him he couldn't live at my house unless he promised to use his
> walker every time he walked. That way, no one would have to know
> that the reason he was using the walker was because he was afraid to
> fall; so his pride wouldn't be affected. I keep the walker right next to
> the bed so he can use it any time he wants.

As the daughter explains in her convoluted logic how what she
is doing is helpful, it may occur to you that her insistence that her
father use the walker which both she—having described it as "horrible"—and her father—who has refused to use it on both his trips to
the front of the house—abhor, may be a major contributing factor to
her father's remaining in bed. Equally possible, however, is that you
are overinterpreting the information you have. At least, you are
uncertain. Rather than tell Beth that she "has it all wrong," you
might want to share with her in a nonconfrontive way that you are
confused—which you are.

> **COUNSELOR:**   I'm going to need your help on this one. I was asking
> what things you'd noticed you'd done that seemed to be helpful in
> getting your dad out of bed. I'm confused, since it sounds to me as if
> insisting your dad use his walker hasn't been helpful. That is, the only
> times he's been observed to actually be out of bed since he came home
> have been without his walker. Maybe I wasn't clear in the way I asked
> you the question, or maybe there is some information I need about what
> your Dad has done or said that makes it seem as if continuing to insist
> he use his walker is getting him out of bed.

Usually, a carefully phrased statement such as the one above will
help your clients to examine the behavioral consequences of their
well-intended assumptions. Suppose that in this case Beth cannot add
any information to what she has told you and continues to believe
that keeping the walker by the bed and insisting on its use is being
helpful. At this point, even though you may disagree with her, it is
best to keep your disagreement to yourself. Your task at this time in
counseling is to gain information. The best way to fail to gain maximum information is to become argumentative. Bide your time until
you know enough about the situation to raise your difference with
the family in a way that will be useful to them.

Remember the Extended Kin Network: Considering Members Who Are Absent from the Counseling Session

Usually more than just the blood relatives of the family have been
trying to alleviate the problem. It is valuable to identify who these
helpers are, as well as to gain some information as to how effective

their advice or behavior has been. Typical helpers are neighbors, in-laws, doctors (and their office nurses), lawyers, long-term friends of the family, and ministers. Since it is impossible to get everyone involved with a problem into the same room at the same time, you will often have to ask the family members actually present for their impression of what others have been doing.

One such approach might be:

> COUNSELOR: I think I have a sense of what the two of you have been doing that has been helpful. I'm wondering what other family members might have said or done that has had a positive effect, or for that matter, any advice or help you might have received from your doctor or minister. Has anyone's help or anyone's advice been helpful in solving this problem?

What Has Not Seemed to Be Helpful?

When you are reasonably certain that you have all the information on what the family has tried that has been helpful in solving their problem, you should next turn to the attempted solutions they have been trying that have not proven helpful. Usually, when clients are asking for help, the number of unsuccessful attempts to solve their problems will greatly exceed the number of successful attempts they have made toward satisfactory problem resolution. If the successes were few, you can be sure that the failures were many. How you react to these long lists of failures will be crucial to the future of your relationship with your clients.

Giving "Failed Solutions" a Thorough and Courteous Hearing

The message a client is sending you via a long list of failed solutions is really not very complicated. The client is only trying to communicate: "Look, I am not a fool. I am not lazy. I really have given this problem my best effort. I want help, but I am embarrassed to have to ask for it. If you find a solution that is quick and obvious, I will be humiliated for not having found it myself. Please, if by chance you can be helpful, try not to damage my pride."

When counselors are sensitive to these needs of their clients, they take great pains to be patient, courteous listeners. Additionally, counselors use reflective listening techniques to probe sensitively yet thoroughly the specifics of each failed solution.

Returning to the example:

COUNSELOR: I wonder if we could turn our attention toward the attempts that have been made to get Doug out of bed that haven't been helpful; in other words, what hasn't worked? I'd like to start with you, Beth.

BETH: I've tried crying, I've tried threatening. I've tried discussing with him the importance of moving around—from a medical point of view. I've tried being nice and cheerful. I've tried being cruel. I've tried having his friends call him. I've tried having the pastor call him. I've even tried telling him I'd have to send him to the rest home if he didn't get out of bed. Nothing has worked.

COUNSELOR: You've given me quite a long list. It certainly must be frustrating to have tried so many things and still not be making any progress [long pause]. I'm going to need more information about what you've just said; I'd like to go over things one at a time. First, and correct me if I'm inaccurate, it sounds as if you've tried pleading with Doug, both with tears and without. How did he respond?

BETH: He just gave me a pained look and turned his head.

COUNSELOR: It must have been awfully difficult for you to feel driven to tears and still not able to get your father to respond to you [long pause]. It also sounds as if you have tried being "rational" with him. By rational, I mean discussing frankly the medical reasons for him to get out of bed. What sort of response did you get from him with that approach?

BETH: He told me very condescendingly that he appreciated my opinion, but that it was his body and he would do with it as he pleased. He also told me that it was easy for me to give advice, since it wasn't my hip that was in excruciating pain at the least movement.

COUNSELOR: How did you feel when he said that?

BETH: Horrible, I wanted to crawl in a hole and die.

COUNSELOR: I don't blame you. It must have been awful to feel blamed for wanting to cause your dad more pain when you were just trying to help him recover [long pause to allow for possible additional comments from Beth]. It also sounds as if you've tried having his pastor and his old friends talk with him. What's happened?

BETH: The same thing, basically. He just tells them that it's a subject he'd rather not discuss, and they are all polite enough to follow his insistence.

COUNSELOR: You also mentioned trying to cheer your dad up. How does that go?

BETH: Well, I've tried to be smiling and pleasant around him. I cook his favorite foods. We subscribe to both the morning and evening paper. I serve all his meals in his room on a clean tray with fresh flowers. Whenever he tells me he doesn't care if he ever recovers—an everyday event—I try to tell him how much he has to live for. It seems like nothing I can do pleases him or ever cheers him up.

COUNSELOR: After all that effort, you must be left with an awfully helpless feeling. How do you keep your spirits up?

BETH: I don't know sometimes . . . [she begins to cry, then stops to wipe her eyes] . . . I guess I'm just determined.

COUNSELOR: Well, I admire your determination, even if when you apply it to cheering your Dad up it doesn't get him out of bed . . . Let's change the topic a bit from being cheerful to being cruel: you mentioned you've been cruel. I know it's difficult to talk about, but could you give me some notion of what you said or did and how Doug seemed affected?

BETH: That was the time I threatened him with the rest home. It was raining and he ordered me to get him cut flowers in his vase. I finally had just had it. I told him in a really cold voice that if he didn't get out of bed within a week I was personally going to drive him to the rest home. I think I actually sounded as if I really did mean business. He looked shocked, then he started to cry. Then I started to cry. When we both stopped crying, I left his room and neither of us has brought it up again.

COUNSELOR: Is there anything else that you can think of that you have tried?

BETH: No, not that comes to mind.

COUNSELOR: What about your husband? Is there anything he has tried that hasn't seemed to be helpful?

BETH: No, my husband is a perfect gentleman in front of my father. It's only when the two of us are in the other room out of earshot from Dad that he opens up on me.

COUNSELOR: Then it sounds as if your husband is being polite to your father, but expressing his dissatisfactions with you, and this isn't working either.

BETH: I hadn't thought of it that way, but you're right.

COUNSELOR: Bob, what about you and your brother? What have you two tried to do to help your grandfather to get out of bed?

BOB: Nothing really, except to politely do what he asks us to do.

Reserving Your Comments

By this point in counseling, in the privacy of your own mind you have begun to develop a picture of what your client family is going through. From the information you have thus far gathered, you may have some initial responses that you will be tempted to share with the family. You should discipline yourself to postpone sharing your observations until you have more carefully organized your perceptions and considered the most effective way to phrase your ideas so as to maximize their usefulness to the family. By way of a *bad* example in this case, you might say to Beth, "Gracious, living the way Doug does, with everyone at his beck and call, why on earth would he ever want to get out of bed?" Equally bad, in a scolding tone you would say, "You know your father can walk when he has to! After all, he walks to the bathroom several times a day. If that weren't bad enough you've also seen him walk to the kitchen table without his walker, and now you know he's come to the living room to watch TV with the boys. You are just spoiling him." By making your observations public so soon—and so insensitively—you make it look too easy. No one wants to admit having missed the obvious, even when coming to you for advice. It is unfair to individuals and families to throw out your observations casually or officiously. No matter how obvious and simple the solution to a problem seems, you must keep your own counsel until you have had an opportunity to gain and digest as much information as possible. By way of warning, if a problem has a simple solution that the family has not discovered, there is usually a complicated reason that prevents them from doing so: no problems are simple that clients believe are complex.

Avoiding the Trap of "What Do You Suggest?"

After a family has given you a list of all the attempts they as individuals and as a group have made, they will usually lean back in their chairs with a look that is both frantic—for a solution—and smug—an understandable defensive reaction to feeling overwhelmed. One member may say to you, "Well, what do you suggest?" Restraint is the response characteristic of professionalism. Just because the family has explicitly asked for your opinion, that does not mean that you immediately give it. On one level, the family may be asking; but at another, deeper level, they are not ready to hear. That is, the individuals in the family system have just told you how they have failed. They are looking for your recognition that their problem is indeed difficult, and not to be solved quickly. In counseling there is seldom a good time to give direct advice, but if there is ever a bad time, it is precisely at the moment when the family has told you of how they have failed and then unconsciously dare you to come up with an "instant cure."

If you are inexperienced enough to accept this dare, giving advice will usually yield a "Yes, but . . ." reply from the family. For
example, suppose you impetuously take the bait and answer: "Obviously, Beth, you should do more of what you know to be successful.
Don't take any more orders from Doug. Refuse to serve him in his
room. If he insists that he is too ill to come to the dinner table, then
you insist he is too ill to get out of bed to go to the bathroom: force
him to use the bedpan! Bob, this same advice applies to you, your
brother, and your father. And for goodness sake, Beth, stop infantilizing him by insisting he use his walker. I wouldn't get out of bed either
if you made me use one of those things. He already has a cane he
knows how to use. Let him use it."

With such an undisciplined, even if invited, statement, you could
predictably expect Beth's reply to be, "Yes, but I couldn't stand to
be so disrespectful to my father. I would feel so guilty by disobeying
him and I just couldn't live with myself knowing how much pain I
was putting him through. To get rid of the walker would be to go
against doctor's orders. What if Dad fell and reinjured his hip in my
home? The doctor has told me that if he reinjures himself he could
be bound to a wheelchair for life. You, of all people, a person who
works with elders, should know of the dangers of falling." After
inviting and getting such a reply you are really stuck. If you were to
argue you would lose even more credibility and give the unalterable
impression that you do not really understand the situation. If you
were to agree, you would be giving your stamp of approval to a
logical system that makes any kind of action to help Doug almost
impossible. Had you disciplined yourself, you would not have offered
your advice or opinion so prematurely in the counseling relationship.

If you should not blurt out all you are thinking, how do you
answer families or insistent individuals who challenge you to come
up with instant solutions after reading you their laundry lists of unsuccessful behaviors? A positive step by the counselor, which many
individuals and families find helpful, would be some personal variation of "I'm not at all sure what you can do to solve your problem at
this point, but I can think of one thing to do that will make sure you'll
never solve the problem [long pause to give the family a chance to
answer; if not]: Keep doing what you have seen doesn't work."

Such a reply at this stage of counseling takes you off the hook of
being "all knowing" and places the responsibility of problem-solving
back where it belongs, with the individual or family. This statement
is particularly useful when a family or its members seem devoted to
repeating almost compulsively behaviors that they "know" will not
solve the problem. In the example:

BETH: Well, now that you know what we've done, what do you suggest?

COUNSELOR: The picture you have drawn for me of the problem that you and your family are facing is certainly complicated. I really don't have any quick or easy answers that would be helpful to you in solving the problem right now. I'm afraid I'm going to need considerably more time and information. Even though I can't tell you what to do to make your problem disappear, I can think of a few things you could do to make sure the problem will *never* disappear. I wonder if either you or Bob might know what those things are?

If Beth and Bob were alert and listening to what you were saying, they will probably arrive at the answer, "Keep doing what we know doesn't work." If after a few seconds Beth and Bob were still silent, you might say: "I don't know what to do yet to change the situation, but I do know what you can do to make sure it never changes: just keep doing what you know doesn't work."

Often such a casual remark from a counselor brings considerable relief to an individual or family. It acknowledges that there is no simple answer to their problem—so the clients are still good people even though they have not been able to solve their problem on their own—and it gives family members permission to stop trying too hard: why keep doing what you "know" does not work? It achieves both of these ends without being confrontive or acting like a sarcastic know-it-all.

Best of all, such a statement allows you, as counselor, to stay clear of the ineffective role of "advice giver," while demonstrating to the family that you do understand their situation and are not trying to make light of it.

9

Determining Goals

When family and individual problems along with attempted solutions have been specified, counselor and clients are ready to identify goals of counseling. The purpose of this chapter is to discuss why establishing goals is important as well as to explore by example how such goal determination takes place.

The Significance of Determining Goals

Goal determination is important for the same reasons that problem determination is important. Specific goals give families and individuals a specific and concrete (as opposed to abstract) yardstick against which to measure their progress. Establishing goals also indicates that counseling is not an eternal process. It points out that when the goals set are reached, the time has arrived to reassess the need for additional counseling.

The Concrete Yardstick

Many families and individuals fail to resolve problematic situations because they try to solve all of their problems at one time. They drain their available energy by trying to do too much. While they may be making small amounts of progress on a wide variety of problems, overall it seems as if they are not really going anywhere. By establishing one specific, realistic goal, family members can focus their energies so that progress becomes palpable. This sense of progress often serves to reverse the vicious circle of failure.

For other families, the problems they face seem to have no possibility of positive outcome. An example of such a situation might be a family in which an elder requires an institutional placement. While members of these families may be accurate in assessing their situation as not having a happy outcome, it may be that the negative impact of the problem can be minimized. Even though it is a bad situation, it may be possible at least to make the best of it. For these families, having a tangible goal provides the opportunity to see that as bad as things are, they can prevent them from becoming worse.

Similarly, some problems may never be solved entirely, but partial progress may be possible. Consider, for example, the elder who is feeling "lonely." It is very unlikely, given the "human condition" so fondly described by existential philosophers, that concerns about loneliness will ever have a complete resolution. On the other hand, an elder might have a sense of making progress against the problem of loneliness if the elder sets a meeting with other people at least three times a week as a specific goal of counseling. Without such a specific goal serving as a concrete yardstick of progress, dealing with loneliness as a counseling issue would be far more difficult.

Goals Identify Limits to Counseling

When counselors set up specific goals with their clients, they are establishing an informal contract to limit the period of counseling to meet these goals. In a sense, establishing goals serves to clarify for both counselors and clients the reasons counseling is taking place. This process serves to keep clients and counselors from unnecessarily floundering about waiting for the clients eventually to report that they have finally achieved "happiness." In other words, goal setting defines the limits of how useful counseling can be expected to be. Without these limits, clients establish false expectations of what they can expect from counseling, while counselors endlessly try to satisfy seemingly insatiable clients.

Specifying Realistic Goals

By the time you get down to determining goals with your clients, you will already have given them the opportunity to specify their particular problems and attempted solutions.

Surprisingly, the goals you may be establishing with families will not always be directly applicable to the presenting problems. The reason for this phenomenon is rather simple: your responsibility is to help your clients establish realistic goals. By realistic, we mean achievable. The problems that clients present are frequently so complex as to be insoluble. Consequently, the goals arrived at by counselor and clients may well appear to be at some distance from the presenting problem, yet still are relevant to the situation.

Counselors work to establish achievable goals with their clients by shifting from the position of "What will need to change in your life so that all of your problems will be solved?" to the more realistic question, "What is the smallest amount of change that could occur in your life that would give you a sense of progress in solving a significant problem?"

What Is the Smallest Amount of Change . . .?

Many of the skills of persistence useful in narrowing down a problem also pertain to narrowing down a goal. An example is useful to illustrate how this process takes place.

Suppose you are a Congressional Aide assigned to work with problems of elders in a Representative's home district office. A woman in her late 60s, Mrs. Lane, calls to express her concern over a matter of federal funding of a school program for her "hyperactive" grandchild. She tells you that the school refuses to help her grandson, Jack, until federal money for educationally handicapped children is made available specifically for her grandson. Hoping to iron out matters as quickly as possible, you tell Mrs. Lane that you will check the matter out for her with the school authorities. You call Jack's school counselor only to be told the following:

SCHOOL COUNSELOR: There's nothing the matter with that 8-year-old kid that a good spanking wouldn't cure. He just craves limits. But our classes have over 33 third-graders in them and our teachers only set limits by putting kids out in the hall. Jack is making passing grades in all subjects, so, frankly, he doesn't qualify for any special programs. The real problem is the grandmother. I talked with her and she is so guilty about having been strict with her daughter that she can't bring herself to exert any kind of control over her grandson—oh, I should mention, her daughter and son-in-law were killed in an automobile accident three years ago; that's how she got custody of the little boy. I suggested she get counseling to work things out on her own about her guilt trip with her daughter, but she got really angry and insisted the little boy had *the problem*, not her. Good luck, you'll need it.

You have made yourself available to both the school and the grandmother and discovered that for the school, the problem is the grandmother, while for the grandmother, the problem is the school.

In a sense, this system is like a family system in which every member is saying, "I don't have the problem, it's the rest of them."

At this point you realize that Mrs. Lane's situation is quite complex. You can deal with it adequately yourself only if you are willing to become more deeply involved and your own work situation allows this. Assuming this is so, you invite Mrs. Lane to come to your office and she accepts. You use your time together to help her specify her problems away from the unproductive "the school is giving me the runaround" to some of the particular behaviors on the part of her grandson that she is finding especially troublesome. Such behaviors on his part include being disruptive in school, refusing to go to bed when asked, and fighting with his friends. Further, you draw out how her grandson's behaviors are affecting her: how her sleeping and eating have been affected, how powerless she feels not being able to get the support she would like from the school system, and the fact that backaches and headaches have become a regular part of her life since her grandson has been so difficult for her to control.

After you have a more specific view of her problem, you explore her attempted solutions. She cooperates by telling you the following:

> **MRS. LANE:** I try so hard to explain to him why he has to mind me and his teachers, but he just can't seem to understand. He tells me he forgets the rules. I've tried so hard to be patient. I've tried to get him tutors. I have tried to get him more involved with his little friends—I drive him over to their houses whenever he wants to go. I have tried everything. It almost seems like the only thing that works is when I grab him and scream right into his face, but then I'm so disgusted with myself for having done such a terrible thing that I try to be more patient next time he begins to act up—and then all he does is takes advantage of my patience. . . . I'm so confused because I never had this kind of problem with his mother, but then I was so strict with her I don't think she ever forgave me.

Piece by piece you go over what she has told you, carefully taking time to give her an opportunity to talk about raising her daughter. As you listen to her talk about her "failures" in raising her daughter, it seems to you that she did a fine job: drawing limits where they needed to be drawn and helping the daughter to leave home to get on with her own life at the right moment. Rather than futilely try to reassure her that she was not "too strict" with her daughter, you simply and compassionately acknowledge that you can understand how she must feel, believing as she does, that she was too strict.

Because this client is so beset with problems—from grieving over her daughter to losing sleep over her grandson's behavior—it is essential that goals be limited so that at least some successful progress can be made to give her a sense of hope:

COUNSELOR: We've talked about a lot of problems, but I wonder now if it wouldn't be most useful to pick a single goal to work toward in order to make some progress in solving of one of the problems you have described. For me, it is usually easiest if we pick a relatively small goal.

MRS. LANE: Well, I'd like the school to do something more with my grandson than just put him in the hallway when he gets into trouble with the other kids.

COUNSELOR: That's certainly a worthwhile goal, but since it seems to involve so many people—the school board, the principal, the teacher, and Jack himself—I wonder if that goal isn't too large to start with? Could you pick a little smaller goal?

MRS. LANE: Well, what about having my grandson learn to listen better around the house?

COUNSELOR: That's a little easier, but I wonder if I could get you to narrow it down even more to something specific that he does that indicates to you he isn't listening.

MRS. LANE: All right, I'd like him to go to bed when I ask him to.

At this point, you have helped your client to narrow down the troublesome, abstract issues she faces to a specific change in behavior against which she can measure her progress. Even though her goal involves a specific change in measurable behavior, it still may be impossible for her to achieve success by meeting her goal. Usually, even the client's most simple goal should be *reduced in magnitude* to maximize the chances for success. In the example, to achieve such a reduction in magnitude the counselor would follow a similar course:

COUNSELOR Getting to bed when asked sounds like a reasonable place to start. I am wondering what would be the smallest amount of change that could occur around bedtime between you and Jack that would give you a sense of progress toward getting him to follow your directions about going to bed?

MRS. LANE: If he went to bed every night when I asked him to.

COUNSELOR: If I were you, I'd feel the same way, but, to be honest, that's a lot of change to start out with. I'm wondering if you would still be able to have a sense of some progress if Jack would go to bed when asked, say, two times a week?

MRS. LANE: Yes, anything would be better than what we have now!

Restraining Your Ambition

Notice how the scope of the discussion between client and counselor has narrowed, from "My grandson is out of control and I can't get the school to help" in the initial telephone contact, to establishing a realistic goal involving the specific behavioral change of getting the grandson in bed at Mrs. Lane's request twice a week. This sort of specificity is essential for success, since it would be almost impossible for client and counselor to take on a problem as broad as "my grandson is out of control" without being set up for failure. Even if you, as the counselor, actually knew all the things to do to bring the grandson into instant "control," it would be impossible for you to communicate these clearly or for your client to remember to carry out all of your instructions.

This point is important to note, since counselors frequently become overambitious in helping their clients select goals. This is particularly likely to occur when counselors believe they have the solutions, even if complex, to their clients' problems. Even when a counselor is "right" about a potential solution and when clients are bright and motivated, overambition in relation to goal setting can be disastrous, because clients inevitably are unable to comprehend and effectively apply large amounts of counselor-supplied information across a broad variety of behavioral situations—for example, being in control of a child's behavior all the time. When clients are unable to follow their counselor's instructions toward achieving sweeping goals, the clients experience a sense of incompetence and despair. As a rule, it is far better for a counselor to underestimate the clients' abilities to achieve goals than to overestimate them.

Recalling Attempted Solutions:
A Precision Reprise

For the same reasons that it is important to establish early in the counseling sessions what clients have been trying to do about their problems, it is essential to inquire what attempts have been made to accomplish the specific goal on which the clients have decided to focus their initial attention. Since the goal is frequently related to one of the previously considered problems, this information gathering usually goes more quickly than earlier in the session. It should be emphasized, however, that information gathered at this point should be sufficiently thorough.

> **COUNSELOR:** Since we have agreed on a goal, I'm going to need some specific information as to what you have been trying with your grandson to get him to go to bed when you ask him to. Has anything worked?

> **MRS. LANE:** About the only thing that even seems to resemble working is exhaustion. When I let him watch TV until he falls asleep, I can carry him upstairs and put him to bed without him ever waking up. Otherwise, it's just a constant battle. I ask him to get ready for bed and he dawdles. It takes forever for him to get into his pajamas, to get him to the bathroom, to brush his teeth, and go to bed. If I do, by some miracle, get him into bed, he asks for water, cocoa, the light to be turned on, and the light to be turned off. This will go on for two or three hours at a time until finally he collapses from exhaustion.

> **COUNSELOR:** I'm confused. It sounds as if when you give in to him he eventually falls asleep on his own. I was thinking more along the lines of what you do that seems to make him go to bed when you tell him to.

> **MRS. LANE:** In that case, nothing.

> **COUNSELOR:** Are you sure? Don't bribes work—you know, things like "I'll take you to the show tomorrow if you go to bed right now," or "I'll buy you some roller skates if you go to bed when I ask you to for a week"—that sort of thing?

> **MRS. LANE:** No. I've tried, but he already gets everything he wants anyway. I must confess, he's a bit spoiled.

> **COUNSELOR:** Well, then would you tell me about the things you have tried to get him to go to bed when you ask him to that do not work? It sounds as if for starters, bribes and "spoiling" haven't worked.

> **MRS. LANE:** True. Explaining doesn't work either, even though all I do is explain to him over and over: I ask him to go to bed; he answers "Why?" I tell him it's important that he get a good night's rest so he'll be bright and alert at school. Then he tells me he hates school and we get off on that for a while—eventually, I tell him, "You have to go to bed now," and he'll start to cry and tell me I'm "mean." Then I explain to him that I'm not "mean" but I'm just telling him to go to bed for his own good. Then he tells me he wishes his mother were alive because he's sure she wouldn't treat him so "mean." When he says that, it just tears me up inside and I start to cry.

> **COUNSELOR:** That must be terribly painful for you. What goes through your mind when he brings up your daughter?

At this point the counselor takes several minutes to listen to Mrs. Lane talk about the difficulty of losing her daughter; how lonely and demoralized she has been trying to raise her grandson the way she believes her daughter would have wanted. When she seems finished and ready to return to the topic of her grandson's bedtime, the counselor resumes:

COUNSELOR: I know this will be a difficult question for you, but how did you and your husband used to get your daughter to go to bed when you asked her?

MRS. LANE: We never asked her, we told her. Every now and then she'd resist, but then my husband and I would both just grab an arm and up the stairs to bed the three of us would go. Even when she went right up, I'll never forget the dirty looks she used to give us. My husband and I used to laugh about it after she had gone to bed. But now, when I think of how joyous her childhood might have been—she was, after all, a very, very good little girl—I am just sick for how strict we were with her.

COUNSELOR: It sounds a bit as if you are getting the same kind of looks from your grandson.

MRS. LANE: Yes, that's the horrible part. It seems as if he is even angrier with me than his mother was. It looks like I can't do it right no matter what I do.

COUNSELOR: It must be a very painful feeling, wanting a loving, mutually supportive relationship with your grandson and not being able to have it, and yet knowing that to bring his behavior under control you will probably make him even angrier at you.

MRS. LANE: It certainly is [a long pause].

COUNSELOR: Let me ask a little more about what hasn't worked. I think you had just told me that explaining doesn't seem to work.

MRS. LANE: No, not at all. I just can't seem to make him understand why it's important for him to go to bed.

COUNSELOR: Have you tried spanking?

MRS. LANE: No, I have never spanked this child, although sometimes I am beginning to wonder if that's not what he really needs. But then, when I start thinking about that, I feel guilty and try to be more patient.

COUNSELOR: Does he have a set bedtime?

MRS. LANE: Yes, I tell him to be in bed by eight o'clock, but that's just when the battle begins. If I remind him what time it is, he gets mad at me and tells me he knows how to tell time. If I wait for eight o'clock to come to remind him, he has always "forgotten" to look.

COUNSELOR: Well, from what you have told me, I certainly can understand why you have been having insomnia, headaches, and back-aches!

Summarizing the Family Situation: Putting Everyone into the Picture

After working on the specific attempted solutions to the specific problem, counselors and family members alike are often feeling disjointed. They have moved so far into specifics that they need an opportunity to review how the specifics are associated with a more global picture. Consequently, it is often valuable for the counselor to take the opportunity at the end of the goal-determination session to summarize the family situation.

This summary should stress how the family and the counselor first made contact, how the family members' behaviors are affecting one another, and what the family members hope to gain from reaching the goal they have agreed upon. The counselor should attempt to communicate, at all levels, empathic understanding and unconditional positive regard for all members of the family. In other words, the counselor reiterates the message: "Everyone is important, everyone counts." In family systems in which only one member is present for counseling, such as in the present example, it remains equally important to stress the interactional aspect of the family system situation.

COUNSELOR: At this point, I'd like to take a few minutes to summarize, mostly for my own benefit, where we seem to be. If something I say doesn't strike you as ringing true, I want you to interrupt me and set me straight.

As I hear it, the problems that you have been having with your grandson include his behavior at home, while playing with his friends, and at school. What brought you in to see me in the first place was your frustration with the school district, which refuses to acknowledge that your grandson has any special problems beyond those that call for him to be put out in the hall as punishment. You have the feeling that the school district, rather than cooperating with you, is blaming you for your grandson's adjustment problems and, if anything, believes that you, not he, should get help. On the other hand, since the school has to resort to putting him out in the hall and sending home notes to you to do something, it seems to you that the school should admit they have a problem and do something about it.

What both the school and you seem to agree on is that there are some problems in your grandson's social adjustment. These problems are clearest to you in your grandson's failure to follow through on your requests and clearest to the school in his disruptive behavior. You have noticed signs of this disruptiveness when he gets into fights and squabbles with his friends.

Looking into the situation from both a quasi-legal and personal point of view, it seems that your grandson's progress and abilities in school are less than what both you and the school would like, yet not bad enough to qualify him for any kind of special attention, beyond being put out in the hall. In a sense, you and your grandson fall between the cracks of the services the school and the federal government provide.

Part of your dilemma, as I see it, is that you can either ignore the situation until your grandson's behavior gets worse, or you can try to do something about it. The fact that you have come to this office tells me that you have decided to do something, but your exact course remains unclear. Based on what you have told me, however, there seem to be some paths you would like to rule out.

One path you no longer wish to follow has to do with the way you have been dealing with your grandson in the past. That is, by continuing to do what you have been doing with him, your sleep will continue to be disrupted and you will get backaches and headaches. In a sense, you are burning out his most valuable resource: you.

Another path you are feeling very hesitant to follow is the path you once used to raise your daughter. While on the one hand you recognize that by being a firm disciplinarian you were able to help your daughter to avoid any severe problems of social adjustment in school or with her peers, the price you paid was a certain amount of antagonism between the two of you. While your husband was alive, that antagonism was easier to deal with because you had your husband for support. With the death of your husband, taking on that antagonism with a new child seems almost overwhelming. In addition, the premature death of your daughter has left you with the feeling that the distance that evolves between a strict parent and a child can never be resolved or reduced as the child comes into adulthood.

Somewhere in the middle, then, you are searching for how you can draw limits for your grandson that will serve to ease his social adjustment in school and with his peers but will not leave him emotionally estranged from you. As an initial goal you have decided to change a small bit of how the two of you interact over his bedtime.

In some ways, working on changing his behavior at bedtime represents an experiment to determine different ways to control his behavior without overcontrolling. You have given me a list of different specifics that you have tried to get him into bed on time, most of which have ended up with both of you feeling misunderstood and unappreciated.

I wonder at this point if what I've just said seems to fit with you?

Examining this summary, it is important to review the key element—sending the message: "Everyone is important, everyone counts." It was important to include in this summary the existence in the system of the school, the grandson, the grandmother, the deceased daughter, and the deceased husband. Even though only the grandmother was physically present, the rest of the family system needed to be acknowledged. This particular example points up that working with families does not always mean that the entire family is present, alive, or even composed of single persons—schools can be family system members, too.

At the conclusion of your summary, you can again expect your clients to press you for suggestions or directions for obtaining the goal you have just worked so long and diligently to establish. *Caution* and *restraint* remain the keywords. Do not set up your families for failure by blurting out the first suggestion that comes to mind. Instead, take some time for yourself to digest the information obtained. This digestion process is the subject of the next chapter.

10

Comprehending the Family System

By the time you have helped your clients to set a realistic goal, you have collected an enormous amount of information. Most of this information is in the form of raw data. Consequently, it is important to take some time out from the counseling session to give yourself the opportunity to digest this information in a meaningful way. The purpose of this chapter is to provide you with a framework with which to organize the information you have gathered.

Taking Time Out from the Counseling Setting

Why Time Alone Is Useful

It is important to take time away from your clients to contemplate what you have learned in the privacy of your own mind. There are several reasons why physically leaving the counseling scene is useful. First, the very act of leaving the room takes time, and time in and of itself is often useful in the process of integration of new material for problem solving. Second, taking a significant amount of time to think about the problem communicates to your clients that the issues raised are not seen by you as simple or easy but instead worthy of thoughtful professional consideration. Third and most important, it is very difficult for most people to think as clearly as they might ordinarily think when under the pressure of a counseling session. This third reason, performance anxiety, is worth further discussion.

The existence of performance anxiety can be a problem for everyone, affecting the quality of behavior in such diverse settings as the putting green and the bedroom. The counseling session is no different. While the family is physically present in the room, counselors often feel the pressure to perform. It is clear from studies conducted over a wide variety of tasks that performance anxiety reduces the ability to be flexible, in thought or action. In counseling, performance anxiety produces a tendency in the counselor to adhere to only one way of looking at a problem. Put another way: when working under pressure, your thoughts may be limited to only your first thoughts.

Making Room for Your Clients and Yourself

There are several alternative methods for excusing yourself from a family or individual to gain some time to think over the situation. The simplest is to end the session after an initial goal has been determined. This is a particularly attractive course of action if the amount of time set aside for the meeting has almost expired. To conclude the session, you might take the approach:

> **COUNSELOR:** I see we're almost out of time—that suits me, because I am going to need more time to think about all the information I have gained today. Between now and our next meeting, I would appreciate it if each of you would not change anything just yet. I'd like to give you a little time to let things settle and to provide an opportunity for each of you to observe rather than try to change the situation that you're in. I find that for almost everyone it is difficult to really examine your situation when you are trying to change it.

Such a statement not only relieves you of your performance anxiety but also relieves the clients of any obligation to act on the information they have gained thus far in the counseling. In a sense, you are giving the family members the message that it is all right with you that the problem not be solved between now and your next meeting. Such a message takes the pressure off the family to "do something now" so that they can muster their energies for whatever useful suggestions you might be able to offer at your next meeting.

When there are 30 or 40 minutes left to run in an appointment, or when some family members are present who will not be present at the next meeting, you may simply need to excuse yourself from the room for a few minutes:

COUNSELOR: At this point I really feel I have a lot of information, but I must confess I need a bit of time by myself to try to put all the pieces together. I wonder if I might call recess in today's meeting, for say 15 minutes, to give me some time to consider what all of you have told me.

After gaining agreement, it is always thoughtful to remember that clients might want to move around in your absence, so that directions as to where they might find a coffee machine or restroom are usually welcome.

First Things First: Does the Family Still Need Counseling?

Once you are alone, or discussing the case with a colleague, the first question that you need to ask is, "Does this family (or individual) need more counseling?" You have already come a long way in the counseling process. Consider that you have acknowledged each person as being a unique human being; you have offered understanding to their problems; and you have provided the family members with an opportunity to share with you and one another their efforts to solve their problems. Additionally, you have helped the family to narrow down their problems from broad, vague, abstract complaints to one specific realistic behavioral goal. There is a good question to consider in each session, which first arises at this point: is any more required?

To answer this question fairly, you must be able to confront squarely your need to be needed: can you let go? No individual or family system is without flaws. Your obligation as counselor is not to stay involved with all your clients until everyone is happy all of the time. The assessment you really must make is whether you have served this family usefully in a way they wanted to be served. If the answer is "Yes," then the issue is really how to say good-bye. This decision is lonely for a counselor, since the family cannot always help. If you have been useful to the family, they may want even more contact with you: the message they might send would be, "If you could help us so much in just two visits, think of what you could do in four!" If your need to be needed is without limits, you will find yourself working with such families beyond the limits of your responsibilities and, frequently, beyond the limits of your expertise.

For example, suppose you are a social worker providing services at a "drop-in center" for elders. You are approached by a frail woman in her late 60s who seeks your advice on how to ensure care for her mother in the event something should happen to her (your client). The client's mother is 90 years old, living independently. You also discover that the client's son and daughter-in-law live within an hour's drive. When you ask your client how they feel about her mother's care, your client begins to weep. After a few minutes of silence, she tells you what is really on her mind: her physician has recommended surgery for her deteriorating arthritic hip. She has been feeling as if she would be a burden to both her mother and her son, based on her interpretation of their responses when she brought up the subject "jokingly" to each. You ask and receive permission to arrange for a family meeting to clarify matters.

You invite your client's mother, son, and daughter-in-law to meet with you and your client in your office the next day. As you listen reflectively and slow down the pace of conversation so that each member of the family has an opportunity to speak, the situation begins to resolve itself as the web of misunderstandings unravels. By the end of the hour, the topic of "mother's care" has given way to a specific discussion of your client's concern in asking her son and daughter-in-law for support during her period of convalescence after the surgery. When the need for support is spelled out, the son and daughter-in-law's response is positive; details are worked out. While the issue of the convalescence is resolved, two new family problems surface in the conversation: first, the grandson is doing poorly in his school; and second, the son and daughter-in-law seem unhappy, but committed, in their marriage.

Does the family need more counseling? In this case, you recognized that your client's initial crying was a request for more than just "help for Mother"; you convened the family and structured the meeting so that real agendas could be addressed; and family members showed willingness to clear up misunderstandings and provide each other with support. The grandson's school problems and the couple's general dissatisfaction with life are really outside of your contract with the family; they were not really identified by the family as issues to be worked on. Moreover, it is always possible that resolution of one problem will have some positive spin-off in dealing with others. In this case, then, you have met your responsibility, so the only thing left is to give the family credit for their progress and terminate counseling. Giving credit and terminating counseling will be explored in a later chapter.

Other Questions You Need to Consider

To begin to comprehend a family system, there are several questions you might want to ask yourself about what you already know. These questions are not necessarily independent of one another, but they do tap in slightly different ways the nature of any family system with which you are working. In a sense, these questions serve as hypothesis builders in that they bring significant points about the family system into explicit focus, as well as help you to order what you already have learned.

What Is the Extent of the Family System?

Put most simply, this question really asks: Who is involved in this family system? How big is it? Who are the members? For example, a family system may include only the nuclear family, the extended family, all blood relatives, no blood relatives, teachers, social workers, ministers, old friends, and neighbors. From the counselor's point of view, it is useful to know the extent of the family system and thereby who and what are involved with the problems being presented.

The most frequent candidates to be overlooked in a family system by the counselor are "non-blood-related" kin. For example, the role of the family physician can be extremely important, particularly when there is the value-laden issue of the "competence" of a family elder. The opinion of a family physician may carry weight with family members, even when by virtue of the nature of the problem the physician's opinion is really personal, not medical. Another type of non-blood kin with extraordinary influence on the family system includes psychologists, psychiatrists, or clinical social workers who may have one of your clients in individual therapy. While individual therapy may, for example, make your client more assertive toward other family members (frequently their parents or children), such assertiveness can also appear as misdirected hostility. This, especially early in therapy, can be more of a hindrance to the family than a help.

As another group of non-blood kin, the importance of longstanding neighbors should be emphasized. Imagine the influence wielded by a "best friend" neighbor when the neighbor offers the advice, usually inappropriate, "For God's sake, whatever you do, don't make the same mistake I did with my folks" (or son or daughter). The existence of this "advice" may never be volunteered by the client.

It is difficult for anyone to admit the loyalty bind: "I'm afraid to insult my best friend by not taking his advice, that's why I am doing what he says instead of what you—and I—want."

The "impersonal" representatives of institutions can also take on the role of being significant non-blood family system members, as was discussed in the previous chapter.

The difficulty with these non-blood family system members is that they are no more without personal flaws and difficulties than obvious, blood-related family members. Everyone has some personal bias in his point of view; what makes these non-blood kin so difficult to deal with is that their personal interests often fail to surface. Therefore, their value judgments are often thought of by at least one family member as being authoritative and thus become internalized into his or her sense of being.

Among blood-related kin, out-of-town relatives are often overlooked as family members. These individuals often exert as much influence through the telephone as local relatives do. As of this writing, before eight o'clock in the morning a three-minute call from coast to coast costs only 53 cents: for $16.00 a month, a "distant relative" can have a daily chat which adds up to an hour and a half monthly. An hour and a half can be a lot of chatting, particularly when pressure is being applied to conform to a norm of behavior not generally known (or accepted) by the rest of the family. Whenever the existence of an out-of-town member of the original nuclear family is known, the counselor should determine, not only how frequently contact is made with local family members, but also how the out-of-town relative participates in family decision making.

Once you realize the full extent of the social system with which you are dealing, you will probably become discouraged. After all, how can you possibly hope to introduce the slightest amount of useful order into such a chaotic and essentially unmanageable social system? The answer is that you can not be expected to control the situation. You might, however, be useful to the family by helping them to recognize the extent of their familial-social ties so that their loyalties and actions will cease to be reflexive and begin to be consciously considered.

Where Is the Counselor in the Family System?

As mentioned in previous chapters, counselors often find themselves becoming tied in as members of the family system. Consequently, it is important to consider how family system members are viewing your role. For example, you may be working with a family in which there has always been a very strong father. The father has died recently and the family members are seeking some kind of solution for what they perceive to be the problems of their widowed mother. If the family is placing you in the authoritative position of replacing Father, then the way you interact with the family will differ considerably from the way you would were you seen by the family as being a "little brother" butting in where he does not belong.

Alliances. Frequently you will find family members attempting to establish an alliance with you. For example, suppose you are working with a family and you are aware that no matter what you say, the oldest daughter always agrees with you. You might want to wonder why. Is she feeling so overwhelmed that she will cling to anything you say? Is she trying to convince other members to place their future in your hands? Is she allying herself with you so that she will be more influential with other family members when you are not present—becoming in a sense your representative to the family? All of these possibilities should be considered if you sense one or more members of the family trying to ally themselves with you.

If you are working as a consultant/counselor in an institutional setting, you may find that staff members will view you as an "ally" if disputes arise between families of patients and staff. You yourself may feel drawn to form an alliance with staff members. Failure to recognize this situation will make it more likely that you will find yourself in the disadvantageous position of looking for "victims" and "perpetrators," and losing sight of the interactional aspect of the problem.

Adversaries. Just as some members of a family system may want to ally themselves with you, others may feel the need to become your adversary. Such family members will argue or disagree with anything you say, even when you are trying assiduously to avoid being argumentative. You should consider why these clients need to take such a position with you. Are they worried that you will usurp their power in the family? Are they worried about what might be the consequences of change in the family—that is, life might get better for some other members but worse for them? Have you done something to put them off? Are you the only person in the family with whom they relate in an adversary fashion?

Thinking about your position in the family system also provides a good opportunity to consider if you are "trying too hard." How much pressure do you feel to "cure" the family? Are you differentially angry or sympathetic to one family member or another? Are you taking sides? If family members are getting you angry or apathetic, you might want to consider how they are doing it. Are they using the same techniques on other members of the family system?

What Are the Family Rules?

Family rules are attitudes and values that families unconsciously adopt to define how family members should interact with one another. Family rules can cover anything from "It's all right to run around naked at home" to "We never explicitly disagree with one another." Family rules are handed down from generation to generation, with each new generation making functional, pragmatic modifications.

Most of us know, without being told, about rules. Probably everyone who reads this book can remember as a child going to a playmate's home to discover that somehow, that family was different from your own. Even though there was not any formal rulebook, things were different. Perhaps your playmate's family did not seem interested in hearing what the children had to say. Or perhaps there was more laughter at the dinner table. In any event, the rules in your playmate's home regarding how family members were expected to interact with one another were probably slightly different from your own.

Blending families and their rules.   When people from different families join to form a new family—usually through marriage—problems occur. In a new marriage, both spouses bring their rules from their own families of origin. When these two sets of family rules are in conflict, they must be negotiated and compromised. Usually this negotiation and compromise takes place implicitly rather than explicitly. In many ways, the high divorce rate among young marrieds can be considered a testimonial to the difficulty of learning to compromise long-held attitudes and values about how family members "should" interact with one another.

In families with elders, obvious complications in making compromises on family rules can occur when elders move in with their children. Longstanding compromises between husband and wife can be upset by the "new" (elder) family member. The same problem can arise through changing patterns of visitation or social support associated with aging.

For example, suppose you are counseling a middle-aged man who complains to you about his mother-in-law. It seems that since her husband's recent death, the mother-in-law comes over to your client's house daily to visit. The visit promptly becomes a "yelling match" with his wife. After meeting with the three of them, it appears to you that his wife and mother-in-law do not perceive any problem to exist. When you get alone to consider the situation you realize that you are dealing with a difference in family rules. The husband was raised in a small nuclear family with only one other sibling. One family rule was "We don't raise our voices with one another." Since that was the family rule, whenever he or his parents did raise their voice, it was usually a frightening event and the situation seemed out of control: in his family, people had to be pushed to the limits of their control before they allowed themselves to raise their voices.

In his wife's home, however, in addition to the two parents there were seven children, a grandparent, and an uncle. To get heard, you had to shout. The family reflected this reality with an implicit rule: "It's all right to shout and get angry as long as you don't call names and do apologize afterwards." Consequently, in the wife's experience, yelling and shouting in anger was frequent, and not at all frightening.

Years before, when the two sets of family rules were joined by marriage, the husband felt his wife raised her voice "too often" and the wife felt her husband was not "expressive enough." Both of their opinions reflected a value system that there actually exists such a thing as "the official right and true amount of emotional expression." As the years passed, a compromise was worked out between the two spouses. But with the death of her husband, the mother-in-law came to visit so much more frequently that the family rules reverted back to those of the wife's family of origin, leaving the husband feeling frightened that the situation was out of control every time voices were raised in anger.

Inflexible family rules.   Family rules also produce problems for families when a rule that has been useful and functional for a long period of time becomes useless or, worse, dysfunctional, and family members are unable to negotiate a change, implicitly or explicitly. Consider, for example, a family that has a rule: "Mother makes the final major decisions for everyone in the family." This rule, though unwritten and unspoken, may have served the family well from the first day of marriage through the birth of all the grandchildren. The spouse and children may not have always been pleased by having to get Mother's approval, but since Mother was more or less a wise, benign despot, no serious difficulties occurred until her stroke. At this crisis point, the rule needs to be changed for the well-being of all members, since Mother can hardly be expected to make major decisions when handicapped with memory loss and aphasia. In a family that remains flexible in relation to family rules in periods of stress, the rule might be changed to "Mother is still important, but now we make our own major decisions." With such flexibility to change family rules, independent decision making would not be seen as disloyal or sick. Therefore, if one of the children had an opportunity to be promoted in her company if she were willing to move to another city, her decision to move would not be interpreted as a "desertion" by the family. In fact, she could expect that the family would support her decision making rather than resent it.

In a family that is inflexible about rule modifications, you might expect a different outcome after the disability of a powerful mother. A family of this type might cling tenaciously, but rather unconsciously, to the rule "Mother makes the final major decisions for everyone in the family." Since Mother would be unable to make decisions, the family would be paralyzed until Mother either improved or died. Under these conditions, the daughter's decision to move to another city would be met with considerable hostility by the family. She would be labeled a "traitor" or "deserter." The family might make its initial contact with you through the father seeking to cut his disloyal daughter and son-in-law out of the will.

If, on the other hand, the daughter sticks to the dysfunctional family rule by refusing her promotion and remaining in her hometown because her mother cannot give her "permission" to leave, she will experience resentment and frustration. To deal with these feelings while maintaining the family rule, the daughter might present to you insisting that her mother's condition was worse than anyone realized and she needed to be institutionalized. In this way, the daughter is aiming to remove Mother from the family scene so the daughter herself can move without breaking the family rule.

Since the number of possible disastrous outcomes for a family with inflexible family rules is endless, the counselor should be alert for the organizing principles of families so as to be able to make explicit—and thus negotiable—these dysfunctional family rules. When, in the course of your consideration of family rules, you believe that you have come across a rule that has been causing a family problem, at your next meeting with the family, it is often useful to check with them to see if your perception of the rule is accurate. More of this technique will be described in the next chapter.

Is There an Identified Patient?

The notion of Identified Patient (I.P.) is fairly straightforward. Whenever a family system is having problems, the members of the family
will focus on one or two members of the system, who will be labeled
by the family as "needing help." Among counselors who work with
families, such labeled individuals are known as the I.P.s. That is, these
individuals have been labeled by their family systems as being the
person with *the problem*. As should be clear by now, we reject the
notion that in any family system there is just one person with *the
problem*. We do believe, however, that the process of labeling an I.P.
provides the counselor with an enormous amount of information as
to how the family system operates.

For example, who is giving the label to the I.P.: is it a parent,
child, sibling, or spouse? Is it a professional person? What do you
assume the motives to be for applying such a label? Is it concern over
bizarre behavior? Is it to distract attention from other, more potentially serious problems in the family? Is it a power play ("Since you're
sick, I must control you"; or "Since I am sick, you have to do what
I want")?

Not only does knowing who initiated the labeling process give
you information about the family, but so does *how* the problem of
the I.P. is discussed. For example, families who discuss the I.P.'s
symptoms or problems kindly and empathetically in the presence of
the I.P. are likely to be acting out of genuine, if misdirected concern.
Families who seem excessively kind and sympathetic (syrupy) may
be communicating the infantilizing nature of their relationship with
the I.P. Families or family members who seem to take delight in
describing the I.P. using graphic clinical terms normally reserved for
members of lower phylogenetic orders are telling you of their anger,
resentment, and guilt about how they are handling the situation.
Family members who are similarly graphic in their clinical description of the I.P. but seem unemotional, aloof, and remote are communicating to you their sense of resignation and despair.

The counselor should also consider how the I.P.'s respond to
their labels. Do they accept being the I.P.? Do they revel in it? Do
they insist that they are being persecuted? How this information can
be put to use in understanding the family system is explored in
greater detail in the following section.

How Is Power Exercised?

Power is your ability to influence the behavior of others. The experience of power, on the other hand, is the sense that you have the

ability to get what you want. In other words, exercising power and experiencing power are not necessarily synonymous. As an example, the most powerful person in the world is probably the 14-year-old girl who runs away from home: everyone her life touches (friends, school counselors, parents) is profoundly affected and controlled by her behavior, yet the act of running away is almost always motivated by the feelings of being misunderstood, abused, and completely powerless.

Indirect vs. direct power.   In families where explicit power is equitably distributed along socially prescribed lines, major transactions involving "getting what you want" are carried out in a straightforward way. Compromise is generally sought in conflicts of interest, and power struggles rarely cause sustained problems. By way of contrast, in most of the families you will see, explicit power will be inequitably distributed, often balanced by implicit and unrecognized power, and family members will be unable to compromise because power transactions will be indirect. In these families, all members will be feeling powerless despite the fact that they all are exercising power indirectly. The reason for this phenomenon is that when straightforward power negotiations are avoided or unsuccessful, clients learn to exercise their power indirectly. While indirect power negotiations have the liability of reducing the chances of getting what you really want—since you can not really say what you want if you are going to be indirect—they do have the advantage of giving you at least something. When the choice is between something and nothing, most people will opt for something.

Indirect power plays.   One of the most widely used methods of indirectly exercising power is through illness, both physical and mental. Individuals who label themselves "ill," or behave so that others do so, can manipulate their family system by playing on the various guilts and sympathies of their significant others. The stereotypes of this sort of power play are the chronic hypochondriacs who constantly call their children to tell them of their latest awful ailments.

Likewise, power can be exercised by relatives by labeling the I.P. as being "ill." Their reasoning is that when people are ill they need to be cared for and directed. This type of caring usually leads to the assumption of personal responsibilities and privileges previously enjoyed by the Identified Patient. Consequently, identifying a family member as the I.P. gives relatives license to exercise power over the Identified Patient.

It is well established that the prevalence of chronic physical disorders increases with age. Since physical illness can be used by either elders or members of their families to marshal power indirectly, it is particularly important to be aware of how the family is relating to an illness of an elder. As you might suspect, elders are most frequently the I.P. since they are most apt to have some kind of physical symptom.

Just as physical illness can be used as a powerful device in a power struggle, so can mental illness. Such use can range from a younger relative claiming that if he does not do something soon about his mother, he will have a "nervous breakdown," to identifying the elder as becoming "senile" or "incompetent." Such mental health labels have a great deal of power in the sense that they can often force change in a family system.

In considering the issue of power, it cannot be emphasized enough that individuals within a family system may be experiencing themselves as being completely powerless when, in fact, they are exercising an enormous amount of power over the family system. Therefore, when you ask yourself about how power in a family is exercised, you will want to avoid the trap of equating apparent "helplessness" with "powerlessness" or overt "assertiveness" with "powerfulness."

Why Has the Problem Not Been Solved?

When the solution perpetuates the problem.   Another question you should consider in trying to understand how a family system operates concerns family interactions that seem to block the family from solving their problem by themselves: what solutions are the family members applying that are perpetuating the problem? The reason this question is important is that generally when family system members are unable to solve a problem, it is not because the problem is impossibly difficult but because the family members proceed with solutions that have the effect of perpetuating the problem instead of resolving it. Stated slightly differently, it is no longer the problem that is the problem, it is the solution that has become the problem.

For example, suppose a middle-aged daughter, with a husband and high-school age children, insists that her mother come to live with her family after the death of the elder's husband. When the mother reluctantly arrives from out of state, she is lonely. She misses her old friends and grieves for her recently deceased husband. When she shares with her daughter how miserable she feels, the daughter feels obligated to do something about her mother's misery. Notice that the mother is not requesting that the daughter take responsibility for resolving her loneliness, but instead is only sharing her feelings of loneliness and frustration at being in a new place after suffering a great loss. Such a self-disclosing statement by an elder might take the form, "I feel so lonely and miserable, sometimes I wish it had been me instead of your father that died. Isn't that a terrible thing to say?"

At this point, if the daughter is able to say something along the lines of, "I know how miserable you must be feeling. I wish there was something I could do to help," there would be no problem; life would go on. The mother would have her feelings validated and be given support by her daughter, and probably would begin to feel better, gradually.

In the case of the solution becoming the problem, the daughter would say, "Oh, Mother, don't talk like that. You have so much to live for. This is such a wonderful town with so many new activities for a person your age that I'm sure your loneliness will go away in just a few days. Just wait till you see what the children and I have planned for you." Such a statement is rarely offered maliciously. The daughter's intentions would be pure. She would only be trying to cheer up her mother. This response is natural for people who believe that it is possible to take responsibility for another person's feelings and directly change how they feel. In this case, the daughter would be feeling responsible for her mother's feelings—probably because she pressured her mother to move in with her after her father's death —and would attempt to talk her mother into changing her feelings.

Observe that at this point a problem would be created where none actually needs to exist. The mother is entitled to feel foreign, lost, and alone in a new city after the recent death of her spouse. Her grief and misery are part of life and not abnormal in the least. If good mental health is characterized by the ability to experience a wide variety of emotions that are appropriate to the setting, then it would be a sign of poor mental health on the part of the mother to feel happy so soon after the death of her husband and before she had created a new social network of friends and acquaintances. The mother is not asking her daughter to take responsibility for how she feels but, instead is just reaching out to share her feelings with some one she loves. Again, a sign of positive mental health.

The daughter, on the other hand, is identifying her mother's statement as a problem. With the best of intentions, she is usurping her mother's right to her own feelings. The problem escalates as the daughter takes on the role of her mother's social director. She begins to introduce her mother to people she believes her mother will take a liking to. She lavishes attention on her mother's every need. She drives or gets her teenage children to drive her mother everywhere. The daughter pushes her mother to join senior citizen clubs and other organizations for elders. The mother objects. She still feels lonely and miserable and out of place. Since she really has not finished grieving over the loss of her husband, her old friends, and neighbors "back home," she is not in the mood to go to parties, or on field trips, or to any of the other activities her daughter is pushing on her.

Since the daughter is trying as hard as she can to change her mother, she reads her mother's inability to change the way she feels as "unhealthy." Usually by this time the daughter's frustrations over failing to cheer up her mother will have spilled over into her relationship with her husband and children. They will begin to complain to her that, "Everything was okay until Grandma came to live with us." Now the daughter will be feeling even more frustrated because she is able to please neither her own family nor her mother.

Labeling her mother's natural grief as "depression," the daughter tries even harder to cheer up her mother. The harder she tries, the more frustrated both feel.

By this time, without her daughter's intervention, the mother would have already begun to make friends of her own in the community; she would have been looking for a place to live and managing her own transportation. These changes would have occurred naturally in response to the cessation of grieving and the natural forces motivating individuals to establish social relationships. These natural forces, however, have been blocked since the mother is now getting used to having her daughter's complete attention. The mother is aware that she is unhappy and lonely, but her daughter's constant attentiveness is dulling the edge of her pain just to the extent that her natural motivation to help herself is lessened. Therefore, the daughter's behavior is not only failing to solve the problem, it is actually making the problem worse.

The daughter is totally unable to see what is happening. Her experience is that she is trying as hard as she can to lift her mother's depression and her mother seems to be getting more depressed. The daughter's dilemma is that she remains convinced that she must try *more of the same:* If only she tries hard enough she can lift her mother's misery—although in reality, the harder she tries, the more depressed her mother becomes. Only by ceasing her efforts will the daughter learn that the situation will right itself. Her mother will then have to reassume responsibility for herself, learn how to get around town, and establish some meaningful relationships. The problem is that the daughter is so certain of her illusion of control that she is unable to let go. She incorrectly, but understandably, reasons: "If I am trying as hard as I am and my mother is still depressed, if I stopped trying she might get so bad she would kill herself." As a consequence the daughter is boxed in. Doing what she is doing is making things worse, but it seems to her that to stop doing what she is doing would end in disaster.

It is at this point that the family will present to you, usually in the person of the daughter, who will be asking your advice about how to deal with her "lonely, complaining, depressed" mother. If you fail to grasp how the solution is perpetuating the problem, then like your clients, you will fall into the same unproductive position of believing that the answer lies with trying more of the same.

What would happen if the family had no problems? What would the family do together? What would the family talk about? Would there be any reason for the family to stay together?

The reason for considering this question is that a family may covertly, often unconsciously, perpetuate a problem because of either an individual or collective fear that the solution of the problem would be more harmful than its continuation. This idea sounds peculiar, since you are considering it in relation to a family that has already come to you for help. You must remember, however, that just because one member of a family is seeking help to solve a problem, this does not necessarily mean that everyone is seeking help to solve it. Even the family member who initiates contact with you may have personal reasons for wanting to appear eager to solve the problem, when in fact he or she will be resisting any solution you might want to suggest for fear of the consequences of resolution of the problem. In such a case, you are the window dressing for the implicit statement, "We're trying to get help, which proves our good intent, but nothing can be done."

There are several reasons why families are reluctant to give up their problems. The first and probably most important reason is that old problems are like old friends: predictable. When you have a real problem, then you have a concrete reason to explain to yourself and the world why you are miserable. On a personal level, this concept is reflected in a statement such as, "If only I were rich (or thin, married, divorced, bigger busted, more athletic, younger, older, *ad infinitum*), then I'd be happy." What excuse does the unhappy poor person have who suddenly becomes rich only to find himself still unhappy? The old excuse is gone and uncertainty has replaced it.

Uncertainty represents new, frightening risks. In family interaction terms, the reluctance to give up predictable misery is reflected in statements such as, "If only my mother were better, then I'd be happy," or "If only my wife would get along with my mother, then our lives would be fine." Again, a family system may be miserable, but at least the misery is predictable and explainable.

From a counselor's point of view, predictable, self-perpetuated misery is at best a nuisance and at worst a disaster. The reason is that self- (or family-) perpetuated misery often obscures other, frightening problems. Such "other problems" that serve as an unconscious motivation on the part of one or more family members to perpetuate a family problem are marital problems, sexual problems, physical or mental illness (in a member of the family who *is not* the I.P.), and alcohol problems, to mention but a few. Consequently, it is important for you as a counselor to realize that within every family system with which you work, even when you are just working with one member, there may be counterpressures being exerted to prevent a problem from being solved. The purpose of considering who might want a problem not to be solved is not to have the information available for purposes of confrontation but, instead, to understand the true nature of why the problem has been so difficult to solve.

11

Mobilizing the Family System

After you have taken time by yourself to comprehend how the family operates, you are ready to proceed with the direct intervention stage of counseling. As the counselor, you do not solve the problem for the family system. You do, however, help the family members mobilize their energies to overcome the obstacles that stand in the way of reaching their goal. You are a coach rather than an athlete; part of the team, but not really a player; part of the family, but not really a member.

The term *mobilize* is particularly important in describing your interaction with the family. Even after a goal has been clarified, family members will be moving in different directions trying to solve the family problems. Most family members either will feel drained of energy or will be acting so anxiously that their energy level is too frantic to be effective. It is your responsibility to mobilize and focus the family energies in such a way that they can be used constructively to meet family goals. To achieve this mobilization, you may work with one member or the whole extended kin network. But the aim of your counseling interventions will be the same: mobilize the family system. The purpose of this chapter is to explore by example specific techniques of counselor intervention shown to be effective at mobilizing family systems with elders.

Reframing: Talking
the Family System's Language

Many families are blocked from meeting their goals because they have "mental blind spots," which, even if the solution to their problem were directly in front of them, would prevent them from grasping it. These families need to view a problem in a slightly different frame of reference to be able to see a solution. To intervene in such cases, the counselor *reframes* problematic situations so that families can see their own solutions. As a counselor, before you can reframe a problematic situation, you must be able to comprehend the problem in its "original frame"; you must be able to recognize the language the family is using to frame the problem. Before getting into a specific example of normal reframing, it is important to give greater consideration to the concept of the *family language*.

Family Language

"Family language" does not refer to syntax or grammar or vocabulary. These points of language are the obvious. Instead, the concept of "family language" refers to the way that the family perceives the world. For example, conservative Republicans usually view the world differently from liberal Democrats; devout Roman Catholics perceive the world differently from iconoclastic atheists; psychologists view the world differently from prison guards. Yet all consider their views as the most accurate, why else would they hold them?

For effective counseling, it is important for you to be able to accept your clients' perceptions as being as legitimate as your own. You must be willing to consider that you are not always "right" about how the world is truly ordered and be willing to bend from time to time to be of maximum usefulness to clients. If you require that your clients change all of their perceptual sets (their ideas of "reality") to match yours, then your chance of being useful to more than a handful of clients is quite limited.

For example, most counselors are "psychologically minded," but most members of the public, particularly elders, are not. If you insist that you will not help your clients until they share *your* insights into their problems, you are really trying to force them to agree that you know the "right and true" way. Consider the unfortunate, yet true, case in which two elders brought their 38-year-old son to a large teaching hospital for psychiatric treatment because at their home he was keeping himself locked in his room, eating his feces, and drinking his urine. After the son was hospitalized, the family was referred to family therapy. This referral offended and frightened both the elders, who from their experience reasoned: Anyone who eats and drinks his own excrement is crazy. Why were they, as parents, being seen in treatment with their son? Naturally, their first question to the therapist was, "Why are we here? It's our son who has *the problem*." The therapist was inexperienced, so rather than explaining the problem in a language the elders could understand and accept, he set off on a long, detailed discourse on family systems theory, which culminated in a brilliant, lucid explanation of the I.P. phenomenon.

When the therapist finished speaking, the father asked, "You mean to tell me that my boy is eating his shit and drinking his piss and yet he doesn't have a problem? You're crazier than he is." With this, the elder arose from his chair, took his wife's hand, and left the hospital, never to return. From the father's frame of reference (perceptual set), he was right. From the therapist's frame of reference, the therapist was right. The help the family needed to get through this crisis was unavailable because the therapist was too inflexible to respond to the perceptions and language needs of the elders.

In essence, if your ideas about how to solve problems are to be of use to a family, then your ideas must make sense from the family's point of view or the family will dismiss you as an educated fool. To avoid being dismissed as a fool, you can either try to make family members think like you—essentially by arguing, though probably cloaked as "expert knowledge"—or you can present your observations and suggestions in a way that makes sense to the family according to their way of viewing the world. Since arguing is almost always doomed to failure, and since persuading a family to think like you is not only presumptuous but generally impossible, in our approach the counselor seeks to make useful observations and suggestions using the client's frame of reference.

The Art of Simple Reframing

Reframing is really composed of two operations. The first is to determine in your own mind what new approaches the family needs to take to reach their mutually agreed-upon goal. Such a determination is usually based on your professional experience as an applied gerontologist. Knowing what your clients should do differently is the easier part. The second, more difficult aspect of reframing is to suggest effectively how the problem might be handled differently in your client's language. The information that you need to reframe a problematic situation successfully in your client's language comes from your comprehension of the particular family system's operation. It is for this reason that interventions should be postponed until you have had an opportunity to comprehend fully the family system with which you are working.

There is one particular language that appears most frequently in counseling elders and their families. If this language could be given a name it might be "I am willing to sacrifice to be a good child." The problem stems from the word *good,* which indicates a definition of values, not simply norms. What makes this language such a problem is that it is regularly associated with good intentions on the part of the child or children. As history can attest, atrocities have often been committed with the best of intentions and the purest of motives: has an army ever marched into combat without the belief that God was on their side? Similarly, middle-aged persons struggling to behave like "good children" often create disastrous problems for their elders, themselves, and the rest of their families by applying dysfunctional solutions to what were initially nonproblems or, at most, ordinary life difficulties of their elders.

As an example of how reframing a problematic situation can be useful when the family language is "I am willing to sacrifice to be a good child," imagine that you are a coordinator of a nutrition site. You notice that one of your elder clients has stopped driving herself and, instead, is now being driven to the site by her daughter. After a few weeks, the elder stops by your office to speak with you about a problem she has been having with her daughter. Since her daughter is going to pick her up in a few minutes, you suggest that the meeting be held then so the daughter can participate. The elder reluctantly agrees; the meeting is set. As the session unfolds it appears that the daughter, after reading an article in *Reader's Digest* concerning age-related sensory deficits, believed that her mother should give up driving. To induce her mother to stop driving, the daughter offered to drive her anywhere she needed to go. The mother disagreed with her daughter's suggestion, but since the daughter was paying for the mother's automobile insurance, the mother felt she had no choice. Three months later, in your office, the mother is feeling angry and resentful and the daughter is feeling overwhelmed, hurt, and abused. *The problem* the mother presents to you, however, is that she disagrees with how her daughter is raising a junior-high-school age grandchild. They have been arguing bitterly over this topic since the elder went into forced retirement in her driving. Since your job description provides that you spend an hour per day "socializing" with your clients, and since you have also arranged to use the hour of "socialization" to apply counseling techniques to problematic situations brought to your attention by your nutrition clients, rather than attempt to refer the mother and daughter elsewhere, you decide to pursue the apparent problem with them.

You proceed until, when you ask them directly about how well the driving arrangement has worked out, each makes a face, and the elder remarks, "What difference does it make?" To this, the daughter replies, "Mother, you know I don't feel as if I have any choice." Asking for clarification, you discover that the daughter feels she has to deny her 68-year-old mother use of her automobile because the article appeared in such a reputable journal, *Reader's Digest.* The daughter's wide, tired eyes suggest that her motives are unselfish, but since she feels she is taking this unpopular stand for her mother's good, backing off from this position would leave her feeling as if she were being a bad daughter—abandoning her poor old mother to certain death on the highways.

A belligerent, aggressive counselor who fails to consider the significance of using the daughter's language to help her accept useful advice might say the following to the daughter:

COUNSELOR: Look, I know you're just trying to be a good daughter. But don't you see that putting your needs first, to avoid the guilt you would feel if something happens to your mother, is demeaning and infantilizing to her? You are reacting too much to something you read in a magazine that is overpopularized and very inaccurate; give her back her car so that you can both get on with your lives.

While such a statement reflects a good suggestion ("give her back her car"), it also reflects the values implicit in the counselor's language: First, that the daughter is putting her needs first (being selfish) by taking the car away from her mother; second, that taking the car away is a demeaning and infantilizing act; and, third, that the *Reader's Digest* is a worthless magazine. Your suggestion to return the car would not be very useful since the daughter would think you presumptuous and stupid: how could she be accused of being selfish considering all the driving she is doing for her mother? From her perspective, she is not treating her mother like a child; her mother is acting like one. Finally, the *Reader's Digest* is the most widely circulated periodical in the world, and the editors certainly would not print something that is not true. In any event, the daughter and the mother would be ill served by such an unreframed suggestion.

A more useful approach, using reframing, might be to meet alone with the daughter and approach the issue along these lines:

COUNSELOR: I see your concern for the safety of your mother, and I appreciate it. These days it's a rare person who is willing to drive her mother almost anywhere just to make sure she is safe. I wanted to see you alone, though, to share with you my concern that your mother's loss of independent mobility might be having some harmful side effects. I've noticed that your mother's mood around here has changed, and from the arguments about the granddaughter you described the other day, it sounds as if her upset is spilling into other areas of her life as well. I'd like to offer you a suggestion that might be useful for your mother, although it would involve some costs for you.

People age at different rates. The *Reader's Digest,* because it is so widely read and influential, must accurately describe the ordinary or average case. But I've noticed that your mother seems to be an exceptional individual in many respects, mental and physical. I'm wondering if it might not be a sound idea to ask your mother to have a very thorough physical exam so that you can get her physician's professional judgment on just how much hazard she poses on the highways either to herself or to others. I realize this is asking you to do more than most children are willing to do for their parents, and since you are doing so much already, it may be really asking too much. I don't have to tell you that physical exams do not come inexpensively—nor do auto insurance premiums.

By reframing your suggestion in this way, you are acknowledging the daughter as being a good person with good intentions. You are also validating her concerns as being worth taking seriously. Rather than invalidating the daughter's feelings by dismissing the *Reader's Digest* as pap, you accept what she has already learned from that source, but in a way which suggests that further information on the matter may need consideration. You are also indicating to her that by following your suggestion to use the physician's opinion she will be sacrificing more. Since she is equating sacrifice with being a good daughter, you are giving her the opportunity to be an even better daughter by sacrificing the money involved for the physical exam, and reinstating the insurance. Since the decision to let her mother drive would now rest with her mother's doctor and is the bigger sacrifice, the daughter could back off the "absolutely no driving" position gracefully without losing face to you, her mother, or herself.

By reframing your suggestion, you have not only given the mother and daughter the opportunity to use your position of being a non-family member to discover a possible solution, but you have presented the proposed solution to the family system (in the person of the daughter) in a way that the family can use.

Complex Reframing: Gently Guiding Neuroses

Most of the work that you do with your clients will involve at least some degree of simple reframing to communicate your ideas usefully in their language. From time to time, however, it may be necessary to go beyond simple reframing to be useful to a family system. This is particularly apt to be the case when you are dealing with a family in which one or more members might be thought of as sufficiently neurotic to require some kind of psychotherapeutic intervention. Such a neurotic individual within a family system, moreover, rarely seeks or accepts a referral for individual psychotherapy, while confrontation of the neurotic behavior by the counselor is likely to be disastrous: this leads to hardening of the neurotic's position far more than does confrontation of an individual living within the limits of good adjustment. In these cases, it is important to learn how to guide a neurotic gently through *complex reframing.*

This task is neither easy nor always possible. Yet when one considers the alternative of abandoning a family because one member is "too mixed up to work with," the effort seems worthwhile. However, you must realize that since neurotics distort their relationships in both behavior and conceptualization, to use their language you will have to distort your suggestions correspondingly, in order to "make sense" to the neurotic. Such clear and obvious distortions made by counselors in order to communicate effectively to disturbed clients, so as to free them to solve situational problems without directly addressing their neuroses, we call *complex reframing.*

An example of how counselors occasionally use complex reframing to free neurotics from repeating destructive behavior is the following: You are a nurse working on a geriatric ward with responsibility for a 75-year-old female patient convalescing from a recently fractured hip. She appears to you to be bright, alert, and quite pleasant. You have noticed, however, that over the last week her relations with her family seem to be deteriorating. It seems to you that her three children are attempting to have her declared incompetent and to have a conservator appointed. By speaking with the sisters, however, you discover that their brother is agitating the entire family by insisting they go along with his plan.

According to the sisters, their brother has been in a "horrible" marriage and is seriously considering divorce. Before their mother's hip-breaking fall, he was constantly calling one or the other of the sisters to complain bitterly about his wife. Since the fall, however, neither has heard a word about the wife. Instead his conversation has turned toward how senile their mother is becoming. Both daughters acknowledge that there is nothing whatever the matter with their mother's mind, but confide to you that they are afraid to side with their mother since their brother has threatened them with lawsuits if they do.

> **OLDER SISTER:**   What are we going to do? If we even breathe a word in front of mother that we might go along with our brother's plan, she begins to sob and tell us that she doesn't want to live if this is how her family is going to treat her. If we take her side against our brother, he threatens to drag all of us into court, which is something that none of us can afford, but he can, since he's a lawyer. We're caught. If we side with mother he'll win by economic attrition; if we side with him, then mother feels betrayed and humiliated. Mother gets destroyed either way.

Since your patient has been physically deteriorating since the son's pressure began, you decide the situation is serious enough to check with her physician. You ask the physician if he would be willing to see the son and perhaps make a psychiatric referral.

To you, the problem is clear: the son's obsession about his mother's "incompetence" is rapidly depleting the physical and psychological resources of the entire family. Worse, the son's behavior threatens to destroy his mother's economic resources as well. These resources may be particularly crucial for the rehabilitation program set up for the mother after she leaves the hospital. For the well-being of all family members, especially the mother, it is essential for the son to back off; but all requests to that effect have made him come on even stronger.

In assessing what you know of his "language," it appears that, first, he desperately feels a need to control emotionally charged situations, and, second, he is angry at his wife, toward whom he seems opposed but on the defensive. To free the son to solve the problem his behavior is creating, you will need to complexly reframe the situation so that he can view changing his posture from that of "attacking general" to "peacemaker" as a move that simultaneously will increase his control over the marital situation by blocking his wife. Consequently, to use complex reframing, you would seek an opportunity to speak with him alone and take the following approach:

> **COUNSELOR:**   I've been thinking about how difficult it must be for you to be caught up in this family quarrel, especially when your wife takes such subtle but evident delight in your plight. I don't know how

you keep your sanity when every time the issue of the conservatorship comes up she seems so quietly amused. It's almost as if she enjoys watching your family get torn apart.

By suggesting to the son that his behavior toward his mother is playing into the hands of his wife, you are providing him with a good reason, within his warped framework, to give up his destructive behavior toward his family. You have freed him to back off by using his "language" to illustrate how he can gain some control over the situation, and especially his wife, by no longer providing her the opportunity to feel amused by his family-shattering quarrels. And if he does so, even the marital situation will be no worse, and possibly a bit more relaxed.

Information-Gathering Assignments

When the time comes for the counselor to give clients direct advice, a crisis often occurs: the clients flatly refuse to take the advice. This situation is most apt to arise when clients seem unable to take any kind of risk or try anything different because of their desperate fears of failure. While such fears are understandable, they are also paralyzing in regard to problem resolution.

Even if clients always followed the counselor's direct advice precisely, there would still be a reason for hedging a bit when giving a family direct advice: the clients may follow your advice to a "tee" and still get no relief from their problems, since you can never be absolutely certain that the advice you give a family will really work. Such an outcome is good for neither family nor counselor morale.

Homework Experiments

One way to deal with the problems associated with giving direct advice is for counselors to reframe advice as "information-gathering assignments." A suggestion to change behavior is reframed as a *homework experiment*—implying that the clients' behaviors be changed only for a short, specified period of time to provide the counselor with more information on how the family system operates.

The advantage in giving advice on "what to do differently" framed as a homework experiment is twofold. First, homework experiments are impossible to fail. Experiments are, by definition, courses of action without known outcomes. Consequently, clients need have no fear of failure. Even when experiments do not alter a problem, they at least provide more definitive information about what does not work. Second, when homework experiments help to resolve a problem (meet a goal), the family has the opportunity to take responsibility for the useful outcome of the experiment. The clients feel that they have contributed to solving their problem rather than that the counselor has done it all for them.

As an example of assigning a homework experiment, suppose you are working with a young newlywed couple who live in the neighborhood of the senior center in which you work as a counselor. They have come to your office because of a problem they are having with the bridegroom's mother. She is constantly meddling in their affairs, calling two or three times a week to lecture the young bride on how to take care of her husband. The bride is hurt and confused because she is unable to satisfy her mother-in-law. The bridegroom confides that he is reluctant to confront his mother over the calls because he feels she is "too fragile" to take any criticism. The couple agree that their goal would be to limit telephone conversations with the mother-in-law to 30 minutes a week. When you inquire as to how often they call her, the bridegroom replies, "Are you kidding, with her calling every other day and talking for 45 minutes at a time, who has anything else to say to her?"

In considering the situation, you suspect that both newlyweds so firmly espouse the family rule "Always be polite to your parents" that they are genuinely stuck on what to do.

It appears upon examination that the problem is being perpetuated because the mother needs reassurance that she can still be useful and important, so she calls her daughter-in-law to give motherly advice. The daughter-in-law will not hang up, but due to her newlywed status is threatened by so much overwhelming advice that her voice betrays her feelings of anger and resentment. The mother reacts to her daughter-in-law's discomfort by becoming more uncertain of herself. When her uncertainty reaches a peak, usually every two or three days, she calls again. Because she calls so frequently, the newlyweds never call, since they are already overwhelmed and view calling her as simply creating more trouble for themselves. Unfortunately, the mother interprets their failure to call her as another message that she is unnecessary, thereby creating in her an even more desperate need to call them.

As a counselor, you realize the solution to breaking this vicious circle is rather straightforward: turn the tables by calling the caller. In your opinion, such a move by the newlyweds would reassure the mother-in-law and break the vicious circle. To free your clients of the risks and fear of failure associated with following your direct advice, you might want to reframe your solution as a homework experiment:

COUNSELOR: Rather than giving you any advice at this time, I'd like the two of you to collect some information for me over the next week. I need to know how your mother will react if every morning at exactly 7:55 you call to ask her the answer to a household problem that you already know. Please limit the call to her to five minutes, no more, no less. I would like you to note on paper for me how, if at all, her evening conversations change. The changes may be in length, content, or emotional expression. Remember in your calls to her to be respectful, but be careful not to ask her any questions about household matters to which you don't already know the answer, since she might not be clear in her answer and the call would run beyond the five minute limit. Remember, this is just an experiment, so it will be important to gain as much information as possible—keep your eyes and ears open.

By giving a suggestion framed in terms of an information-gathering assignment, not only have you limited any possibility of failure, but you have also framed your suggestion in a way that is compatible for the newlyweds. By insisting they treat the mother with respect, you are not attacking their family rule. By instructing the daughter to ask only a question to which she already knows the answer, you are acknowledging her competence as a person who does not really need her mother-in-law's advice, so that she feels more equal and thus more free to relate to her mother-in-law as a person.

If your information-gathering assignment is useful, the newlyweds will discover the value of calling the mother-in-law on their own and continue to use the technique without further prompting. If initiating telephone calls on their part is not successful, then you will have gained some information about the nature of the problem without the clients losing confidence in either themselves or you. The ability to give a suggestion in such a way that the clients do not feel useless even when the suggestion does not prove immediately useful is a mark of a true professional.

Symptom Prescription:
Providing the Opportunity for Insight
into Personal Freedom and Responsibility

A more complex variation of the information-gathering assignment than the homework experiment is the intervention technique of *symptom prescription*. With symptom prescription, a counselor instructs the clients to do more of whatever they are already doing to create and perpetuate their problems. For example, families whose chief complaint is that they are quarreling too much are encouraged to quarrel more. While symptom prescription is not always the first treatment of choice, at times it may be the only effective intervention.

The reason symptom prescription is occasionally the only effective counseling intervention rests in the fact that some family systems are absolutely unable, without outside help, to achieve insight as to how they perpetuate their problems by pursuing dysfunctional solutions. Without such insight it is impossible for system members to recognize their individual roles and responsibilities in sustaining their problems, and thus to effect any meaningful personal change.

Along these lines, possibly the most rewarding use of symptom prescription is enabling family members to achieve insights into themselves and their interactions by leading them to the discovery that in almost every family interaction each member has a freedom of choice. Frequently one or more family members feel that another family member (or coalition of members) is controlling them. They feel they have no choice in how they must respond. Obviously, they feel powerless.

By way of example of a problematic situation in which symptom prescription would be useful, consider the three-generation household in which the first (oldest) and third (youngest) generation seem to be in constant disagreement. As open hostility becomes "inevitably" more frequent, the couple in the second generation feels helplessly trapped as children and parents petition them for support. The grandparents feel miserable because they are not getting what they want; the grandchildren feel miserable because they are not getting what they want. The parents feel miserable because they are caught between people they love in a no-win situation.

Usually, in such families, each of the "fighters" blames his or her antisocial, hostile behavior on another family member. Thus, Grandfather believes he had no choice when he called his grandson a "slob" because of the way the boy was dressed to go out for dinner at a nice restaurant. Grandfather's reasoning was, "My grandson knows perfectly well how I feel about being properly attired in an expensive restaurant. His sloppy appearance was aimed to insult me. I merely responded in kind by calling him a slob." Grandson believes he had no alternative but to defend his honor by telling Grandfather to "get screwed," his reasoning being, "I wouldn't have said it if Grandfather hadn't called me a name first." The fight escalates into a name-calling orgy of major proportions until finally the parents cancel dinner plans altogether since everyone is suffering from an upset stomach.

Under these circumstances, Grandfather will not admit publicly —or, most importantly, even to himself—that he could have prevented the fight by either withholding his comments on his grandson's attire or, failing that, refusing to retaliate after his grandson told him to "get screwed." Likewise, Grandson will not admit that he could have prevented the fight by either getting dressed to his grandfather's standards, or, failing that, refusing to rise to his grandfather's bait about looking like a "slob."

Similarly, the parents, who are feeling trapped and pulled apart, are unwilling to admit that they could have stopped the fight by siding consistently and promptly with either Grandfather or Grandson so that this and almost every other fight's outcome could be predicted even before it started. For example, if the parents consistently sided with Grandfather, the son would rapidly learn that three against one makes fighting unworthwhile and would go out of his way to avoid a fight; similarly, Grandfather would face an analogous situation should the parents decide to side consistently and promptly with their son. In any event, all members of the family are feeling powerless, despite the fact that each possesses the power to end the fighting at any time by refusing to fight.

Being aware of such a family system, you might want to invoke symptom prescription along these lines:

> **COUNSELOR:** It's clear to me that your family is being torn apart by all the fighting and quarreling that is going on. I think I may be able to help you, but I need more information about how the fights start and how they keep going. What I'm going to ask you all to do for me will sound strange, I know, but it will produce information I need to have if I am going to be of further use to you. I would like each one of you to start at least one fight each day, intentionally. Notice, I'm asking you to start a fight intentionally so that instead of being so emotionally involved in the fight that your powers of observation naturally are impaired, you'll be able to be a cooler, more objective observer of what is going on. After the fight you start, I'd like you to record the date, time of the day, topic, and duration of the fight. Also, please do not disclose to the person with whom you are fighting that this fight is for the homework assignment. You may suspect from time to time that you are being led into a fight, but go ahead and allow your adversary to suck you into the fight anyway. I know you parents normally haven't been directly involved in these fights, so rather than actually get directly into a fight, I'd prefer if each of you would observe what you can do *intentionally* to intensify a fight between your father and your son after it begins. Again, no matter how bitter the quarrel becomes, don't tell them, even afterwards, that you are intensifying the fight for the purpose of the homework. Are there any questions?

You can be almost certain there will be! Usually family members will complain that they came to you to fight less, not more. Since initially because of old habits it will be easier for them to fight more rather than less, by being insistent that they must fight more *before* they fight less you are maximizing their opportunity to discover that they can control the frequency of their fighting. Any move toward control is important for quarreling families because once the members admit to themselves that they do know how to start more fights with each other, then on each subsequent occasion in which they behave in a way they know will start a fight, they must take responsibility for the fact that they are fighting intentionally. Their ideas of helpless innocence—"I didn't want to fight, you *made* me"—become plainly untenable.

An additional benefit of symptom prescription is that family members learn to observe the behavior of one another more closely. Once an individual recognizes his own power to create problems, he or she becomes more aware of how other members of the family system use their power to create problems. In the example, as the grandson discovers that he can stop himself from provoking a fight with his grandfather, he also discovers how he allows his grandfather to provoke him into a fight. Fighting then becomes a voluntary, as opposed to reflexive, act.

Finally, symptom prescription as a variation of an information-gathering assignment is useful because it allows the family to give up its dysfunctional symptoms slowly. If a fighting family is told, "I know you can control yourselves. Go home and be more patient and loving with each other," then any breach of the peace is labeled a failure. If, however, the fighting is prescribed, then the old habit does not have to disappear overnight and relapses into quarreling are not necessarily read by family members as an indicator of hopelessness. Giving a family time for change is very important. Symptom prescription gives this time while allowing the family to set its own pace. Since the pace of progress is so important, it is the topic of the next section.

Pacing Progress: Problems and Interventions Associated with "Going Too Fast"

Potential Problems from "Going Too Fast"

The concept that family members can make too much progress too quickly is often difficult even for experienced counselors to grasp. Does a family not come for counseling to solve their problems in the shortest period of time? It would seem that the shorter the period of time it takes to actually reach their goal, the happier clients would be. In reality, the opposite is frequently true: when the problem begins to be solved, much familiarity or certainty in the family system begins to disappear. Although the original situation is improving, anxiety rather than elation is the result. People always need time to adapt to change, even when it is positive. Consequently, counselors must be prepared to intervene when they recognize that their clients are experiencing difficulties associated with solving problems too rapidly.

For a specific example of how rapid problem solution can pose difficulties for a family, let us reconsider the family that is experiencing the intergenerational conflict between Grandfather and Grandson. Assume the symptom prescription intervention has been successful in allowing all three generations to accept more conscious responsibility on how the fights start, are sustained, and are ended. Correspondingly, hostility between grandson and grandfather has been drastically reduced. This change has introduced an enormous amount of uncertainty into the household. For example, over the last year the parents were spending 30 to 50 percent of their private conversations discussing the problem between Grandson and Grandfather. What are they going to talk about now? Similarly, if Grandfather and Grandson are no longer spending all their time together fighting, they now could be talking with one another; what are they going to talk about? In general, where is all of the energy previously expended by the family to try to stop the fighting now going to go?

Another change caused by the cessation of fighting is alteration of the family power structure. Neither Grandson nor Grandfather can now control the middle generation or one another. Where does everyone stand? Decisions the parents might have been basing on the behavior of Grandson and Grandfather are no longer valid. For example, the parents might have been regularly dining out by themselves, to "escape from the chaos." What should they do now that there is no chaos? How can they explain spending so much money on themselves without this excuse?

Still another frightening situation that can arise from rapid problem resolution is that family members have time to take up "old business" with one another that had been left aside because of the overwhelming proportions of the original problem. In the example, as Grandson and Grandfather repair their relationship, the level of conflict between the parents might increase as they return to old, unsettled matters in their own relationship.

Enjoining Families to Give Up
Their Symptoms More Slowly

When family interactions continue to change rapidly, family members may experience more and more uncertainty, until at some point at least one family member will feel so overwhelmed by the uncertainty that his or her behavior changes so as to bring the family back to the original problem. In other words, the most anxious client may subvert the change (usually unconsciously) to return to painful, but at least familiar, ground. Recognizing this phenomenon, there is a saying in family counseling that "slow change is far more reliable than fast change"; if clients can get better overnight, then they can get worse the next night. Families need to be aware that all change involves new problems, and so it is preferable to change slowly.

Getting down to specifics of how such a message is delivered, let us continue with the family that has virtually eliminated the fighting between Grandson and Grandfather in response to symptom prescription. In the privacy of your own mind, you are pleased that your intervention has been so successful so soon, but you are aware that the rapid changes are resulting in new stresses now acting upon all members. To give the message to slow down, you might want to take the approach:

> **COUNSELOR:** I'm pleased to hear that you've been quarreling less, but I'm concerned that you're moving too quickly. My experience is that when families change too rapidly they find it's "too good to be true." After all, progress in almost every endeavor in life is punctuated by steps backward. I would prefer that rather than give up your fighting behavior altogether, that you do it in a much more slow, orderly fashion. Remember, your family has been using a lot of energy in dealing with these fights; if the fights stop, then that energy needs to find another place to go. Such a process takes time. Since it seems from what you've told me you are unwilling to each start one fight each day, how would each of you feel about a compromise in which you only have to start three fights a week?

By using such a statement, you are assuring the family that any steps backward—fights, in the example—do not have to be labeled total failures. You also are warning your clients that even if the fighting stops, everything else will not be perfect. Additionally, you are providing a realistic pace at which they can give up their problems without becoming too anxious to get on with their lives. Under the circumstances cited in the example, you could expect to find the family members angry with you for trying to slow down their rate of progress. They would probably complain to you that they do not really want to fight at all, and question why they should do so just to please you. It is important that you not let their pleas move you from your position that they must slow down their rate of progress. *It is far better to lean in the direction of moving too slowly than too quickly.* If the family system members are experiencing no anxiety from rapid change, they will be unmoved by your pleas to go slowly; if they are experiencing anxiety, then your request to proceed slowly will be welcomed.

Sometimes clients will recognize the wisdom of moving slowly, but frequently they will not. When you cannot stop your clients from moving too quickly, you can at least warn them. If you are empathic and supportive in your warning, then a subsequent slowing in progress need not result in a sense of failure. Sometimes, when families are particularly insistent about moving as fast as they possibly can, the best you can do by way of a warning is to give a message similar to the following:

> COUNSELOR: Well, I know that you are all feeling the need to move as fast as possible, but since all change requires time for adaptation, I would like to make one simple request: if at any time you find yourself asking, "Am I going too fast or too slow?" then I would like you to choose the lesser error of going too slow. In other words, if in doubt: Go Slow!

When Families Slip Backwards

Families will often ignore your advice, go as fast as they can toward solving their family and personal problems, and do quite well. They will be none the worse for ignoring your injunction to move more slowly. More often, however, families that insist on moving too rapidly do, in fact, find themselves overwhelmed by the uncertainty of change and suffer a setback. Staying with the example, suppose Grandson and Grandfather immediately stop fighting for two weeks, then suddenly have such an enormous battle that even their previous performances are eclipsed. These clients appear at their next appointment discouraged and feeling as if their predicament is even worse than before. You can be useful to such a family by providing an explanation as to what may be happening:

> COUNSELOR: I'm really sorry to hear that you've taken a step backward, but I must confess I'm not surprised. After all, you folks have been seeing the problem of the fighting build up for over a year. I don't think it would be very realistic to expect it to disappear overnight. I interpret

this one big fight after two weeks of relative peace as a sign that you
need to slow down your progress on not fighting. This fight, or step back,
is a sign to me that the energy you were freeing up by not fighting hasn't
yet found a constructive place to go. Maybe we need to take a little time
to discuss where that energy might go so it could be used constructively.
Another thing we may need to discuss is the possibility that when you
folks aren't fighting or talking about fighting, you aren't interacting at
all. Sometimes families find that fighting is a better interaction than no
interaction at all. I'm curious, what were you doing during the period
of peace?

In almost every case with which you deal, you will find that it
is more appropriate that a family proceed slowly rather than quickly.
Moreover, the families presenting the greatest apparent need to
change quickly—"Things can't go on like this a day longer"—are
especially likely to be the families that in reality have the greatest
need to proceed slowly. Such families suffer from the second type of
problem associated with going too fast and are discussed below.

Families Frightened by the Idea of Success:
Slipping Backward before Moving Forward

Many of your clients will not even appear in your office until they are
feeling in a state of emergency. In their minds they not only need
to do something, they needed to have done it yesterday. These clients
present the picture of trying to do everything at once. Typically,
their experience of running in circles leads them to feel angry and
miserable about their inability to change things now. They are perpetuating their problem by being impatient: if the solutions they
have tried have not been 100 percent successful immediately, they
have become discouraged and tried something else. Since almost
nothing is 100 percent successful immediately, they have ensured
their failures in advance.

These clients are giving you the implicit message that they are
frightened, usually quite unconsciously, by the possibility of success.
As difficult as it may be to believe, for these clients even the prospect
of success is so overwhelming and anxiety-producing that they will
act in every way to try to prevent the possibility of actual success.
The most frequent sign that a family is afraid of success is their failure
to carry out a modest task, such as to complete a simple information-
gathering assignment. In effect,they are communicating to the counselor: "Slow down, you are going too fast, don't ask us to give up our
familiar problem so quickly." Rather than scold such a family for not
following your suggestion or accuse them of not being serious about

wanting to change, you best serve these clients' interests when you reassure them implicitly by accepting responsibility for assigning an inappropriate task:

> **COUNSELOR:** There's no way for you to fail my homework assignments. I always learn about a family whether or not assigned tasks are completed. In this case, it looks to me as if I made an error in judgment as to how fast change could take place, picking a homework task that asked you to move too fast. I believe that the pacing of problem solving is crucial, and, frankly, it is much safer for progress to be too slow than too fast. It looks as if we need to reconsider your homework, and perhaps goals, to enable you to move at a more comfortable speed. I'm at least glad that your collective wisdom to move slowly and cautiously prevailed over my impulsiveness to do too much too soon.

12

Winding Up: Giving Credit and Getting Out

How a counseling relationship is terminated, even when the relationship is very informal, greatly influences the long-term outcome of counseling. The purpose of this chapter is to explore how to decide to terminate counseling; how to allow the family to take credit for their own solutions; how to help the family anticipate what might go wrong in the future; and how to restrain your own optimism usefully at the end of the final session. In other words, this chapter addresses how to wrap up, give credit, and get out.

The Decision to Terminate Counseling

Reluctance on the Part of the Family

For the family being counseled, reluctance to face the unknown without the counselor is understandable. From the family's point of view, if things are getting better, it is good common sense to change the environment as little as possible and to hope that life will continue to improve. Therefore, it is not surprising that individuals and families who have been in counseling are often quite reluctant to give up regular—or impromptu—meetings *even though they have managed to solve most of their original problems.*

With such families it will be important for the counselor to address the issue of how difficult it is to say good-bye.

Reluctance on the Part of the Counselor

Surprisingly, the biggest obstacle to winding up counseling usually comes from counselors rather than their clients. When clients express the desire to consolidate their gains and get on with their lives without regular counseling sessions, many counselors find themselves simultaneously gratified and anxious. The reasons for feelings of gratification are obvious; the feelings of anxiety are more subtle, since they stem from the counselor's inner struggle to answer the question: "Are they really ready?" This is an unnecessary question, since it can be answered only by the clients. It is their life, their decision. When counselors undertake to make this decision for a family, they almost inevitably conclude that their clients are not *really* ready to leave counseling.

There are three major personal reasons why it is difficult for counselors to wind up counseling with their clients. First, after working closely with a family or individual, even if briefly, counselors become attached to their clients, particularly when the clients have worked hard and made progress. The end of counseling represents the end of the special relationship. It means having to say good-bye. Many counselors have difficulty saying good-bye. Unfortunately, counselors' problems with farewells become the clients' problems when counseling is continued unnecessarily.

A second reason that it is difficult for counselors to wind up counseling is that letting go of a family, particularly at the counselor's initiation, is sending the message: "I've done the best I can in the time I've had." It is very difficult for many counselors to admit that while they have tried their best, their ability to help has limits. While counselors are human beings and may be overzealous in their attempt to strive for perfection, when they allow this flaw to spill into their professional lives, their demand for perfection in themselves inadvertently becomes demand for perfection in their clients. Not only are these demands unrealistic, they are also destructive to the self-esteem of clients. Consequently, counselors must use extra self-restraint when considering termination to avoid placing such demands on their clients.

Still a third reason that it is difficult for some counselors to conclude counseling is that ending regular counseling sessions is an implicit admission by counselors that they are no longer *indispensable* to the well-being of the family system. Counselors who oppose their clients' wishes to terminate, or refuse to initiate the termination of counseling after the presenting problems are solved because they believe their clients unable to make it on their own, have actually fallen into the trap of being more concerned about their clients than their clients are for themselves. It is unlikely that continued counseling from such an untenable position would be of use to the clients anyway.

Whatever counselors' personal reasons to prolong counseling unnecessarily may be, the most frequent public reason given for continuing counseling after the initial problem has been solved or goal has been achieved is that the progress made thus far has really "just scratched the surface" of the problems. This statement is always true, since no one is without problems and everyone's life could stand some improvement. Therefore, such a statement has no real meaning. Your responsibility, remember, is not that of a psychologist, psychiatrist, or psychoanalyst; your obligation to your clients is to help them live without you in the shortest period of time, not to be a crutch for them for the rest of their lives nor to lead them to the promised land before they leave you. Consequently, the excuse, "We've only just scratched the surface of the problems," is not sufficient to continue counseling beyond meeting the first set of goals. If significant doubt remains, a reasonable trial period apart may be the best indicator of whether a family is able to proceed with life without you, needs further counseling on situational problems, or needs your informed advice on a referral to long-term treatment.

Once you and the family have decided that it is time to wind up counseling (at least for a few weeks, months, or until time tells whether any further crisis is likely), then the termination process has begun. In your final meeting with your clients you will probably want to include three elements: giving credit, anticipating problems, and dealing with optimism.

Giving Credit: Allowing Family Members to Take Responsibility for Their Own Solutions

It is important for you to extend credit to the family for the progress made. This is important for two reasons. First, giving family members the opportunity to take credit for their own solutions gives the family a sense of accomplishment. Second, when clients can acknowledge their responsibility for fortunate events, it is more likely that in the future they will be able to acknowledge their responsibility for unfortunate events. Both these reasons require additional discussion.

The Sense of Accomplishment

Each of us enjoys a sense of accomplishment. The sense of accomplishment is synonymous with the experience of power. Clients who feel effective feel powerful. They feel in control of their own lives. They no longer feel defeated. The old saying: "When you're hot, you're hot; when you're not, you're not," is an acknowledgment from folk wisdom that a positive attitude (or sense of power) creates positive events, while a negative attitude creates negative events. Since the cycle can be self-perpetuating, clients who come into counseling feeling overwhelmed and defeated but now enjoy a sense of power and control over their lives have begun to change their downward spirals into upward spirals. The more your clients can feel responsible for their progress, the more powerful they will feel. The more powerful they feel, the more likely they will be to influence future events positively.

Families or individuals will often be reluctant to accept credit for their efforts. Such a situation typically occurs in a family in which "modesty" is a family rule. Such families will be apt to give you all the credit for the improvement in their lives. For example, suppose you help solve the quarreling and bickering between a head nurse and a patient's family in a convalescent hospital. After three rather informal meetings, the family switches from being antagonistically disruptive toward the staff—in particular, the head nurse—to being appreciative of the work the hospital is doing, while the head nurse switches from a threatening, accusatory posture to one of understanding and compassion. Essentially, your role was to bring the "warring" factions together in neutral territory (your office) and to slow down the pace of communication so that each side could have a chance to listen to what the other was saying before responding with a counterattack. As the misunderstandings between family members and staff had an opportunity to be cleared up, goal clarification demonstrated that both family members and the head nurse wanted the same things for the patient. When you announced this meeting would be the last, at least for a while, both the family members and the head nurse made statements to the effect that you, as the counselor, were entirely responsible for solving their problems.

Rather than simply bask in the limelight, a more useful approach for the clients might be the following:

> **COUNSELOR:** I really appreciate the credit you folks are giving me. As a matter of fact, I love praise and am more than happy to take my share. But I feel all of you should also take your share. After all, each

of you has had to make some rather major changes to enable the progress that you've made to occur. For example, Mrs. Anderson, I know that as head nurse it is very difficult to get time to come to these meetings, yet I've noticed that you've been staying a little later on the days we meet so that you can come and still complete your duties. You also were the person who first brought the problem to my attention. I know that it isn't always easy to ask for help, particularly when you are in the professional role of being a "helper" yourself.

Mr. Jones, I know that you too have had to make sacrifices to make room for both your work and these meetings. I know that when we first met, you were feeling rather skeptical about the chance of anything positive coming out of our meetings, but you came anyway and were willing to be honest about your feelings. You deserve a lot of credit for that.

Mrs. Jones, I know that you have worked very hard too, being the one who spends most of the time in the hospital visiting your father and having to be running messages back and forth between all of us. Without your efforts, we would never even have found a time when all of us could get together.

I also think it's important to mention that all of you stayed with the meetings, and if you agreed to do something differently, you stayed with your agreements until the next meeting when it could be discussed. I also know that some of the things that were said in here were difficult to say—and often even more difficult to hear. But you all did it just the same. While I appreciate the credit you've given me, I think it's important that each of you take some credit yourselves; after all, you're the ones who took the risk to do things differently, not me.

Such a statement recognizes the effort of all family system members involved in the counseling. It also points out that many small but significant different behaviors have to change if progress is to be made. For example, rearranging work schedules may be a very important step because it usually requires a great deal of personal inconvenience. Yet many clients may not be aware that their willingness to show concern and to compromise by inconveniencing themselves at work has affected the outcome of counseling until you point it out to them in an acknowledging way. The list of small but significant changes that individuals in a family system often must make for a change to take place is almost limitless, but some frequent examples include the following: additional driving, additional housework, admitting to having a problem, asking for help, being on time, being a patient listener, acting in good faith, following through on agreements, saying things that are not comfortable to say, doing things that feel awkward or embarrassing, having less money to spend, being socially inconvenienced, having less time for personal matters, and continuing to come to sessions even when it seems as if no progress is being made.

Resumption of Responsibility for Life's Events

The second reason it is important that clients take credit for the progress they make is that only by accepting credit, or responsibility, for positive change can clients accept accountability, again, responsibility, for negative change. If clients will not accept credit when their lives become better, then they will not accept responsibility when their lives become worse. Therefore, when dealing with clients who seem unable to take any kind of credit for the changes in their lives, it is useful to point out for them some of the things they could have done either to prevent change from occurring or to ruin the progress made to that point.

Staying with the middle-aged couple and nurse presented in the example above, suppose you suspect that rather than a sense of modesty, the reason they all are having trouble accepting credit for their progress is that, at some level, there is a shared reluctance to accept responsibility for one's actions, good or bad. In other words, you have the impression that there is a subconscious conspiracy among the three of them to perpetuate the myth: "We don't know how we got into this mess and we don't know how we got out, but we know we couldn't have done it without you." Under these conditions, you might want to take an approach similar to the following:

> **COUNSELOR:** I think you folks are saying that I played an important role in making things better, and I appreciate that credit. I have a sense that you are all feeling as if you didn't play much of a role in making things different. I'm not comfortable with that, since after all, we're talking about your lives and your future. Sometimes I find that when my clients have difficulty taking credit for the positive actions they have taken to make things better, it is a little easier for them to recognize the little things they didn't do that would have made things worse. For example, Mrs. Anderson, you could have refused to acknowledge that a problem existed. Better still, if the problem had been brought to my attention by someone else, you could have said that you didn't have time to come in and discuss it with Mr. and Mrs. Jones. Even if you had come in, you could have sat in that chair in body, but not in spirit.
>
> Mr. Jones, in some ways the same thing applies to you. You could have made the decision that your work schedule was more important than trying to solve the problem. Or you could have come to the meet-

ings and refused to say anything, and then later complained to your wife about how useless the meetings were.

Mrs. Jones, you could have just stopped coming to the hospital instead of tenaciously hanging in there when things were rough. Or you could have avoided taking responsibility for setting up the meeting time that made it possible for the four of us to get together.

If any of you had wanted to stop our progress, you could have made commitments in our meetings that you knew you wouldn't be able to keep, or not said something that you knew was important to be said. But none of you did any of those things, and I think you all must take credit for the work you have done.

Taking Care of Yourself

Not infrequently, and perhaps when you have been the most useful to a family, one or more members will initiate the termination of counseling by saying something like, "Well, things are better, but counseling doesn't seem to be doing much of anything, so I think it's time we stop coming in." Statements like this are characteristic of clients who are taking all of the credit themselves and giving none of it to you. These clients differ from those discussed above in that instead of needing credit, these clients have taken more than they seem to deserve: they have taken the counselor's due credit! At first, this sort of termination stings a counselor's ego. It is nice to get some recognition for your efforts. On a deeper viewing, however, such an expression from a family is probably the ultimate compliment: the clients are now functioning on their own, taking responsibility for their problems and their progress.

This process is fine for the clients, but what about their counselors? Counselors need their share of credit for the same reasons clients do. As in all conflicts of interest over immediate personal gratification, it is important to put clients first. How then can you take care of yourself, as well as your clients? We suggest that rather than seeking acknowledgment from your clients that you have been skillful and useful, it is much better for your clients if you present any such claims to your fellow workers. In fact, we believe *it is essential to have fellow workers with whom you can confide how "brilliant" you have been so that you can avoid destructive bragging in front of your clients.* Then, in turn, you can recognize their successes and ask their help with difficult cases.

For an example of how to take care of both your clients and yourself when the clients insist on taking all the credit themselves, consider the following situation. In a counseling setting, you have been working with a middle-aged woman and her mother. Both women are highly verbal and have argued with considerable gusto since the daughter's second birthday. This type of interaction was tolerable until the widowed mother's osteoporosis (loss of bone) "forced" her to live with her divorced daughter. The problem of intergenerational conflict became serious enough that the daughter approached you about an institutional placement for her mother. You employed the technique of symptom prescription because you believed that both mother and daughter needed an opportunity to assume more responsibility for their argumentative behavior. At the third session, they reported they had not had a fight. After the fourth session, they had one fight. At the fifth and what subsequently proved to be the last session, both mother and daughter tell you that they will not come to see you again because your suggestions are not "helping." Although they are polite, their message is clear: "Things are better at home, but no thanks to you and your stupid suggestion to fight more!"

For many counselors, situations of this nature precipitate crises. These counselors feel attacked and discounted by clients they believe should be grateful for the help they have received. To salve their wounded pride, such counselors often fall into the course, disastrous for the clients, of explaining what competent and clever counselors they actually are. In this case, the extreme form such a statement might take would be the following:

> **COUNSELOR:** How can you say I haven't helped you [looking at the daughter]? Two months ago you were ready to put your mother in an institution. [Looking at the mother]: Did you know she was thinking of that! Since you've seen me, you've had a total of four fights, and only one of them within the last month. The technique I used was *symptom prescription* and it worked like a charm. Instead of criticizing me you both ought to be thanking me.

Obviously such a defense/offense, even when less aggressively phrased, serves only to put down the clients and provide the shallowest of unprofessional victories for the counselor.

Under the same circumstances, you might take an approach far more useful to the clients by saying, "I'm glad to hear the fighting has stopped, even though it doesn't seem as though our work together mattered in that. I'm wondering what the two of you are doing differently to stop the fights." Such a response on your part allows both clients to tell you (and one another) what they have done to break the fight cycle. In other words, you provide the clients with an opportunity to elaborate on the positive behavioral changes they have made in their interactions with one another and for which they are assuming total credit.

After the conclusion of such a session, the time has arrived to take care of yourself. Congratulate yourself out loud. Let yourself experience the pride that accompanies the satisfactory completion of a difficult task. Talk to your counseling supervisor or, staying within the bounds of confidentiality, call or visit a colleague with whom you feel sufficient comfort to boast openly about your success. Clients are not the only people who need recognition and a sense of achievement!

Anticipating What Could Go Wrong

After giving credit, the next important aspect of terminating formal or informal counseling is to anticipate with your clients what might go wrong in the future. Clients are usually not particularly eager to anticipate future problems. Many people subscribe to the rather naive notion of "Out of sight, out of mind" or the foolish superstition "If you don't think it, it won't happen." This ostrich approach to life is rarely useful, because it eliminates the possibility of a prophylactic (preventative) posture toward possible impending life difficulties. Aside from being useful as a device to avoid these potential pitfalls, anticipating problems with clients also serves the useful function of identifying and discouraging intentional or unintentional sabotage of achieved progress. Both of these functions are discussed below.

Setting a Realistic Stage in Order to Avoid Pitfalls

A good reason for anticipating problems with clients is that such a process prepares them for the realistic eventuality that today's success will not last forever. It is hardly realistic to believe that the solution of one problem will prevent another from ever taking place. Yet many counselors discount this fact by avoiding the matter of problem anticipation, because they detect their clients' enthusiasm and are reluctant to dampen it by discussing future prospects realistically. Unfortunately, the temporary optimism these clients thus enjoy is only the calm before a painful storm of new, real problems. Consequently, counselors who fail to explore probable future problems are really failing their clients.

For an example of how counselors can usefully anticipate problems with their clients, suppose you are working with a three-generation family in which the grandfather was presented as the I.P. by his daughter-in-law, who described him as "senile." Through your primary investigations you discovered that the grandfather's apparent confusion was due to sensory deficits: he needed cataract surgery and a hearing aid. When his sensory problems were solved, his confusion was eliminated, and the spirits of all members of the household seemed at an all-time high. Rather than leave the family with the unrealistic expectation that they would now all live a utopian existence, it would be more useful to take this approach:

> **COUNSELOR:**   I can sense how good you are all feeling and I'm feeling good too. It's always gratifying to me when what seems to be a hopeless situation has a happy ending. But it also occurs to me that it might be useful for us to take some time away from how excited we are to consider for a few minutes some problems that might arise now that Mr. Peterson has his sight and hearing back. After all, every change, even changes for the better, bring new stresses and problems. I'm wondering if any of you can anticipate any problems that now might arise?

Usually no one in the family will want to be the first to consider how things might turn sour. Carrying on with your responsibility, you would choose to anticipate some problems yourself:

> **COUNSELOR:**   Without trying to be a pessimist, I can think of some things. For example, now that you can hear and see what's going on, Mr. Peterson, I wouldn't be at all surprised if some of what you hear or see won't be completely to your liking. So it would make sense to me if the level of conflict between you and the rest of the family went up a bit, at least temporarily. And my guess is that when the level of conflict between you and, say, your grandchildren goes up, probably the tension between your son and daughter-in-law will also go up. Another problem that certainly isn't rare for families who have just solved a serious crisis is that the husband and wife end up quarreling more for a while. It isn't surprising, since a crisis tends to make a couple put small, but significant, everyday differences on the "back burner" until the crisis is over. Since your crisis has been solved, my guess would be that the two of you [looking at son and daughter-in-law] will probably find yourself feeling a bit strained at times as you deal with the old business you need to catch up on.

There are, after all, literally thousands of stressful events that all families must endure whether they are happy or not. Among the events that usually are stressful, in addition to those mentioned above, are deaths of significant others, marriages, job changes, moves, children leaving home, new babies, and retirement. The reason for mentioning and anticipating problems associated with each of these life events is simply to remind the family that life is not always easy or pleasant. Hence, should they find themselves feeling that life is becoming more difficult or unpleasant, they need not assume the difficulty is necessarily such a problem that they need to rush back to you immediately for more counseling.

Identifying and Discouraging Potential Saboteurs

The second reason it is useful to anticipate problems with a family before terminating counseling is that frequently problem anticipation can be used as a technique to identify different ways that family members might sabotage progress the family has made. While most clients are pleased when family problems are solved, you may recall from the previous chapter that frequently they are frightened by their success. Consequently, either intentionally or unintentionally, some clients will sabotage the progress that has been made by returning to earlier, dysfunctional patterns of interaction. A variation on the technique of anticipating problems can be very useful to these families in identifying and discouraging such behavior in a way that is not only palatable to the clients, but almost fun.

For example, suppose you are working with three elders, two brothers and a sister. The sister has had a rather severe stroke and requires skilled nursing along with some physical and speech therapy. Her two healthy bachelor brothers refuse to put her into an institution where she can get the care she needs; they insist on caring for her in their home. You are called to the case through the District Attorney's office. It seems the sister's daughter, who lives out of town, is pressuring the District Attorney to do something. By earning the trust and respect of all three elders and the out-of-town daughter (via the telephone), you facilitate discussion of the unpleasant but realistic alternatives to providing adequate care for the failing sister. In this atmosphere, the stroke victim, who has been afraid to confront her brothers openly, confesses that she would prefer to be in a good hospital, at least for a while. She admits that she feels caught living with her brothers because the level of care they are providing is inadequate—she has bedsores and an infected urethra to prove it—yet she is afraid she will appear ungrateful if she says anything. Even more on her mind is the possibility one or both of her brothers might injure themselves while caring for her. She also confesses that she shared these feelings with her daughter, but when her daughter confronted the brothers with her mother's request, the sister denied having spoken with her daughter. The stroke victim was afraid to be direct, because she thought her brothers' feelings would be hurt and that they would be so angry with her they would not visit her in the hospital.

With your help, the two elder brothers find an institution for their sister with which they all feel reasonably satisfied. Since all three elders are now back on speaking terms with the daughter, they arrange to share the expenses. While all the problems associated with having the stroke are not solved, at least life is as good as can be expected under the circumstances; everyone is feeling much better. In your final meeting with the three elders, you feel it is important to anticipate how a new crisis might develop, since from your experience the oldest brother seems to thrive on being in a crisis—that is, it gives him something to do. To attempt to prevent any obvious acts of sabotage you would want to say something along these lines:

> **COUNSELOR:**   One of the things that I was wondering about as I came over today is what could each of you do if somehow you wanted the situation to go back to what it was before the three of us first met together?

If no one volunteered, you might continue with something like the following:

> **COUNSELOR:**   I have some guesses—not that you would ever do any of these things intentionally, but sometimes making guesses helps to stop things from happening unintentionally. For example, Betty, right after your stroke you were pretty quiet about what you were feeling. My guess is that if you went back to never telling anybody what you wanted, then things could get worse for you in a hurry. Bill, I'll bet you could make things worse by getting your lawyer to write another threatening letter to Betty's daughter. George, my guess is you could make things worse by complaining to Bill about Betty's daughter or the nursing home instead of doing something about it yourself. There, that's a start. Can't any of you think of some things you could do to bring things back to a crisis point?

Usually clients will be willing to volunteer some information at this point, which puts them on the record as knowing ahead of time what behaviors they could exercise to sabotage progress. The tone of such a discussion should be light, not heavy. After all, the clients are feeling good; and there is an element of creativity in thinking of ways to be a great saboteur.

Restraining Optimism

If counseling has gone well, the final session you have with your clients will usually be positive and optimistic: life has become better, and this change is reflected in the mood of your clients. Experienced counselors prefer that their clients leave their final counseling session with some sense of the impending and unavoidable emotional let-down that occurs after a positive change in life. This differs from anticipating problems in that the focus is on the general rather than the specific.

Of all the things you convey to your clients, one of the most important is the image of future reality you leave with them in their final session. Remember, your clients' feelings about themselves to a large extent will be formed in comparison to your expectations of how they will fare when they stop seeing you. If they sense that you expect them to live a euphoric, utopian existence, then they will respond to the inevitable heartbreaks and disappointments that normally accompany life by defining themselves as failures. It is obviously far better for clients to remember you as being too pessimistic about their future rather than too optimistic, and to exceed your indicated expectations rather than to fall short of them.

To implement this philosophy means, however, that in the closing minutes of your last session with a family, you will need to give some very guarded predictions about the future. In a sense, you take a little air out of your clients' optimistic balloon. If you cannot put aside your desires for recognition and admiration, you will find this task particularly difficult. While for the present your clients may resent you for warning them about the future, they will eventually be grateful for your restraint and professionalism.

How then should you end your final session with a family in a way that your optimism can be useful in the long run to your clients? You might want to take the following approach:

COUNSELOR: We've had an opportunity today to take a look at how you each have made some changes that have resulted in a positive change in all of your lives. We've anticipated some problems that might come up and we've had some fun discussing some ways you could create problems if you wanted to, which I'm sure none of you want to do! I guess I'd like to end this session, our final meeting, with a bit of a cautious note. You've made some big steps and a lot of progress. It is not uncommon after making a change like you've made to find yourself slipping back a bit—sometimes even a lot. I want each of you to be waiting for the slippage to happen, because it almost always does. But when it does happen, rather than panic, I'd like you to simply recognize it as a temporary but necessary part of your growth as individuals and as a family.

I can assure you that in the weeks and months ahead, there will be times—although fewer as time goes along—when you will be feeling as if no change ever took place. Again, rather than viewing these feelings as an irrevocable step backward or as a sign of personal or family failure or weakness, I'd like you to try to consider the situation as a mountaineer considers stepping back from time to time as he climbs a mountain. Every now and then, all mountaineers, no matter how great, find themselves caught somewhere on their climb where they wish they weren't. At that time, they have no choice but to retrace their steps back down the mountain to where they can once again find a firm familiar footing from which they can get on with their business of climbing the mountain, this time wiser for their previous experience.

If you find yourselves stuck again, and despite your best efforts nothing seems to be happening over a period of a few weeks or months, then give me a call. In fact, if things continue to go well, give me a call too. I enjoy hearing that people I know are dealing successfully with the vicissitudes of life!

When working with a family, it is best to say good-bye to each member individually. A direct look, a firm handshake, or a sincere hug may fit the occasion.

Part III

Case Examples

13

Introduction to the Case Examples

Two things should be made clear before presenting the following chapters, each of which discusses a common type of aging problem briefly and offers a concrete example of how such a problem might be appropriately handled utilizing the family viewpoint and approach, which up to now we have been describing mainly in terms of general principles and techniques.

The Nature of the Case Problems

While the six types of common problems, or problem areas, listed are indeed likely to be met often in gerontological practice and to be readily identifiable by these labels, there is nothing absolute about this classification—or any other. It is simply one convenient way to proceed with a necessary task of division and organization of experience in order to convey information about it. Its use does not mean that all problems met will necessarily fall neatly within one of these six categories. Some unusual problems may not fit any of them well, and many problems may overlap one or more of them. But this is all right. It may even be of use as a reminder that we always impose order on the wholeness and fluidity of life, which does not itself come prepackaged; that each case has its own uniqueness, to which more general principles must be adapted; and that categorization and specialization are tools whose usefulness is limited, or even lost, when they are grasped too tightly.

The Nature of the Case "Dialogues"

While the case examples presented are real in one sense, they are ideal in another. They are based on actual cases—that is, the events described actually happened—but they are by no means verbatim transcripts. Compared to the source interviews, the "dialogues" given here are excerpted and clarified—in short, considerably condensed and cleaned up. While we also believe that the study of verbatim materials on counseling sessions (full transcripts or tape recordings) can be very useful and even necessary for some purposes, we have chosen a different course here for two reasons. First, even for brief counseling, actual transcripts are lengthy; condensation is essential if a number of typical examples are to be given. Second, and still more important, even with skillful counselors and cooperative clients, actual interviews always contain large amounts of discourse inessential to the main course of treatment—repetition, multiplication of examples, sidetracks, hemming and hawing. Therefore, selection is essential to make what is basic in this approach to problem resolution stand out plainly.

Thus, you should be warned that your experience in actual counseling will be very different from the "condensed, cleaned up" versions of actual cases that you are about to read. On the one hand, actuality will be more disorderly and difficult. Do not let the discrepancies between your real life experiences and our expository examples modified from real life discourage you from sustaining your effort in learning to be personally effective with your aging clients and their families.

On another hand, while these examples are based on real cases, condensation and clarification inevitably reduce the immediacy and authenticity one feels with direct experience. We can only hope that some of this sense of real life will still come through in the written accounts that follow.

14

Confusion

General Remarks

Among the potential problems that a family system might present to you, a heartbreaking, difficult, and yet potentially rewarding problem is that of *confusion* in an elder member. Frequently the family system will present to you labeling the confused behavior of the elder as "senile." The family will want to know "what to do." Usually the "senile" elder will not be present when the problem is first broached. The family, or a selected member, will generally insist on meeting with you alone to discuss the problem because in the minds of the family members nothing can be gained by speaking directly with the confused elder.

In previous chapters, the term "senility" has been examined and implications of its use by frustrated, strained family members explained. Obviously, whenever any family member suggests to you that an elder relative is becoming "senile," then seeks your advice on what to do, it is imperative that you make an opportunity to speak with the I.P. elder before you give any advice. The reason for this strong injunction is simple: family members are often very unreliable and subjective in their allegedly objective reports of their confused elder's behavior. For example, we were once asked for advice by an angry son-in-law on what to do with his "hopelessly senile" mother-in-law. She was currently immured in a local extended care facility, but was making such an enormous ruckus that the administrator had threatened to discharge her. Before giving advice, we insisted we needed more information; we asked to visit the elder. We were again angrily assured that she was "hopelessly senile" and that our proposed visit would be of absolutely no value. When our insistence prevailed, we walked into the elder's room to discover her reading a copy of the 1000-plus page novel, *Centennial*. She was perfectly well-oriented, bright and interesting. Not surprisingly, with the same stubborn insistence with which her son-in-law labeled her "hopelessly senile," she labeled him as being "petulantly paranoid, obviously suffering from intractable stupidity."

Regrettably, not all labeling of "senile" or "confused" stems from what is clearly an intergenerational power struggle. Confusion at least in some degree is often actually present. Family members may recognize and be alarmed by signs in their elders of forgetful periods (which may occur as memory blackouts or episodes of wandering), inappropriate outbursts of anger or sadness, or changes in sexual behavior (overt expressions of sexuality) or attitude (making false, apparently irrational accusations of sexual misconduct in others). Such signs indicate the possibility that the elder may be experiencing some kind of impaired mental status. In your meetings with elders who have been labeled as acting confused, there is some information you should have about their mental status to give yourself some idea as to how credible family reports of confusion actually are.

Basically, in your work with elders who are reported to be confused, you will want to learn if they are aware of *where they are* (city and state); *who they are* (name, age, and birthdate), *the day of the week, the date,* and *the year*. Some clinical gerontologists find it useful to ask, "Who is the President of the United States?" followed by, "Who was President before him?" If an elder can successfully answer eight or more of these questions, then the "confusion" reported by the family is more likely a consequence of dysfunctional family interaction than impaired mental status on the part of the elder. Even when elders are unable to answer your questions satisfactorily, however, dysfunctional family interactions *should not be ruled out as a possible cause*—even for the most impaired mental status of an elder.

Obviously, gaining this mental status information should not come from an interrogation of the elder. Such an approach not only lacks respect; it also biases the results. Much of this information can simply come from the flow of conversation between elder and counselor. While it is certainly beyond a counselor's usual training or expertise to make a differential diagnosis on the condition of any "confused" elder you might be seeing, it is important to gain a sense of what factors, physical (organic), psychological, and interactional, might be contributing to this confusion.

Physiological (Organic) Reasons
for Confused Behavior

Organic brain syndrome (OBS) is a technical term indicating that an individual's behavior can be accounted for by some kind of physiological change in the brain. OBS can be divided into two types: the brief and reversible *acute brain syndrome* (ABS) and the long-term, irreversible *chronic brain syndrome* (CBS).

Acute brain syndromes. ABS affects both young and old. Almost everyone suffers from ABS at some time or another. For example, when you have a severe case of the flu and have a fever of 102 degrees, you probably are behaving in a way that would suggest to those who know you that you are not "acting normal." You probably feel dizzy, your usual enthusiasm is subdued, and your concentration is severely affected. If you were given a test of intellectual functioning (IQ), your performance would be viewed as being impaired. If your fever goes very far above 102 degrees, you may even hear or see things that are not real.

Another familiar sort of ABS accompanies drug reactions. In this case, your thought processes are altered by the chemicals you ingest. One classic example is a "martini overdose," in which the ABS may last well into the next morning: how would you like to take an IQ test (or try to remember where you left your car the night before) while your brain tries to recover from an extraordinarily debilitating hangover? Almost all drugs, especially prescription drugs, have the potential for causing ABS through either predictable or idiosyncratic side effects, or through potentiation of one drug or another when the drugs are mixed. For example, a frequent cause of ABS in both young and old is the potentiation of sleeping pills by ethyl alcohol (liquor).

While physical illness and drug reaction (or interaction) are common causes of ABS for young and old alike, they more frequently cause ABS among elders.

Fortunately for both young and old, ABS is reversible. When the agent that disrupted the body and brain physiology is removed, behavior returns to normal.

Chronic brain syndrome. The other type of OBS, however, is almost never reversible. Chronic brain syndrome is usually the result of trauma (such as a gunshot wound or a blow to the head), cerebral-vascular disease (strokes), or some form of viral and/or degenerative disease of the nervous system. For elders, CBS usually stems from the latter two causes. In the case of stroke, small arteries or arterioles in the brain become occluded (plugged up) such that brain tissue receives an insufficient amount of oxygen-carrying blood to continue to function. When such an occlusion is major and occurs rapidly, it is easily diagnosed by physicians as a stroke. But this "hardening of the arteries" often occurs very slowly, so that discrete strokes are imperceptible.

Degenerative diseases of the nervous system are thought to be caused by either genetic predisposition (heredity) or a slow virus (which may take 30 years to damage the nervous system) or a combination of both. In any event, areas of the brain begin to atrophy (shrink away) and behavior is usually affected.

Confusion between the terms OBS, ABS, and CBS. Unfortunately, it is often assumed by those who should know much better (nurses and physicians) that organic brain syndrome (either ABS or CBS) means chronic brain syndrome. Worse still, since the incidence of CBS is greatest among elders, reversible ABS is frequently misdiagnosed as irreversible CBS. Exploring the implications of such error, let us consider the case in which an elder might develop peculiar or even bizarre behavior in response to a very mild bladder infection (causing ABS). Because of his behavior, he might be institutionalized in a mental hospital with a misdiagnosis of CBS. When his bladder infection finally gets treatment, his ABS would be "cured," yet because of his age, previous abnormal behavior, and incorrect initial diagnosis, the elder would be committed to an institution, his possessions given away (or into the hands of a county appointed "conservator"), and his relatives resigned to his "incurable" state. Because of the poor prognosis associated with CBS, he would receive custodial, as opposed to rehabilitative, staff attention. Should he insist that he be released, he would probably be given medication to make him more "manageable." Under these circumstances, it would be surprising if he did not become depressed, his symptoms of depression being interpreted by the staff as additional proof of his CBS. This example is not pure fantasy. Unfortunately, there are many such elders now residing in institutions, most of whom were "placed" when the rights of patients were given considerably less attention than today.

All of the above is by way of urging that even in the most extreme case, when family members come to you with genuine compassion and concern over an elder or when by your own personal observation you discover the elder to be behaving in as confused and bizarre a way as you could imagine, DO NOT ASSUME CHRONIC BRAIN SYNDROME. Instead, attempt to connect the elder and his family to a responsible member of the medical community.

First, urge the family to get the elder a thorough physical examination, not just a cursory office visit. A thorough physical exam includes at least a history, sight and hearing tests, comprehensive tests on blood samples, an electrocardiogram, and a physician who does not resent spending time with elder patients. Not infrequently, elders have more than one physician. It is important to the elder to make certain that the physician giving the physical examination is aware of any other physicians the elder has seen in the last five years. While the step of encouraging a thorough physical exam is far from a cure-all, it does give the family the message that old age is not synonymous with "senility," and reassures you that as far as humanly possible, physical disease can be ruled out as a reason for the elder's disturbed behavior.

The second step is to reassure yourself that the elder's behavioral problems are not a result of a drug-induced ABS. To accomplish this step, the elder's medicine cabinet needs to be considered. An elder will frequently accumulate a virtual pharmacy of half-used prescriptions. Many of the drugs are outdated so that at best they are ineffective and at worst are now dangerous. Given the availability of the drugs and the urge to save money, elders frequently self-medicate their symptoms. This self-medication creates a problem long recognized among physicians—"A doctor who treats himself has a fool for a patient." Aside from the obvious problem of knowing what to take, self-medication may lead to using formerly prescribed drugs that dangerously interact with currently prescribed drugs. That is, a doctor may prescribe a medication after first checking with the elder as to the other medications currently being taken. Since *that day* the elder was taking no other medications, the physician may well have thought the prescription to be safe, when in fact the elder's bathroom pharmacy was plentifully filled with drugs, many of which would result in a dangerous (ABS-producing) interaction with the "safe" newly prescribed drug.

When considering the medicine cabinet of a confused elder, the best procedure to follow is to take *all* the drugs in the cabinet (prescription and nonprescription) to the physician when the elder goes for the physical examination. This approach has three advantages: First, the examining physician knows what drugs the elder may have been taking. This information may suggest pertinent facts in the elder's medical history and suggest areas of investigation. Second, the prescription labels show the date the prescription was filled and the name of the prescribing physician, so the examining physician knows who else has been seeing the elder. Third and finally, future prescriptions will result in less risk to the elder since the medicine cabinet will now be emptied, and responsibility for managing the drugs—in this case, taking away the nonessentials—will be in the physician's hands.

Psychological and Interactional Reasons for "Confused" Behavior

Certainly a discourse on the psychological causes of regressing into a state of confusion is beyond the scope and intent of this work. It is our belief, however, that all behavioral problems, no matter how great or small, have an interactional element to them. Even if a seriously confused elder is unable to participate in family sessions, we believe that how the family reacts to this confusion will affect the elder, as well as each other member of the family system. Consequently, we see the role of the counselor in this problematic situation as in all others: to be useful to the family system as an agent of mobilization of system energy so family members may deal as constructively as possible with life's difficulties.

Case Example

This case was chosen for several reasons. First, it is a good demonstration of how tortuous the path to approaching the family system often can be—and may need to be. Second, it illustrates the significance of the extended family network of elders who are institutionalized. Third, it provides a striking example of how totally unpredictable, positive results can come from working with even the most "confused" clients.

Certainly a case like the following is not average. Its outcome was so thoroughly positive as to be almost miraculous. Do not expect such results often; yet they may serve as a useful reminder of what positive change can be possible.

Approaching the Family System

The counselor was a graduate student in an applied gerontology program doing a field placement at a large hospital. To earn some money on the side, she took a job as a "gerontological consultant" at a local convalescent hospital. This arrangement met the counselor's need to make a few extra dollars and met the convalescent hospital administrator's need to boast to the families of potential patients that, "This facility even employs a gerontological consultant." In other words, the serious intentions of the counselor were not shared by the hospital's administrator. This lack of administrative determination to make real use of the new consultant became apparent at the first of the inservice meetings with the staff the counselor was to lead. The staff, for understandable reasons, reflected an underwhelming amount of enthusiasm when they discovered that their lounge was being appropriated for inservice work at the end of the shift. But if the staff was unenthusiastic at the notion of a young, naive graduate student telling them how to help their elder patients, they became downright hostile when they noticed the absence of all their supervisors, who were now free to take a break instead of leading the in-service meetings themselves.

The questions asked at the first meeting were all aimed at bowel and bladder control. A psychoanalytic interpretation of such a response on the part of the staff could provide delightful grist for the Freudian mill. Alas, the young counselor had no one to make this aside, so she continued to listen to the questions, recognizing that the behavioral techniques for teaching bowel and bladder control are well-known by members of the nursing profession, particularly by those working in the area of convalescent extended care. In her own thinking, the counselor usefully interpreted the staff's questions as asking: "How do we know we can trust you?" Such a question was to be expected under the circumstances: the staff was composed mostly of semiliterate older women who were at the bottom of the socioeconomic ladder; most were ethnic minorities; the counselor was a WASPish young woman, 24 years old, experienced only in degree garnering. Why in fact should the staff trust her? How could they know if she was serious about working with them or if she was really just looking down her nose at them?

Because the counselor realized that in any extended care or skilled nursing institution staff become influential members of all the patients' family systems, she knew that in her work with elders at this institution she had to have the confidence of the staff. Rather than taking the staff's rebuff personally, she accepted it as a natural part of being available to the family system. Rather than accuse the staff of being unmotivated or only motivated to make a fool of her by asking her embarrassing questions about bowel and bladder training, she addressed the question of trust in a language that she knew the staff would understand:

COUNSELOR: It occurs to me from your questions that I'm skating on pretty thin ice. I really don't know much about bowel and bladder training. It would be pretty high-hat of me to tell you what to do when I've never been closer to a bedpan than seeing one in a book. Before we go any further, I wonder if I might ask one of you to get me a set of whites and to show me how to change a bedpan and clean up a few soiled patients. Even then, I'm not sure what ideas I could offer, but at least I'd know more on a personal basis what you are up against.

The staff was taken off guard, but soon a white uniform appeared and the counselor went out on the floor and was taken to the most unmanageable patients (in terms of bowel and bladder behavior) in the hospital. After about two hours of changing bedpans, sheets, and diapers, the staff got the message that they could trust her: she had made herself available.

The lack of administrative and supervisorial enthusiasm continued to be a problem. Rather than being confrontive, the counselor took the position with the charge nurses, head nurse, and administrator:

COUNSELOR: At least for the first few meetings, it would certainly make it *easier for me* if I could have you there. I doubt that there will be much for you to learn, but I do think that if the staff noticed your presence, it would make them more responsive to me.

By reframing the problem of the supervisorial attendance as being a problem of the counselor, the supervisors were free to attend the next meeting without having to admit that they might learn something—a difficult admission on the part of any supervisor. Consequently, the counselor was now available to all the staff, including the supervisors.

Determining the Problem

COUNSELOR: Now that we're all together, I wonder if anyone is having any particular problem with one of the patients' families?

MRS. BLAIRE, LVN: I've got one. It's Mr. Carrow. He threatened to report me today because his mother's toenails are too long and one of her sweaters is missing. He was so angry I thought he was going to have a heart attack. I wish he had.

COUNSELOR: Why is his mother in the hospital?

MR. CONN, RN: I can answer that. I have the charts right here. She was admitted two months ago. Six months ago her husband died in bed, beside her. She didn't discover he was dead until she tried to wake him up in the morning. So then she went to live with her younger sister. She was in her 70s, I guess. While she was living with her sister, Mrs. Carrow had a double cataract operation. She was back from the hospital less than a week when her sister died. This is really a horrible story: she still had her eyes bandaged when she discovered her sister was dead. As her son tells it, after shouting for her sister to wake up, she crawled over to her sister's bed and found her cold to the touch. I guess at that point she just couldn't handle it and started to scream. The neighbors called the police, who took her to the emergency room at Mercy Hospital. The hospital kept her a day to sedate her; then, because of costs, her son tried a couple of other places and finally transferred her here. Since she's been here, her cataract surgery has healed nicely, but otherwise she's just a mess. Even heavily medicated, all she does is scream and moan and cry. She is incontinent and refuses the bed pan. All in all, it's a sad case.

COUNSELOR: Aside from her eyes, what's the admitting diagnosis?

MR. CONN, RN: OBS.

COUNSELOR: What's the diagnosis based on?

MR. CONN, RN: Behavioral observation. She's obviously senile.

COUNSELOR: I wasn't questioning the diagnosis. I haven't even seen her. I guess what I was really asking is does there seem to be any sign of a stroke, like paralysis?

MR. CONN, RN: I haven't noticed anything, has anyone else? [No response.] But, you know, just because they don't show any physical signs doesn't mean anything. I told you, she's obviously senile. What difference does it make whether or not she had a stroke or her brain is just shriveling up from old age?

COUNSELOR: I have a feeling you are getting mad at me.

MR. CONN, RN [Laughing]: No, I'm not mad at you. I'm just frustrated because cases like this seem so hopeless.

COUNSELOR: I'm glad you're not angry now, but I imagine eventually you will be because I'm sure I'm going to say lots of stupid things before we finish working together. I will feel really uncomfortable if every time I ask anybody a question they take it as an accusation. Would you all be willing to make an agreement that if I do start coming on too strong you'll tell me? Maybe I need to check first to make sure you all feel comfortable enough with me to tell me if it seems like I'm coming on too strong [makes eye contact with everyone in the room]. If we're agreed that you'll let me know when I'm getting outrageous, I guess I'd like to get back to Mr. Carrow. Has anyone besides Mrs. Blaire had any problems with him?

MRS. WITTER, NA: He has bawled me out lots of times for her fingernails being dirty.

MR. ERWIN, NA: He once asked me in a real snotty tone of voice what we were doing to his mother. He said she was much better before he brought her here.

COUNSELOR: Let me see if I have all of this straight. Mrs. Carrow came to the hospital after a couple of experiences with death that would probably drive anybody crazy. Her son, apparently, can only see the negative aspects of her hospitalization. By that I mean, rather than appreciating the staff for feeding, bathing, and constantly cleaning and changing his mother, he seems intent on attacking the staff about petty things.

I wonder, do any of you have any idea why he is coming on the way he is?

Here the counselor is attempting to draw out something from the staff rather than say it for them.

MRS. BLAIRE, LVN: I think I know. From some of the things he's said to me, I think he's guilty she isn't living at home with him. Besides, whenever situations are hopeless, relatives pick one small thing and make a big deal out of it. That way they feel like they're doing something. The trouble is, just because I understand why Mr. Carrow is a pain in the ass doesn't make him stop being a pain in the ass. Have you got any suggestions?

COUNSELOR: I wish I did have some good suggestions, but I'm afraid at this point I don't have enough information to be very useful. I would like to follow up on something you said, though. Do the rest of you agree that Mr. Carrow seems to be motivated out of guilt and frustration?

MRS. WITTER, NA: Yeah, he's guilty, frustrated, and a pain in the ass! [General laughter.]

COUNSELOR: Sounds as if I need to meet the Carrows; I wonder if I could ask one of you to introduce me to Mrs. Carrow?

MR. CONN, RN: I'll take you down there, but she's at a point where introductions don't make much sense.

When the counselor approached Mrs. Carrow's room, she could hear her crying. The noise was disruptively loud and most pathetic. Mrs. Carrow was lying in bed, without her glasses or her false teeth. She was unresponsive to any questioning and seemed unaware of what was going on in the room. Seeing her, the counselor felt discouraged and depressed. The woman seemed genuinely beyond hope. Even though the counselor subscribed to the notion that, although many of the problems of aging cannot be "cured," at least the quality of remaining life can be improved, the sight of Mrs. Carrow pathetically moaning and rolling her head from side to side left the counselor feeling quite powerless. Recognizing her feeling of power-lessness, however, she refused to yield to it.

Since the son, Mr. Carrow, visited at regular hours, the counselor made arrangements to meet him at his next visit. She greeted him in his mother's room and was surprised to find that the old woman could respond to her son, although she seemed to be obsessed with the idea that her late husband was still alive. Whenever Mrs. Carrow would demand that her son bring her husband to visit her, Mr. Carrow would sit silently and sadly, shaking his head. Knowing the administrator had gone home, the counselor suggested to Mr. Carrow that the two of them might go to the administrator's office where they could speak in privacy.

> **COUNSELOR:** I was watching you when your mother asked you to bring your father in to visit. I could see on your face how painful that experience was for you. I wish there were something I could do. . . .
>
> **MR. CARROW:** It is discouraging. She was doing so well until her sister died. It was just too much for her. I brought her here because she needed someone to watch her and to provide medical care. But ever since she's been here she's gone downhill. I'd like to take her home, but they tell me her condition is hopeless and I'm not in a position to put my wife and teenage kids through this kind of ordeal. God, I hope I never get old . . . [a minute of silence elapses].
>
> I'll bet you got your earful from the nurses. We have a perpetual war. Most of them aren't competent to tend ice cubes in a blizzard!
>
> **COUNSELOR:** How are you managing? You have a couple of kids and a wife who must be making demands on you. And now this problem with your mother. How are you getting through all this?
>
> **MR. CARROW:** Not very well, believe me. When I come here the nurses are teed off at me, and when I go home the family is teed off at me. But that's nothing compared to what my mother is going through. If only I could help.
>
> **COUNSELOR:** You mentioned that before her sister's death, your mother was doing quite well. Will you tell me a little more about that?
>
> **MR. CARROW:** Sure. Mother took Dad's death quite hard, but after a month, she began to get back on her feet. She decided that if she didn't have Dad to read the paper for her every morning, she would have to get her cataracts removed so she could read it herself. She'd put off the operation because the doctors had told her to postpone the surgery until she really needed it. When she decided to have it, she insisted that both eyes be done at once. My mother was quite a determined woman.
>
> Anyway, the surgery went well, but the healing process took a bit longer than expected. Mother is 88 and her younger sister was only 78. Her death, and finding her the way she did, was a terrible shock. The

neighbors said her screams could be heard for blocks around. When
they got her to the hospital, all they could do to calm her down was to
knock her out with drugs. Every time the sedation began to wear off,
she began to get agitated, so they medicated her some more. Finally,
it got to the point where her Medicare wouldn't cover keeping her at
an acute hospital. They insisted she be transferred somewhere else. This
is the third convalescent hospital I've tried, and each time she moves
she seems to get worse.

Everyone tells me that it's just a case of "senility" and that she's
lucky to have had as many good years as she has had. Maybe so, but
when it's your own mother that's hard to accept. Nobody will tell me
how it happened so suddenly. Nobody seems to know. Her ophthalmic
surgeon gave me what he called his best guess: that the shock of finding
her sister may have caused her to have a stroke in the area of her brain
that affected her thinking and reasoning but not her movement. I'm not
sure that I can accept that, because when she and I talk, she seems a
bit delirious but not unable to reason. To me, it's more like she's just
given up.

COUNSELOR: So it sounds as if you are the only one who hasn't
entirely lost hope: that must put even more pressure on you.

MR. CARROW: Why do you think I visit so often?

COUNSELOR: Let me summarize then what I think I've been hearing you say today—if I'm inaccurate, be sure to let me know. It sounds
as if your mother was doing quite well despite the death of your dad—
that is, she was alert, ambulatory and able to enjoy life. But with the
death of your aunt, your mother seemed to fall to pieces. Everyone is
acting rather vague on why she suddenly is behaving so differently.
While the medical types are guessing that she has some kind of irreversible brain damage, it seems to you, from your conversations with her,
that it's more of a matter that she has given up. In any event, her
behavior at worst is disoriented and confused; and at best, deliriously
melancholy.

Making it even harder, her best behavior seems to occur when you
are in her room with her; her worst behavior occurs when you are away
from the hospital. As I think I hear it, much of your anger toward the
staff even though it may be over topics such as missing sweaters, fingernails, and toenails is really about the fact that they seem to have given
up any hope for your mother while you have not. Is that accurate?

MR. CARROW: I'm not sure. But I will say I'm a hell of a lot more
concerned about their attitude that she's hopeless than I am about her
fingernails. But I want you to know that personal hygiene is important
to me [long pause].

COUNSELOR: It was nice to have had a chance to talk with you. I
hope we can get together next week after I've had a chance to get some
more information from the staff. Take care of yourself; you are your
mother's most valuable resource, you know. You won't be doing her
much good if you burn yourself out!

Determining Attempted Solutions

At the next inservice meeting, the counselor summarized the last session:

COUNSELOR: Let me take a couple of minutes to refresh my mind as to where we were last meeting. As I recall, we were discussing Mrs. Carrow and her son. There were really two issues that we were dealing with. The first issue was Mrs. Carrow herself. That is, her behavior is quite disruptive to the normal flow of activities of the staff. She is very noisy and unwilling or unable to use the bedpan or bathroom, which makes her even more demanding in terms of staff time.

The second problem we were considering was the difficult behavior of Mrs. Carrow's son. His constant threats and quarrels are also disruptive to the staff. His obvious hostility is certainly not helpful to the staff—that is, not showing any appreciation for the work you are doing for his mother—nor is it successfully meeting his own needs to feel as if he is doing something constructive for his mother.

Does what I've just described seem right to most of you? [Heads nod in affirmation.]

All right. Then, I'd also like to know more about what you have been trying to do to make Mrs. Carrow a bit less disruptive.

MR. CONN, RN: A better question would be, what haven't we done? Let's go over the medications first. Her doctors, and she has three of them, an ophthalmic surgeon, an internist, and a G.P., have given us a multitude of orders: she can get up to three psychotropic drugs: an antidepressant, Elavil; a major tranquilizer, Thorazine; and a minor tranquilizer, Valium. Her internist has given us orders for two different blood pressure meds plus nitroglycerin for angina (chest pain). Her ophthalmic surgeon still has an order for an antibiotic for the low-grade infection in her eye. The antidepressant, blood pressure, and antibiotic prescriptions are administered regularly, while the other prescriptions are prn—as needed. Depending on the shifts, and how disruptive she is, she gets varying amounts of Valium or Thorazine every day.

Really, she's just like most patients in this convalescent hospital; her doctors have just left us with a long list of prescription drugs we can administer if in our judgment she needs them. For example, she has prescriptions for sleeping medication—either chloral hydrate or Seconal; an aspirin with codeine preparation for when her arthritis flares up; and some corticosteroids for her chronic bursitis. Of course she gets a laxative suppository every day. Let's see, just by glancing at her medication record, it looks as if yesterday she got her antidepressant, antibiotics, antihypertensive, and laxative as usual; in addition, she got pain meds twice, tranquilizers three times, and a sleeper before bed.

COUNSELOR: How often do her physicians come to visit her and to review her medications?

MR. CONN, RN: According to our records, the ophthalmic surgeon came once to remove her bandages, and her G.P. came once to admit her. The internist's orders were by telephone since his meds were the same that she was taking before she came to the hospital. There really hasn't been any need for them to come; her condition has remained stable.

COUNSELOR: What about her screaming? Aside from medication, what sorts of things have you tried? I would especially be interested in hearing from the aides on this point.

MRS. BROWN, NA: I've tried not to upset her. For example, she doesn't like to wear her teeth or her glasses, so I haven't made her put them on. I don't think anybody else has either.

MR. VERDUCCI, NA: Whenever I get any free time I try to sit with her. That quiets her down a bit, but it only lasts as long as I am there.

COUNSELOR: How have you dealt with her when she calls out for her dead husband?

MRS. WITTER, NA: Oh, I've tried a couple of things for that. Sometimes I tell her not to worry, that he'll be coming to visit her the next day. Sometimes that quiets her down for a while. But not for too long.

MRS. ERWIN, NA: I've tried something that works pretty well, that the PM and night shift nurses taught me. I get one of the old men in a wheelchair to go in quietly to sit with her; I tell her that her husband has come to hold her hand. That works real well until the wheelchair patient has to be moved out. Then the screaming begins again.

COUNSELOR: Doesn't she know he's not her husband?

MRS. ERWIN, NA: No, at least she doesn't act like it. After all, she's blind without her glasses, and the old men don't talk to her.

The session continued with the counselor moving the focus to what attempts had been made to pacify the son. All the staff said that they had explained and explained to him everything from why his mother's case was hopeless to why her fingernails were dirty, but as nearly as all the staff could discern, he seemed immune to reason. The counselor also discovered that the staff was trying to minimize the conflicts between themselves and Mr. Carrow by avoiding him whenever they could.

A subsequent session with Mr. Carrow was very similar. He, too, felt that the staff was completely unable to fathom the logic of his arguments. He was spending more and more time dwelling on small points like finger- and toenails because he believed that the staff was so poorly educated and unintelligent that they could understand only concrete demands.

Determining Goals

At the next staff meeting, the counselor worked to determine goals. There was a general consensus that staff would have a sense of progress in working with Mr. Carrow and his mother if the following conditions were met: First, a staff member could walk into Mrs. Carrow's room with Mr. Carrow present without being criticized by Mr. Carrow more than half the time; and, second, Mrs. Carrow could sit quietly in her room for one hour without crying, screaming, soiling herself, or otherwise being disruptive to normal staff functions.

At a separate meeting, Mr. Carrow told the counselor that he would be satisfied that some progress was being made if when she was awake, his mother was sitting up in bed when he came to visit her.

COUNSELOR: That would certainly be a change in your mother's behavior, but I am wondering how that would make things different for you?

MR. CARROW: I'm not sure what you mean.

COUNSELOR: Well, if you had some sense that your mother was making at least some progress, how would you be feeling differently?

MR. CARROW: I wouldn't feel the horrible dread in my stomach I do now every time I come to the convalescent hospital.

COUNSELOR: Then one of the ways you would know that the situation was getting some better would be that the uncomfortable knot in your stomach would no longer develop when you come to visit your mother. I wonder if it might be possible for your mother to still not be able to sit up in bed but that the knot in your stomach be relieved. That is, having your mother sit up in bed may be too big a change to hope for in the short run, but perhaps getting rid of the knot in your stomach might be an easier first step.

MR. CARROW: That's probably true. I can tell you when it hits me: as soon as I walk in the door and see the nurses running for cover trying to avoid me. Christ! I feel like I have the plague.

COUNSELOR: Then if I hear you right, one of the ways you might be able to postpone getting the knot, from at least the front door to your mother's room, would be if you could at least get a cordial rather than evasive greeting from the nurses.

MR. CARROW: Yeah. That's right. At least then I wouldn't feel as if I were in enemy territory.

Comprehending the Family System

What is the extent of the family system? This family system includes at least mother, son, convalescent hospital staff, and the three physicians. In many ways, the convalescent hospital staff are in competition with the son to decide who is really the family. Staffs in hospitals frequently come to see families as outsiders who have abandoned their elders to the hospital. Family members pick up on staff attitudes and feel justifiably defensive. A power struggle often results. To exclude the staff as a fundamental part of this family system would be preposterous, since no successful solution will be attainable without the staff's willingness to change how they are interacting with the rest of the family system.

Where is the counselor in the family system? The counselor realizes that her position as a paid employee of the hospital—and thus indirectly, staff—places her in the staff's eyes as being on their side; therefore, she is particularly careful to avoid saying or doing anything to suggest to them that she is taking Mr. Carrow's side, since that would appear to the staff's heightened sensitivity as a desertion or betrayal. The counselor is consequently trying to appear out of the middle of the power struggle between staff and son, since being in the middle will be perceived by both sides (especially staff's) as taking the opposite side. To stay "out of the middle," the counselor avoids trying to "defend" staff to son, or son to staff. Eventual suggestions of trying things differently will have to be framed in a way that does not appear to lay blame or take the other side. To achieve this "out of the middle" position without appearing inconsistent, the counselor is meeting with the opposite sides separately. In this way, understanding one person's position and feelings cannot be misinterpreted by another as approval of those feelings or actions.

What are the family rules? In any institutional setting the family rules include not only the written rules that govern the institution, but the unwritten ones as well. For example, in most long-term care facilities, there is a rule that "You don't bother the doctor." Physicians reciprocate by ordering a long list of "prn" medications—medications the doctor has prescribed to be dispensed only when, in the staff's opinion, the drugs are needed. This long list of prn medications leaves the staff members authorized, in effect, to dispense drugs, free to practice medicine within the range of the prn list. In this case, the family rule that results in such a long list of prn orders may be impairing the cognitive functioning of Mrs. Carrow. Realizing that all family systems become discomforted when family rules change, the counselor must look for a way to modify the rule in this situation without so frightening the staff or Mrs. Carrow's physicians that they defensively withdraw or subvert any change.

Another institutional rule is that "Patients should not be noisy or disruptive." Noisy, disruptive patients are medicated and/or placated until they are no longer noisy and disruptive. In this case, keeping the family rule has resulted in both medication and placation to keep Mrs. Carrow quiet. Unfortunately both approaches may be preventing her from becoming better-oriented. Therefore, another family rule that may have to be relaxed for a while relates to noise and disruption.

In the Carrow family it is not difficult to surmise a family rule such as, "We are persistent, no matter what the odds." Mr. Carrow's persistence is clearly misdirected, but this rule may ultimately be advantageous to the family system provided his persistence finds a constructive target.

Is there an identified patient? There are two I.P.'s. The first is the mother, the second the son. By identifying Mr. Carrow as an unreasonable troublemaker, the staff are able to get one up on him in their power struggle. If Mr. Carrow were not an I.P., then the staff would have to take his needs and requests more seriously. The staff are similarly protecting themselves with Mrs. Carrow. They have labeled her as "hopelessly senile." As long as she bears this label, the staff does not have to consider the possibility that they might be able to do better for her.

Why has the problem not been solved? Since there are really two problems, they need to be examined individually. In the case of the staff–son problem, it is probably safe to assume that the son is feeling powerless and misunderstood. The more powerless and misunderstood he feels, the harder he tries to do something. The "something" he has been trying to do has been to pressure the staff. The staff have responded by feeling threatened. The more threatened the staff become, the more apt they are to attack or ignore the son. Then the son feels even more powerless and misunderstood, so he escalates his effort by being even more demanding. Under these circumstances, the vicious circle continues to build.

The problem of Mrs. Carrow's disruptiveness may in fact have only one reason for not having been solved: she may well be suffering from an irreversible chronic brain syndrome from which there will be no relief until death.

If, rather than assume the worst, the counselor is willing to consider other possibilities, then there is a plausible alternative explanation as to how the staff's attempted solutions have perpetuated and intensified Mrs. Carrow's manifest problems: First, because of unwritten institutional rules, she has been medicated into relative submission, and most probably into disorientation. This medication may have been begun appropriately at the time she was first brought to the acute hospital in an understandably hysterical condition: who would not be hysterical after going through the experience of finding a loved one dead in the morning twice within two months? The solution began to become the problem when every time she began to come out of the medication she showed signs of disorientation and fright. Her screams for attention were interpreted as screams of dementia. Her behavior was interpreted as OBS because of her age and because patients with OBS do let out with disoriented screams.

Since she came in blind and overwhelmed with grief and fright, no one at the acute hospital, with the exception of her son, had ever seen Mrs. Carrow well-oriented. Accordingly, her condition was assumed to be chronic—although the diagnosis still read "OBS" and she was transferred to a convalescent hospital for long-term care. Because her condition was viewed as being organic and hopeless, she continued to be medicated whenever she became noisy. Similarly, she was never properly oriented to the convalescent hospital. When the bandages were taken off of her eyes, she was never required to wear her glasses—"she just keeps knocking them off"—so she was denied the opportunity of visually orienting herself. Because the staff assumed from the admission data that she was "senile," Mrs. Carrow was placated by infantilizing techniques, such as placing an old man in the room each time she would call out for her husband. These infantilizing placations simply intensified the confusion and disorientation she was experiencing in her almost blind, overmedicated state.

Additionally, she was on a soft food diet, since the staff felt it was not worth the battle to have her wear her false teeth. In many ways, she was in a state of sensory deprivation since she could not see, was medicated to a state of semiconsciousness, and was able to eat only soft, tasteless food. Her only real contacts with the outside world were when she was with her son, when being changed after soiling herself, or when she cried out for her dead husband and at least someone would hold her hand.

The system and symptoms were self-perpetuating because Mrs. Carrow was disoriented and frightened—for very good reasons—and her behavior reflected it. But since her behavior was disruptive, she was treated medically and behaviorally in ways that quieted her but left her even more disoriented and frightened. The staff could not let her become more disruptive; and she could not become less disruptive without first becoming more disruptive.

Does the family still need a counselor? It is rather plain from the above discussion that the family system most certainly does still need a counselor, since the bad situation that now exists gives every indication that it will continue to get worse unless some kind of intervention takes place.

Mobilizing the Family System

In the privacy of the counselor's own mind, it was clear that several rather dramatic changes needed to occur, but in an undramatic way. In terms of the staff's behavior, the counselor wanted, first, a competent and comprehensive review of the overmedication problem; second, an end to placating, infantilizing behavior toward Mrs. Carrow; and, third, a change in the policy of ignoring Mrs. Carrow's prosthetic devices (false teeth and glasses), which may be resulting in sensory deprivation. In regard to the son, the counselor was looking to give him a useful outlet for his need "to do something," as a more constructive alternative than venting his frustration on the nurses.

There were several courses of action open to the counselor. The most obvious was to report the entire episode of mismanagement to the administrator. Such a move would have probably been counterproductive since the administrator would either ignore the counselor or act in a way (authoritarian confrontation) that would lead the staff to feeling rightfully betrayed, thus precluding the counselor from being useful in the future. The counselor could also provide the staff with a didactic lecture on proper patient management, but this course would also not be useful since it would, accurately, be interpreted by the staff as criticism.

Since the language of the staff seems to be "Mr. Carrow is a pain in the ass even though we understand why," and "Mrs. Carrow is hopeless," a potentially more useful approach to mobilizing the energies of the staff to make the changes the counselor feels necessary would be to use the family systems language, and the technique of *simple reframing,* to suggest to the staff that the only way Mr. Carrow will ever understand the terrible condition his mother is actually in and recognize the staff's efforts is to see her at her worst: unmedicated and unplacated.

Notice in the following statement how carefully the counselor avoids appearing to take the side of the Carrows, lest she accidentally invalidate the feelings of the staff members.

COUNSELOR: I've been giving some thought to Mrs. Carrow and her son, and I must confess, I don't particularly feel optimistic. I do, however, have some ideas that I would like to share with all of you.

It seems to me that a major part of the problem with Mr. Carrow is that he just can't accept that his mother is being cared for as well as possible. As I understand it, from his point of view, his mother was fine until she went into shock from finding her sister. His problem, it seems to me, is that since he has never seen how his mother would be if she were not being cared for, he has no accurate basis for comparison for how she is now. So he blames you for her condition even though she arrived in about the same shape from another convalescent hospital.

Before I go on with my ideas, I want to share with you a sense of reluctance I feel. Since I am just a student and really rather inexperienced when it comes to handling people, especially compared to all of you, I am feeling very presumptuous and terribly afraid that anything I might say by way of trying something different might be interpreted by you folks as a criticism of what you have done so far. . . .

MR. CONN, RN: If we weren't willing to try something else, we wouldn't have brought up the case to you. Go ahead, we can always reject what you say [general laughter].

COUNSELOR: Well, that's for sure [sharing in laughter]—after all, this place is your hospital and the patients are your responsibility. . . . If we're agreed so far, I'll go on. But if anyone begins to feel criticized, it's important for me that you let me know.

In considering the case, I was looking for things an outsider might notice but an insider wouldn't have time to think about. For example, in regard to medication, I noticed that the prn orders for medication were rather extensive. I understand the rationale for that; God forbid if every prescription that was occasionally dispensed had to have a signed or telephoned order from a doctor. But it also occurred to me that Mrs. Carrow is under a lot of medication, and has been ever since she entered the hospital. As a consequence, her son has never really seen her at her worst, say in the middle of the night when the medications wear off a bit, nor has she really ever had a chance to interact with anyone free of her medications.

There is no question that medications are important for maintaining order. I guess where I'm stuck is that I don't know how Mrs. Carrow might behave at this point if all but her essential medications were lifted for, say, a week. I have my hypothesis, Mr. Carrow I'm sure would have his hypothesis, and I'm sure that each of you has your hypothesis. But the fact is, we just don't have any concrete information.

The only other area I could think of applies to something that you are doing to help calm Mrs. Carrow that may only be postponing her next outburst. Several of you have told me that whenever she cries out for her husband, you bring in one of the other male patients to sit with her. While this probably is comforting to her in the short run, it may also be confusing to her in the long run. That is, she may actually believe her husband is there even though she knows he has died. Without her glasses to see for herself who is holding her hand, this might really be confusing.

I know I have been doing a lot of talking, so let me get right down to my suggestions of how we might get some more information about the Carrows.

First, I would like to have an opportunity to see, and I would especially like Mr. Carrow to have an opportunity to see, exactly how his mother's behavior is affected by the withdrawal of all nonessential medications. I'd like to put his excess energy to work, by getting him to contact his mother's internist to get him down here to review all the drugs and write new orders for which he will be held responsible.

Second, I would like to ask you, just for a while, to not wheel in another patient to stand in for Mrs. Carrow's deceased husband just because she calls out for him. Instead, I'd like you to answer her demands by compassionately but firmly saying, "I'm sorry, Mrs. Carrow, but your husband passed away four months ago. Now you're staying at the Vermillion Convalescent Hospital."

Third and finally, I am going to have to ask you for your patience. Because I want Mr. Carrow to really see the true state of his mother's condition without the psychotropic drugs, I have in mind asking him to be here as frequently as possible over the next week so that he can do his share in the process of attempting to reorient his mother, by reminding her who and where she is, and to keep her teeth in and glasses on and see what happens. Having Mr. Carrow around more—say, from after his work until midnight—certainly would be a strain on all of you.

My goal in this next week is to gain more information. First, we will have a better idea of how manageable Mrs. Carrow can be without drugs. I'm not too optimistic. But more importantly, Mr. Carrow will have an opportunity to share the same observations—in fact, he'll *have* to. If she improves at all, all of us can be happy. If she remains the same or gets worse, then at least Mr. Carrow will have to understand at a more fundamental level the difficulties of providing care for his mother, and maybe he can begin to develop an appreciation of how hard you are trying.

Of course, it's easy to have big ideas, but it is you folks who would have to do the real work, and more important, put up with what could be uncomfortable consequences. I wonder how this strikes you?

In general, the group was suspicious, but supportive. Even though they really did not believe any of the proposed changes would improve Mrs. Carrow, the possibility that they could prove to her son that they really were doing a good job, by showing him how bad she could get, appealed to them. The staff seemed especially pleased that Mr. Carrow's "excess energies" would be put to use pressuring the doctor, since generally an attempt to do the same thing on the part of their nurses would result in being ignored at best, or being scoffed at for being so insistent at worst. The staff took particular delight in the idea of Mr. Carrow being made responsible for his mother's teeth and glasses being in place, since that task was particularly difficult and discouraging for them and they assumed would be the same for him—a fitting punishment for a "pain in the ass."

The rest of the session was spent role-playing how each staff member would approach Mrs. Carrow when she called out for her dead husband. Also role-played was the "highly unlikely" situation in which Mrs. Carrow ceased to be disruptive—how the staff could relate positively through touch and speech. After the day shift was excused, the counselor waited until she could hold a similar meeting with the PM shift. The PM shift was enormously flattered that anyone would bother to stay to talk to them! They were very cooperative and responsive in their gratitude for being recognized as important and contributing members of the staff. Through members of the PM shift, an arrangement was made to pass the information from the meeting on to the night shift. In this way, all three shifts were prepared to cooperate.

On the next day, the counselor met with Mr. Carrow. She told him that the hospital staff wanted to be "more understanding" of his position and, therefore, was willing to try things differently for a week. A change in Mr. Carrow's attitude came about almost immediately: he felt he had finally been heard. Instead of complaining, he asked if there was something he might do. The counselor gave him instructions to contact his mother's internist to ask him to review the medications and suspend as rapidly as possible orders for the nonessential (psychotropic) drugs.

When Mr. Carrow asked if there was anything else he might do, the counselor explained to him her ideas about possible sensory deprivation and resulting disorientation. Subsequently she took the following approach:

> **COUNSELOR:** I appreciate your offer of additional help and in fact would like to request your cooperation in the rather time-consuming, discouraging tasks of keeping your mother's teeth and glasses in place while she is awake. Additionally, to help her in her period of reorientation, it would be optimal if you could repeatedly remind her of who and where she is. To really give this experiment a fair trial, I think it would be important for you to be at your mother's bedside from the time you leave work in the afternoon until midnight—I'd like to say until she falls

asleep, but since she may awaken several times during the night without her sleeping medication, I'd like you to be there for her as much of the time as possible.

The counselor called the hospital the next day to get a progress report from the staff. The charge nurse reported that the internist had reviewed all the medications by telephone, made many changes, and was very cooperative in all respects but one. The doctor told the nurse that she was crazy not to have a prn order for the major tranquilizer and insisted it remain. The nurse assured the counselor, however, that the major tranquilizer would be used only if Mrs. Carrow became a danger to herself or others.

On her next regular weekly visit, the counselor was amazed to discover Mrs. Carrow sitting up in bed, reading the newspaper accounts of the Watergate hearings.

Winding Up: Giving Credit and Getting Out

At the next inservice meeting, the staff were obviously impressed. Rather than blindly accepting the praise, the counselor made certain that each member of the staff was recognized for being willing to try something new and being willing to put up with what eventually proved to be 16 hours of nonstop noise-making by Mrs. Carrow. The counselor made certain to wait for the shift change so she could also congratulate the PM shift for their flexibility and tolerance. A personal note of congratulations was also left for the night crew.

Since the inservice meetings were to be ongoing, the counselor took extra pains to warn the staff that this kind of "cure" was very rare, and that in all likelihood in the rest of their work together they would never again accomplish such a dramatic change in a patient in such a short period of time.

To wind up with the son, the counselor spent considerable time praising him for his flexibility and courage in facing what had been a most difficult situation. She warned him that since the progress had been so rapid, some slipping back could be expected. The counselor also warned Mr. Carrow that other problems (difficulties with his wife, kids, job, and so on) would probably be popping back up in his life now that the energy-consuming problem of his mother was under better control. Finally, the counselor noticed out loud how Mr. Carrow seemed to be getting along much better with the staff. When he agreed with her observation, the counselor lightheartedly asked him what he could do or say now to the staff so that their currently good relations would return to where they had been when he got a knot in his stomach when he walked in the hospital door.

In closing, the counselor observed that since his mother had made so much progress, the question of alternative housing might be coming up. She told Mr. Carrow that she would be available should his family run into difficulties "working out a solution that everyone can live with."

15

Overt Intergenerational Conflicts

General Remarks

Intergenerational conflicts are primarily power struggles involving members of different generations, although these power struggles may take many forms. Some of these forms are covert, as when elders come to believe that they are invalids to gain the attention of their children. Others are more overt, one good example being a physical fight between middle-aged father and teenage son over whether or not the son can drive the car that evening. For the most part, however, overt power struggles are verbal. Generally, they are experienced as being painful and destructive. There are two notable and instructional exceptions to this rule, however, which need specific mention.

Fights for Fun

Some intergenerational families *simply enjoy fighting.* Occasionally such fighting is physical, more often verbal, sometimes nonverbal (e.g., provocative actions), but it is always fighting. Typically, these families enjoy being in conflict. For example, they may repeatedly argue religion, politics, or morality—three topics that most resist conversion—knowing at an unconscious level that there will never be a resolution on the topic argued. They seemingly fight not to win but because most of the members of these families enjoy the sensation of pumping adrenalin, to the point that any argument is worthwhile. At the conclusion of such arguments, inevitably, someone will remark, "Well at least we agree we disagree," or "It's a good thing it isn't up to our family to solve all the problems in the world," or some other remark that indicates, first, that the fight is over and, second, that no one has won or lost.

Another example of fighting that does not necessarily have a painful or destructive conclusion consists of families in which the members pick on very personal topics and seemingly relentlessly attack one another, complete with cursing and perhaps a physical shove or two. Allowing such a scenario to develop a bit, you might imagine a family discussion over "changing sexual mores" developing into a bitter personal argument that culminates in the grandmother calling her granddaughter a "shameful person" and the granddaughter retaliating by calling her grandmother a "narrowminded old fool." Again, the adrenalin is pumping, everyone is challenged, but instead of withdrawing from one another, the combatants continue to engage until one, followed promptly by the others, apologizes profusely—often exuding copious quantities of tears and remorse. After the fight, the family members seem to feel closer than before. Apparently, family members are willing to put up with fighting because making up is so good. Again, in this kind of system, the fighting behavior is terminated clearly so that, first, everyone knows the fight is over and, second, no one has won or lost.

Certainly mental health experts could debate endlessly about how healthy or unhealthy these sorts of fights for fun actually are. Pragmatically, families who find either of these styles of expression meeting their needs will seldom if ever come knocking on your door. Instead, the clients who will seek your attention are involved in family struggles that always seem to require a clear winner and loser, yet perhaps for that very reason never seem to end.

Fights for Blood

These two features, *no clear demarcation of when the fight is over,* and *an unwillingness to stop fighting until there is a clear winner or loser,* characterize overt destructive family power struggles being acted out through relentless family quarrels.

To an observer of such a power struggle, the content of the discussion will often border on the ludicrous. For example, families who are really deeply into conflict will find themselves disagreeing over virtually everything. In response to the question, "Why are you here?" it is very common to be told by one of the members, "Because we fight too much," and by another, "We hardly ever fight." Such a family finds itself in the preposterous position of arguing over whether they argue!

From a safe distance, such family gyrations might be seen as amusing. Up close, for the parties involved, the circumstances often are excruciating. When family members are fighting relentlessly to win, members can become quite brutal toward one another, even to the point of what seems to be their own self-destruction. Lawyers see such fighting carried to the extreme when their clients self-destructively want to sue fellow family members "no matter what the consequences."

Aging and Fights for Blood

As families age, there are certain changes that can result in power struggles. For example, heads of families become ill and die. Who will become the new heads of these families? How will this decision be made? In the jockeying for power, severe family squabbles often arise.

There is another area of change that often results in power struggles. As elders' economic and physical powers begin to wane with advancing age, it is not infrequent for their children, who in the past have had a difficult time confronting their parents, to become more assertive. Since being assertive is new to these previously passive children, they often act more aggressive than assertive as they seek new ways of interacting with their less powerful parents. This pattern is most frequently seen in "role reversal" families in which middle-aged children assume responsibility for their elder parents. As these elder parents are treated like young adolescents, they understandably often begin to act the part. One consequence of this interaction is the same kind of bitter bickering many families with adolescent children know all too well.

The consequences to elders of fights for blood. Regardless of the causes of fights for blood, endless fighting, particularly in families not accustomed to fighting, can destroy the very fabric of the family system. Unresolved quarrels cause changes in economic and social support patterns. Because the socioeconomic conditions of elders are often tenuous, changes in social and economic support patterns generally have the most pronounced effect on elders. Therefore, elders usually are the greatest losers in prolonged family power struggles.

Sometimes changes in the family social support system due to prolonged intergenerational conflict occur slowly. For example, one or more family members may simply tire of the fight and begin to withdraw from the family. Their withdrawal could take the form of calling other family members less frequently or staying away from traditional family functions. Sometimes withdrawal from the family is more precipitous: after a major family argument, one member concludes "enough is enough" and decides to move to a different neighborhood, city, or state. Sometimes, rather than a member withdrawing, the family extrudes one or more of the major combatants. Such a case might result in an elder being moved into a "home" or an adolescent being sent to a boarding school.

From an economic point of view, support patterns are often changed when economic deprivation becomes a major retaliatory tactic.

The task of the counselor in fights for blood. For the counselor, the task is simple, the technique more complicated. Families who are destroying themselves by fighting must stop fighting. To stop fighting, these families need to accept, first, that whenever fights have—or, more objectively, are mutually defined as having—winners and losers, everybody loses; and, second, all fights can be prevented or ended at will. "It takes two to tango"—or to have a fight. For the psychotherapist, perhaps, it is important to determine why it seems so essential for some family members to fight and to win. For the gerontological counselor, it must be a sufficient goal simply to change the combative behavior that is destroying the family.

For some families, the only technique required is to provide the family members with an opportunity to listen and speak calmly to one another. This technique is quite rewarding when family members have been so busy rehearsing retaliatory remarks that each has never really had a chance to hear what the others have to say. By providing each family member with an opportunity to speak, misunderstandings can be clarified so family members discover that they are not really so far apart.

More frequently, unfortunately, even when families discover that they are not that far apart, they are so habitual in their fighting that the bitterest of quarrels develop almost reflexively. The fight has begun and the combatants are engaged; the recurrent battle to determine a winner and loser seems hopeless to end. To be useful amidst the already serious destructive consequences of this sort of interaction, counselors generally must employ the *symptom prescription* intervention. This can be difficult, since on the surface this may look like adding fuel to a raging fire; yet adherence to basic principles is even more important in extreme cases.

Case Example

The lengthy example that follows was selected for several reasons. First, this case is of interest because while the elder is the most vulnerable member of the family, he does not present as the Identified Patient. This situation is sufficiently common that gerontological counselors should be aware of its existence. Second, although "condensed and cleaned up," the dialogue illustrates how to be persistent without being offensive. Third, the case illustrates the initial and continued employment of symptom prescription as a useful intervention in a very difficult situation.

Initially, this case presented very similarly to other cases. A nervous mother, 50 years old, brought in her only child, a 17-year-old girl starting her senior year in high school. Mildred, the mother, complained of the usual difficulties that many parents have with their about-to-leave-the-nest female children: "She won't wear a bra, she's taking birth control pills, her boyfriend is a degenerate, her friends are leading her astray, she won't listen to what I tell her, she is cutting school, and she lies to me." As Mildred recited her list of grievances, her daughter, Sally, sat looking bored and unimpressed. Sally, when questioned, limited her answers to "yes," "no," and "I don't know."

With a bit of historical probing, it turned out that Sally was reared by her aunt and grandfather, the three of them living together in a different state. Just after Sally's 16th birthday, Sally's aunt (Mildred's sister) had died suddenly in an automobile accident, leaving Sally's grandfather, Henry (Mildred's father), as her guardian. After ten months of bitter quarreling, the grandfather gave up; he sent Sally to live with her biological mother. After four months of living and fighting with Sally, Mildred brought Sally in for counseling.

"How was it Sally was raised by your father and your sister instead of by you, Mildred?" the counselor wondered out loud. Mildred replied that Sally had been born out of wedlock and that, "My family decided it would be best if she stayed with them." When the counselor pursued how that decision was made (since simple arithmetic indicated that Mildred was 33 years old when Sally was born), Mildred seemed genuinely uncertain.

Since Sally had lived with her mother for only four months out of her 17 years, it seemed to the counselor that if he were to pursue a family systems approach, he needed to know more about the rest of Sally and Mildred's family.

Approaching the Family System

> **COUNSELOR:** From what the two of you have told me so far, it sounds to me as if we are missing an important member of this family, namely Sally's grandfather, who is also your father, Mildred. I'm wondering if either of you would mind if between now and the next time we meet I give him a call to find out a bit more about the two of you, and something about him?
>
> **MILDRED:** You don't even have to call. He's coming here at the end of the week to stay for a while to help us with some repairs and remodeling around the house. I could get him to call you then.
>
> **COUNSELOR:** If he's going to be here, it would be even more useful to me than a phone call if he could come in with you and Sally next week. Would that be all right with you?
>
> **MILDRED:** Sure. I know he would be very eager to talk to you about Sally's problems. He's very worried.
>
> **COUNSELOR:** What about you, Sally? How would you feel about your grandfather coming in next week?
>
> **SALLY:** Doesn't make any difference to me.
>
> **COUNSELOR:** Fine. Then, Mildred, you'll ask him?
>
> **MILDRED:** Yes.

The next week, Henry came to the meeting with his daughter and granddaughter. He was short, with dark wavy hair and very intense brown eyes.

> **COUNSELOR:** How do you do, sir. I'd like to be on a first name basis with you if that would be comfortable, but I'm aware that you are quite a bit my senior and I don't want to take any liberties without your permission.
>
> **HENRY:** My Christian name is "Henry," Pastor, and I'd be pleased if you'd call me that.
>
> **COUNSELOR:** Thank you. My Christian name is "Steve," and if that would feel comfortable to you, I'd like you to go ahead and call me by it; otherwise "Pastor" is fine.

Determining the Problem

> **COUNSELOR:** What brings you to this part of the country, Henry?
>
> **HENRY:** Well, there are some things around Mildred's house that have been needing to be fixed for some time, so since I'm alone now, I thought this would be a good time to stop promising her I was going to do them, and do them.

COUNSELOR: From what Mildred and Sally told me last week, I guess there have been a lot of changes in your life in the last couple of years.

HENRY: You can say that again. You know, my wife died the year after I retired, that was two years ago March. Then almost exactly a year ago, my oldest daughter, Mildred's sister Grace, passed way—automobile accident, she never came home from her trip to the market. Then four months ago I had to give up Sally, I just couldn't handle her anymore. . . .

SALLY: That's because I didn't need to be handled!

HENRY: You be quiet, girl. Speak when spoken to.

SALLY: You can't make me be quiet. I'll talk when I want to.

HENRY: Who taught you to talk like that? Your good for nothing juvenile delinquent friends?

MILDRED: You know she still calls them long distance every night when I'm at work. Then she lies to me when I confront her with the telephone bill.

HENRY: What's the matter with you, Sally?

COUNSELOR: Help! I'm lost. I thought, Henry, that you and I were talking about the changes that had taken place in your life and now suddenly we're in the middle of a quarrel and have managed to be talking about telephone bills. What happened? [The counselor looks each member in the eye to underscore that the question—What happened?—is aimed at everyone.]

Instead of blaming or accusing the family for rudely interrupting one another, the counselor assumes responsibility for the topic change by asking the family for "help." By asking "what happened?" the counselor helps the family to learn how to comment on what is happening rather than simply be controlled by the flow of events.

HENRY: I don't know. But this sort of thing happens a lot.

COUNSELOR: I'm curious, Sally and Mildred, does this sort of argument seem as familiar to the two of you as it does to Henry? [Sally and Mildred nod affirmatively.]
      Maybe we ought to just make a mental note of that, and then return to you, Henry. I think you were telling me that in the last two years you have lost three very important people to you: your wife, your oldest daughter, and your granddaughter. I'm wondering what you've done to keep yourself going?

The counselor attempts to personalize the I.P.'s problem to Henry's life —that is, fighting with Sally has meant losing Sally, which has resulted in feeling lonely.

HENRY: Well, I guess I haven't been doing that well. It's awful lonesome around the house. I guess that's another reason why I'm here.

COUNSELOR: Did you know that your grandfather was here because he missed you, Sally?

The counselor reframes Henry's loneliness in personal terms for Sally ("He missed you").

SALLY: Yeah, I missed him too. I know he loves me.

HENRY: Then why don't you mind me? You were brought up to know right from wrong.

SALLY: 'Cause I don't have to mind you. I'm old enough to take care of myself. You don't understand me!

HENRY: I understand enough. I understand you won't tell me the truth. I understand you'd sneak out of the house at night and then lie to me about it the next morning.

SALLY: It was none of your business. Besides, what were you doing checking up on me in the middle of the night anyway? If you'd trusted me more then maybe I wouldn't have had to sneak out. So there!

COUNSELOR: It's happening again. We were talking about how much you, Henry, missed you, Sally, when suddenly the topic changed so that before we could finish with the thought of what it was like for you to be missing Sally, and what that was like for Sally, we were arguing over whether or not Sally used to sneak out of the house.

The fight is interrupted by the counselor to point out the process of how the fight is happening, but not to scold or accuse anyone of having let it occur.

HENRY: We do argue a lot, don't we? [Looks toward the counselor.]

COUNSELOR: I'm not sure; are you asking me a question or making a statement?

HENRY: I guess I'm making a statement.

COUNSELOR: I don't even know if arguing a lot is a problem for the three of you, but I do know that I'm not here to create problems that don't exist. So I guess I'm wondering why it is that the three of you are all here together right now? What problem do the three of you have in common that has brought you here together?

MILDRED: All Sally and I ever do is argue. If I tell Sally to be in by ten o'clock, she makes it a point to be in no earlier than eleven. Then there is a fight. If I ask her to pick up her room, she won't do it until I scream at her. I am sick to death of the hassles, and I have only had Sally for four months.

COUNSELOR: What do you think is the problem, Sally?

SALLY: They both pick on me. They won't let me do anything that I want. None of my friends' parents are as unreasonable. Grandpa and Mom don't even want to try to understand me.

COUNSELOR: What about you, Henry? What do you see as the problem?

HENRY: The girl is headstrong, that's all. She's too headstrong for her own good.

SALLY: I am not!

MILDRED: You are too!

SALLY: That's bull!

HENRY: Don't talk back to your mother.

SALLY: I'll talk back to anybody I want to. You can't stop me. I proved that.

HENRY: [turning toward the counselor]: See what I mean? The girl is too headstrong for her own good.

COUNSELOR: Is there anybody else in the family like that?

HENRY: [smiling sheepishly]: Well, I guess I do have a bit of a stubborn streak myself . . .

MILDRED: A bit—that's an understatement!

HENRY: Well, you're just as stubborn.

COUNSELOR: Whoa! Let's not get started on an argument about who is the most stubborn. [Smiling] It sounds and looks to me like all of you are rather forceful. [Mildred and Henry smile and nod.] [Looking at Sally] It sounds a bit to me, Sally, as if you take after your mother and your grandfather more than they'd like you to in the stubbornness department. How does that seem to you?

The counselor reframes Sally's attitude from "quarrelsome" to "stubborn." Since Henry and Mildred admit to being "stubborn" themselves: this reframing suggests how stubbornness as well as insolence can create and perpetuate a family quarrel.

SALLY: It's okay for them to be stubborn. They're the adults. But if I stick up for myself, then there's trouble.

HENRY: It's different when you are 17.

SALLY: It is not!

MILDRED: How many times have I told you not to talk back to your elders?

COUNSELOR: Here we go again! I need for you folks to speak one at a time. The three of you are used to communicating like this, but I'm not. Bear with me; I'm a little slow, and I need more time to think over what each of you is saying. . . . To catch up, let me summarize where I think we are, but if I summarize your position inaccurately, be sure to tell me. It sounds to me that each of you is feeling frustrated because it seems as if no matter what you do, some kind of conflict arises. From Henry and Mildred's point of view, it seems that Sally is starting all the problems by not cooperating with what you ask her to do, whether it is coming home at a certain time or keeping long distance telephone conversations to an arranged limit.

Sally, it sounds as if you are feeling that no matter what you do, you won't really be able to please your mother and grandfather. So you have made up your mind not to tell them what you are really thinking and feeling because you feel hassled whether you tell them the truth or whether you don't. [Sally nods approvingly.]

Let me ask you each the same difficult question: What would happen if I had a magic wand that could make the problem go away? That is, suppose I waved my wand and suddenly there was no more quarreling in your family. Mildred, for you and Henry that would mean that whenever either of you asked Sally to do something, she would do it without question; while for you, Sally, that would mean that Henry and Mildred would only ask you to do things that you agreed were reasonable. Suppose I could make that condition exist. How would your lives change? Henry?

"Sally's problem" is generalized to a family problem and then reduced so each family member can appreciate how he or she is being affected in personal terms. This technique lightens Sally's label of Identified Patient.

HENRY: Well, I might not have to take so many nitroglycerin pills for my heart condition. I'm sure I'd sleep better at night not wondering what kind of mischief Sally was in.

COUNSELOR: What about you, Sally? How would your life change?

SALLY: Well, my friends would be able to come over when Mom was home. I could go out more without having to feel so guilty. But it will never happen.

COUNSELOR: The nice thing about playing "what if" is that nothing has to happen to be able to talk about it.

What about you, Mildred, how do you think your life would change if there was an absence of conflict?

MILDRED: Well, then I'd be able to work better without always having to jump when the telephone rings. That would be a relief. I'd certainly have more money, since I would save all the money I've had to spend on long distance telephone calls to Dad over all the crises in the last four months.

COUNSELOR: So both you and Sally get into telephone problems when you're feeling stuck and lonely and need some support.

There is one thing that is missing for me in what you all have told me. It sounds as if the energy that you would free up should you all decide to give up arguing would go into individual activities. In other words, if you stopped arguing with each other, you would stop talking and relating to one another.

For example, Henry, I could see you stuck at home feeling very unnecessary and unneeded by both Sally and Mildred. Mildred, when you said you would stop calling your father so much if the arguing stopped, it sounded to me as if you would be losing some of the contact and close relationship you now have with him. Sally, when you said you'd be spending more time with your friends and being away from home more, I had the same sense of the family bonds growing weaker.

In my experience, it usually seems as if families would rather fight with one another than have no contact at all. So I'm afraid I have some concern for the three of you, thinking that as long as you have no constructive activities planned into which your energy could go to keep you connected as a family, all of you will be feeling a need, although perhaps unconsciously, to keep the fighting going. I guess what I'm saying is that frequently families have an easier time giving up their quarrels if they have in mind some activities that would be possible if they had extra energy to invest—the extra energy coming from the energy they were previously wasting on the old destructive quarrels.

At any rate, you all need to be aware that if you give up fighting with one another, you will have to relate to one another in a different way than you are doing now. Maybe it will be better or maybe worse, but it surely will be different.

Determining Attempted Solutions

COUNSELOR: I'm curious; what have the three of you been trying to do to keep the fighting down? That is, what have you tried that has worked and what have you tried that hasn't? What do you say we start with what has worked?

SALLY: Nothing works.

MILDRED: Nothing works.

HENRY: Nothing works.

COUNSELOR: Well, at least you have all finally agreed on something. That's a start! What about what hasn't worked, then? Sally, what have you tried to do to stop the arguments that hasn't worked?

SALLY: Nothing works. Even if I give in and do what they say, they just start up right away on something else.

COUNSELOR: So giving in doesn't work.

SALLY: Right.

COUNSELOR: What else doesn't work?

SALLY: Arguing with them.

COUNSELOR: So more arguing doesn't stop the arguments. What else?

SALLY: Telling them the truth.

COUNSELOR: What happens when you tell them the truth?

SALLY: They tell me how I shouldn't think that way or something dumb like that.

COUNSELOR: So telling your mother or grandfather what you really think doesn't work to stop the arguments?

SALLY: Right. Another thing that doesn't work is running away from home. I tried that once, but it was stupid. Anyway, it didn't change how they treated me.

COUNSELOR: So running away didn't help.

SALLY: That's all I can think of.

COUNSELOR: That's quite a lot. Thank you, Sally, you've been very helpful. What about you, Henry, what have you tried to get Sally to do what you ask her to that hasn't worked?

HENRY: Well, I've tried locking her in her room, but she jumps out the window.

COUNSELOR: So locking Sally in her room hasn't worked.

HENRY: I even tried sending her back to her mother, but that didn't work.

COUNSELOR: So having Sally move out didn't work.

HENRY: I've tried reasoning with her.

COUNSELOR: So reasoning didn't work.

HENRY: I've tried restricting all of her privileges until she didn't have anything left, but that didn't work.

COUNSELOR: So restricting her privileges didn't work.

HENRY: I've tried bribes, but they didn't work either.

COUNSELOR: Bribes?

HENRY: You know, if you will do such and such, I'll buy you a car, or a stereo, or things like that.

COUNSELOR: So bribes haven't worked. Can you think of anything else that was unsuccessful or maybe even just partially successful at slowing up the fighting?

HENRY: Every now and then I just lose control and scream. That seems to work for a while, but with my heart I can't afford to lose control like that very often.

COUNSELOR: So all things considered, losing control and screaming doesn't work either?

HENRY: I guess I have to say that.

COUNSELOR: What about you, Mildred? What have you tried that hasn't worked to slow up the quarreling?

MILDRED: Basically the same things as my father. I'm rather new at this whole "mothering thing," you know. For a while I tried letting Sally do anything she wanted, but that didn't work: we would just end up arguing over what television show to watch.

COUNSELOR: So giving Sally free rein hasn't worked?

MILDRED: I'm afraid not.

Determining Goals

COUNSELOR: One of the things that I'm rather concerned with right now and feel I should share with you is that it seems as if you have tried almost everything in an attempt to get along better, yet nothing works. I almost wonder if, under the circumstances, the three of you really want to be a family?

HENRY: I certainly do. That's why I'm here.

MILDRED: I do.

SALLY: I guess so.

COUNSELOR: Well, at least that's a good start, but I'm afraid good intentions aren't always enough to change old destructive behavior patterns. Assuming for a minute that your situation isn't completely hopeless, I'm wondering, what would be the smallest amount of change in your family situation that would give each of you the sense that you were making progress toward a more peaceful existence together?

MILDRED: I'd know things were better if we stopped fighting.

COUNSELOR: That's an awfully big order to start with. I was thinking of something far more conservative; for example, cutting back to three separate quarrels a day instead of the constant argument that you seem to have now.

MILDRED: Well, I'd know we were doing better if we only had one fight a week.

COUNSELOR: That still seems a big change. I'm looking for the smallest amount of change you would need *to begin to have a sense of progress* toward growing closer together as a family.

MILDRED: I don't even know how much we fight each day. All I know is that it is too much.

COUNSELOR: I can understand how you feel, but what you say suggests that before you can make an estimate of how much change you would need, you probably need to get an accurate measure of exactly how much fighting goes on.

What about you, Henry, can you think of some personal measure that might change if you had a sense the family was making progress?

HENRY: I wouldn't feel so tensed up all the time.

COUNSELOR: Does how tense you are feeling seem related to how many nitroglycerin tablets you need to take each day?

HENRY: I guess it is.

COUNSELOR: Then how many are you taking each day now?

HENRY: Maybe three or four.

COUNSELOR: You don't have a good record then?

HENRY: No, not really.

COUNSELOR: It sounds to me that before you're ready to set any goals you need some more information as to how many nitroglycerin tablets you are taking, and when you are taking them. In other words, do they relate in some way to the bickering and distress in the family?

What about you, Sally? What would be the smallest amount of change in your life that would give you a sense that things were improving, even if the improvement were slow?

SALLY: Things would be better if they stopped picking on my friends.

COUNSELOR: How often do your mother and grandfather make remarks about your friends?

SALLY: All the time.

COUNSELOR: It's hard for me to put a number on that. I guess I need for you to be more exact if I'm going to be useful to you.

SALLY: Well, I can't tell you exactly. But I'll bet they put down my friends at least six times a day.

COUNSELOR: So you feel it's too much, but you don't really have a count against which we might compare, so you would have some indication that progress was being made. . . . Well, it sounds, then, as if each of you has at least a general notion of what would constitute progress for the family, but that each of you needs a bit more information before you can really get down to measuring specifics. Just to make sure I have it straight—as I understand it, Sally, you would know there was progress if your grandfather and mother criticized your friends less, but as of now you really don't know how often that occurs or for that matter how much is too much. I wonder if during the next week you would be willing to keep a record of how many times each day you feel as if either Henry or Mildred criticizes your friends?

SALLY: Just keep count?

COUNSELOR: That would be fine.

Mildred, it sounds as if you would know that there was progress if there were fewer fights each day, but presently you don't know exactly how many fights there really are. Would you be willing to keep a journal about how many fights there are each day? I'd like you to keep track of *date, time, topic,* and the *length* of each fight. Would you be willing to do that?

MILDRED: I'll do anything if you think it will help.

COUNSELOR: I appreciate your willingness to expend some energy trying something new, but I should make clear to you that just keeping track of what's happening isn't supposed to make for any changes. It is simply a preliminary step. What are you going to record, then?

MILDRED: Date, time, subject, and length.

COUNSELOR: Fine.

Henry, would you be willing to keep an accurate log of how many nitroglycerin tablets you are taking each day?

HENRY: Well, I'm not sure how much good it will do, but if you say so, I'll do it.

COUNSELOR: I'm not sure how much good it will do either, Henry. At best it will give me some more information with which to work. At worst, it may just be a plain waste of time.

HENRY: Well, time's something I've got plenty of, unfortunately.

COUNSELOR: Then what I'd like you to keep track of is the *date, time of day,* and *what is happening*—are you fishing, fighting, reading —every time your chest pains get bad enough to take a pill. Have you got that?

HENRY: You want to know the time, date, and circumstances every time I need a pill.

COUNSELOR: Right.

There is one thing more I need to ask you to do by way of completing your homework. I would like each of you not to change in any way how you are dealing with each other. By that I mean, Henry, I don't want you suddenly to stop arguing just because you are aware that if you continue to get mad you will need a pill. Go ahead and argue, take the pill, and note it in your book.

Mildred, the same with you. Halfway through the week, you may detect a pattern of what's happening when Sally draws you into fighting with her. Rather than change your normal behavior in any way, I want you to go ahead and have the fight so that we'll have a record for an average week.

Sally, the same applies to you. I don't want you suddenly to stop arguing, or become instantly respectful toward your grandfather and mother. If you feel either one of them trying to suck you into a fight, go ahead and *be sucked in.* If you know that doing something they disapprove of will make them say something that will start a fight, go ahead and do it just as you normally would.

I know that it sounds strange to ask you to not change anything for a week, but I have my reasons. First, *it is very difficult to change your family and observe it at the same time,* so I would like you just to observe this week so that I have accurate information about you for next week.

Second, I think you folks *have been through a lot* of major changes in your lives lately and I think *you all deserve a week's rest.* Henry, you've lost three women from your home that you really loved, your wife, your oldest daughter, and now your granddaughter. Mildred, you've had to adapt to becoming Sally's instant mother after 17 years of separation. That's enough to wear anybody out. And, Sally, you've had to adjust to the deaths of your grandmother and your aunt—which is really like trying to adjust to the death of two mothers. In the last four months, you've moved hundreds of miles away from your old friends and now have to start all over again getting used to a new school and new friends. You certainly have earned a week off from trying to make everything different.

What I'm saying is that all three of you have been through a lot. You all need some time away from trying to change so that you will have some time for some new energy to build up.

Finally, the third reason I don't want you to act any differently toward one another is that I can tell just from the interaction that you have described so far that the three of you spend a lot of time together for support. I could wish that you had some other joint activities besides making demands and quarreling, but under the circumstances, I think it's better for all of you to be together quarreling than quietly drifting apart from one another.

I realize I've been talking a lot and might have overloaded you. I wonder if I could ask you each to tell me what you just heard me say so I'll be sure I got my points across.

The counselor then allowed the family members to have an opportunity to reflect back what each had just heard him say. Essentially, the counselor wanted to make certain that the three family members understood that they should keep doing what they had been doing because, first, they needed an opportunity to observe what they were doing; second, they needed a rest from trying to change because of all the other recent changes in their lives; and, third, they needed to continue to support one another even though that support now took the form of arguing.

Comprehending the Family System

What is the extent of the family system? This family system clearly includes mother, daughter, and grandfather. The importance of the elder in this family cannot be overemphasized: it is Henry who provided and lived in the same home in which Sally grew up, it is Henry who has recently gone through the same losses as Sally, and it is Henry who left his home in a different state to be with Sally in her new home at Mildred's. Henry's feelings will have to be counted if counseling is going to be successful.

There is a natural temptation to exclude family members who do not live permanently in the immediate geographical area from one's idea of what constitutes the family system. After all, including a distant relative certainly complicates matters. In this case, it might seem particularly tempting to exclude Henry since he is terribly opinionated, stubborn, and rather demanding of attention. There are many indications, however, that even though Henry claims he is going to move back home after Mildred's house is repaired, he will still remain very influential in the family system. Consider first that he raised both Sally and Mildred. In a sense, he is father to both of them. Second, Mildred reports that she frequently communicates with her father by telephone when she feels uncertain; this behavior again shows the significance of Henry's connection to the family system. Finally, Henry has at least temporarily physically moved himself to the scene of the action—presumably to "try again" with Sally. All of these clues tell the counselor that Henry is a full-fledged member of this family system.

Where is the counselor in the family system? Another way of looking at this question is to ask, "What is the counselor doing with the family?" In this case, the answer is rather clear. Most of the counselor's time is spent stopping arguments. The counselor has been drawn into the family system as a sort of verbal policeman. When in this role, the counselor experienced himself siding with Sally (the "victim") against her demanding, moralistic, stubborn grandfather (the "perpetrator"). He used this information to recognize how this family system made it difficult for anyone, even a counselor, to remain neutral while discussing any topic.

The counselor used the information as to *how* he was being drawn into the family situation in two ways. First, he recognized that the family was placing all the responsibility for preventing or halting a quarrel on him. That is, the family members were interrupting one another, reading each other's minds ("You are a liar because I know what you are really thinking"), and discounting each other through topic changes as if they bore no personal responsibility for the "inevitable" fight that followed. Therefore, the counselor realized that before this family could make any progress in getting closer, they would first have to learn to police themselves—to monitor and eventually control their own predictably provocative behavior.

Second, the counselor moved away from the position that Sally was "right" and Henry was "wrong." In the privacy of his own mind, he tried to examine what it must be like to be Henry. That is, what would it be like to view yourself as a religious, moral man, yet have both your daughter and granddaughter violate your codes? The counselor tried to imagine the sense of failure Henry would have experienced when his daughter had a baby out of wedlock as he was trying to maintain a sense of stature within his church. Now, even given the opportunity to try again with another generation (Sally), Henry still is unable to control the standards and values of his off-spring. The counselor tried to imagine Henry's sense of powerless-ness.

Intensifying Henry's pain and frustration are the loss of his wife and other daughter within a two-year period. Again, he finds himself unable to control the important events taking place in his life. The counselor tried to imagine how the sense of loss of control would feel.

What are the family rules? As with most families who are fighting, the family rule is, "We don't talk to each other about what is really important." Another way of putting this rule is, "We keep our personal troubles to ourselves." In other words, these families fight with each other so they will not have to share their personal feelings with each other. What such a rule means is that this family may feel very awkward when the fighting stops because Henry, Mildred, and Sally will not know what to say to one another. There-fore, the family needs to move slowly enough for the members to make an initial transition from quarreling to neutral topics such as recipes, movies, and television shows, rather than move all at once from fighting to holding meaningful conversations about personal topics.

Is there an Identified Patient? Sally is this family's Identified Patient. The family needs an I.P. to explain why they are having trouble living together. Besides, if there were no I.P., Henry would have to admit to his unhappiness, isolation, and profound sense of failure; Mildred would have to admit to her guilt for conceiving and abandoning Sally; and Sally would have to admit to her hurt and resentment about being abandoned by her mother, her aunt (through death), and her grandfather (through uproar). Sally would also have to deal with her loneliness and isolation while trying to adjust to a new school at a time when most older adolescents have already formed strong social bonds with one another. Consequently, having Sally bear the label of I.P. serves a purpose in protecting all members of the family, Sally included.

How is power exercised?   Henry is exercising his power by using moralistic denunciations. His most recent power move was to extrude Sally from his out-of-state home—to attempt to prove to her that he really could control some aspect of her behavior. Mildred is exercising her power by coming on as an "incompetent"; by acting in this way, she is able to coerce her father into assuming responsibility for Sally that rightfully Mildred must exercise. Sally is expressing her power by acting out of control.

Why has the problem not been solved?   Everyone in the family is feeling very powerless and victimized. The worse the three of them feel, the more they retreat into behaviors that give at least some sense of power. That is, each one does or says something to get a reaction from the others. The reactions may be negative, but at least provoking reactions is controlling something. The negative reactions lead to fighting, which in turn precludes the possibility of the establishment of any positive relations. As long as each continues to fight so as to keep from feeling powerless, none of them can ever gain a positive sense of what it means to feel powerful (getting what you *really* want) from living in a supportive family.

Does the family still need a counselor?   Certainly, yes. Henry, particularly, given his losses of the last two years and what can be deduced to be the general state of his health—nitroglycerin is not a casual medication for disease—is clearly in need of a reduction in the level of stress. In some ways, the constant quarreling poses a life-and-death situation for Henry. Even speaking conservatively, of all the members of the family, Henry is really the most vulnerable since he is in the process of losing what is left of his family after already having lost his health and his job. Because he is the most vulnerable—and thus desperate—he will probably be the most difficult member of the family with whom to deal. This example clearly demonstrates how the I.P. is often not the client most in need. Yet the mother and daughter also are in bad straits, after only four months together, which are likely to get even worse.

Mobilizing the Family System

Speaking the family's language.   In working with a family system in which the predominant problem is verbal conflict, the system usually communicates in the language of "negativism." In other words, no matter what you as counselor say, the entire family system is apt to take issue with you. When, for example, you give homework, they are as likely to be uncooperative with you—by not following through on their assignments—as they are to be uncooperative with one another. This behavior can be a problem for counselors who are insensitive to the language the family is speaking. Suppose such a counselor decides that the family should start being more friendly with one another and makes a suggestion that they declare a truce at the dinner table; this family would probably report that the biggest fights during the succeeding week occurred during dinner! For some counselors faced with the language of negativism, it is easiest to label the family "resistant" or "impossible" and terminate counseling at once.

Other counselors can accept families who speak in negativism. Rather than set these families and themselves up for certain disaster by issuing behavioral injunctions (homework directions) requiring the language of "cooperation" to be useful, such flexible counselors will concentrate on giving behavioral injunctions that will effectively meet and fit the family's language of negativism.

In this case, for example, the counselor's goal is to help the family members stop fighting with one another so they have an opportunity to develop deeper and more straightforward relationships of support with one another. Knowing their language to be negativism, he will ask the family members to do homework assignments that will be *useful to them if they do them,* but *even more useful to them if they do not*—that is, if the members "negate" the counselor's requests as they do each other's. Along these lines, the counselor asked the family members to collect information for him about the frequency and effects of the family quarrels, but most importantly he specifically instructed them that they were not to fight less, or even try to fight less, over the next week. If, in fact, they cooperate with his instructions and do not change, then they will each have collected a valuable behavioral record providing insight into how and when they start, continue, and end their family fights, as well as indicating that they can all follow a request. Therefore, if they cooperate with the counselor, the effect will be useful.

If, on the other hand, they use their normal negativism language, they will "quarrel" with the counselor by refusing to cooperate in either the recording of data or the perpetuation of fighting. Generally, negativism families follow true to form by refusing either to record data or to fight.

Because most families who use negativism find it such a compelling language, there is one technique of phrasing used by skillful counselors to reframe negativism to make room for peace. This phrase is specifically introduced to the family during the homework assignment. Each family member is told, "Go ahead and allow your-self *to get sucked into the fights.*" This behavioral injunction is partic-ularly powerful because it permits the family members for the first time to experience being powerful by choosing not to fight. For a particularly negativistic individual, the opportunity to defeat both a fellow family member and the counselor simultaneously by refusing to fight is almost irresistible.

Therefore, the counselor decided to use the technique of *symp-tom prescription* for this family, since by either following his instruc-tions or subverting his instructions—thus allowing peace to break out —the outcome would be useful to the family.

> **COUNSELOR:** You folks were going to collect some information for me for this week. How did that go?
>
> **HENRY:** Well, I needed to take four or five pills, but those seemed more related to exercise than arguments.
>
> **COUNSELOR:** You didn't keep a written record?
>
> **HENRY:** No, like I say, there really wasn't anything to write down that I couldn't remember to tell you.
>
> **COUNSELOR:** What about you, Sally? Did you keep a record of all the times that your grandfather and mother criticized your friends?
>
> **SALLY:** Yes, but it only happened once. I even forget what it was about.
>
> **COUNSELOR:** What about you, Mildred? You were supposed to keep a record of fights for the entire family.
>
> **MILDRED:** I made the list, but I left it at home. There was really only one fight worth talking about and that was when I asked Sally to feed the dog.
>
> **COUNSELOR:** I'd rather go by written information, but if we don't have it then we'll have to go by what you remember.
>
> **MILDRED:** It took place Wednesday, before dinner. I asked Sally if she would please feed the dog and she said she wouldn't do it.
>
> **SALLY:** That's not the way it happened.
>
> **COUNSELOR:** I understand that you both may remember what hap-pened differently, and I'll try to make sure that you both get a chance to be heard from. But for right now, Mildred, I'd like to stay with how you recall what happened. Do you remember exactly what Sally said?
>
> **MILDRED:** She said, "Not now, after dinner."
>
> **COUNSELOR:** So you asked Sally to feed the dog and she told you she would do it after dinner, is that right?

MILDRED: Right.

COUNSELOR: Then at that point, what did you do to keep the fight going?

MILDRED: What do you mean?

COUNSELOR: I'm trying to get a sense of how you responded to Sally. Can you tell me how you felt when Sally said, "I'll feed the dog after dinner"?

MILDRED: I felt like she wouldn't listen to me.

COUNSELOR: You felt ignored?

MILDRED: Yes, ignored.

COUNSELOR: And how did you feel when you felt ignored?

MILDRED: Angry.

COUNSELOR: So when Sally told you that she would feed the dog after dinner when you asked her to feed the dog, you felt ignored and angry.
  [Turning to Sally] I'm curious, Sally, did you mean at that point for your mother to feel ignored and angry?

SALLY: No.

COUNSELOR: So, Sally, you didn't mean for your mother to feel ignored and angry, but that was the way you [looking at Mildred] were feeling. At that point, Mildred, how did you allow your anger and frustration from feeling ignored to keep the fight going?

MILDRED: I'm still not sure what you want me to say next.

COUNSELOR: What did you say next to Sally?

MILDRED: I told her she was "lazy" and "good for nothing," and told her I shouldn't have even bothered to ask her anyway.

COUNSELOR: So feeling angry and ignored, you kept the fight going by calling Sally names, like "lazy" and "good for nothing."

MILDRED: I'm still not sure what you mean by saying I kept the fight going. Are you saying I could have stopped the fight?

COUNSELOR: You weren't supposed to stop the fight. I'm glad you didn't. That's how we're getting this valuable information—what I meant by "what did you do to keep the fight going" is that there might have been another course of action you could have followed to end the fight. For example, you might have fed the dog yourself, or waited to see if she really did it after dinner. Or you might have shared with Sally how angry and ignored you were feeling when she didn't do what you asked her to do. I'm certainly not saying you should have done anything different from what you did. All I'm trying to do is find out what is keeping the fighting going. Does that answer your question?

MILDRED: Yes, I thought you were saying that I was *intentionally* trying to keep the fight going.

COUNSELOR [turning to Sally]: Sally, at that point in the argument when your mother called you "lazy" and "good for nothing," what were you feeling?

SALLY: I was feeling: "Here we go again."

COUNSELOR: Are you saying you were feeling resigned and hopeless?

SALLY: Yeah, I guess you could say that.

COUNSELOR: Did you know that was how Sally was feeling?

MILDRED: No, I thought she was feeling smug and satisfied that she had gotten me mad.

COUNSELOR: So you thought she was feeling good when actually she was feeling bad. [To both Mildred and Sally] That's interesting to me, since at this point in the fight, both of you thought the other was feeling quite differently than she actually was. [Turning to Sally] But rather than tell your mother how you actually were feeling, or feeding the dog, you acted on your feelings of resignation and hopelessness to keep the fight going by saying back to your mother . . .

SALLY: I told her I thought she was a "bitch" and "I wish I lived in a foster home."

COUNSELOR: How were you feeling then, Mildred?

MILDRED: I was feeling totally defeated, so I began to cry.

HENRY: Then I stepped in and told Sally that she couldn't talk that way to her mother.

COUNSELOR: So, Henry, you stepped in between Mildred and Sally and turned the fight into your fight by taking Mildred's side?

HENRY: I hadn't thought of it like that, but I guess you could say so. Anyway, using your logic, I guess "it worked" because Sally and I got into it . . .

The counselor continued with the same line of questioning and reflecting: asking at each point in the fight how each family member felt and what each family member did to keep the fight going. The counselor continued very casually to mention strategies they might have used to stop the fighting—had they wanted to. By using the language, "What did you do next to keep the fight going," the counselor implicitly emphasized the element of *choice* that is always present, even when reacting to the most provocative of incidents. After dissecting the fight from beginning to end, the counselor cut the interview short:

COUNSELOR: Well, I'm glad we've had one fight to discuss, but frankly it just isn't enough. Of course, it's more pleasant that you weren't hassling with one another as much this week, but I'm sure that's just a temporary phenomenon. I think it's only reasonable to expect that next week your conflict level will probably go back to where it was before you came in here.

Sometimes, unfortunately, families may have a natural "lull in the battle" for a couple of weeks at a time. That sort of thing gets in the way of doing the work we need to do in here to find out more about the fighting. Just to cover that possibility, I'm going to ask you each to do something you may, at first, think peculiar: I'm going to ask each of you to intentionally start one family fight a day. In this way, you will each have an opportunity to observe what you all do to keep a fight going when, in fact, the fight isn't real to begin with. Is that clear?

HENRY: You're telling us to have, let's see . . . three fights a day in addition to the ones we are already having? We came here to fight less, not more.

COUNSELOR: I can see your point that what I've said sounds peculiar. The problem is that if you are not having fights spontaneously, then we are wasting our time meeting together; there is no material to work on. I wish as a family you were at a point where we could begin to talk about how you might now use the time you used to spend fighting to be nice to one another, even if this only meant that you could all go to a movie together, or sit down together during a meal and talk about school, or hobbies, or whatever. But though I'd like to, there is no reason yet to believe that you folks are ready to work on treating each other well—as well, say, as you might treat one of your own friends or a distinguished stranger. So for now we need to keep working on the fighting.

MILDRED: Three fights a day extra really does seem like a lot. Couldn't we fight less . . . say, each of us start just one fight during the next week?

COUNSELOR: What do you think of that, Sally?

SALLY: I want to fight less, not more.

COUNSELOR: I'd like to go along with you, but I really don't see how I can get enough information about your fighting in just three experimental fights during the next week. Let's compromise so you each intentionally start a minimum of three fights a week. Sally, that means you'll pick three fights with either your mother or your grandfather. Henry, you should pick one fight with Sally on your own and then intentionally take over two fights for Mildred. Mildred, I would like you to pick one fight with Sally and then in two others, I'd like you to get your Dad to come to your rescue.

One other thing, and this point is very important, I'd like you not to identify which fights are "experimental" and which are "real" until next week.

HENRY: That's still nine intentional fights for next week. That's just too much.

COUNSELOR: You've been fighting much more than that anyway.

HENRY: But these are *additional.* Couldn't we just have, say, one experimental fight a week?

COUNSELOR: I'd like to say Yes, Henry, but we really need the information about how you fight and I just don't think you or Sally or Mildred are ready to spend peaceful, supportive time with one another yet. I'm sorry.

HENRY: Well, I don't know . . .

COUNSELOR: It's important you give it a try.

HENRY: Well, I'll try.

COUNSELOR: How about the rest of you?

At this point, both Mildred and Sally assured the counselor that despite the fact that there was too much fighting for their tastes, they would "try." The counselor then went over in detail the fighting and record-keeping procedures so that each family member understood exactly what was *assigned* to have happen. A new appointment was set for the following week.

When the family returned the following week, they had not done their homework. Again, they reported only one fight—it was spontaneous—which the counselor dissected in a similar way to the fight over "feeding the dog" in the previous session. When the counselor informed the family that if they expected to make any progress they still needed to fight more, he was met with an impressive, unified wall of resistance. Henry, Sally, and Mildred each felt that the counselor was mistaken in asking them to fight more. Henry, acting as spokesman, informed the counselor that they were now ready to be nice to each other. As if to offer proof, he stated that they had gone not only to a show together but to church together as well. The family was clearly unified on something: defeating the instructions of the counselor.

In the privacy of his own mind, the counselor interpreted the family's position as a definite sign of progress: before the family had been fighting among themselves; at least now they were unified enough to fight someone else. Behaviorally it was also clear that the family was capable of getting along when they stopped fighting since they had actually gone out together on two occasions. Given such rapid progress, a counselor can be tempted to switch to the language of "cooperation," or even to brag to the family how clever he was in his use of symptom prescription. Instead, fortunately, the counselor recognized that since the intervention he was using was being helpful to the family, he should *continue* to use it:

> **COUNSELOR:** Henry, Mildred, Sally: I hear what you are all saying. I know it feels better now that you have somehow reduced arguing, but I really don't think that you are ready to start treating one another like friends. For instance, Sally, I would love you to be able to share with your mother what's going on at school; whom you would like to meet; the challenges and frustrations of your life. Mildred, I would love for you to be able to share with your daughter and your father about your life, the disappointments and the victories. I'd especially like for you to be able to share with Sally what it was like for you to have to give her up and what a joy it was for you to finally have her back as a daughter after all these years. Henry, I would give anything to believe that you were ready to share with Sally and Mildred the wisdom of your years, and that you could feel comfortable sharing with them the history of the family so that they could have a sense of continuity of how their lives fit in with yours. But I really just don't think you are ready yet. There has just been too much change too quickly. I'm sure you'll have a big upset next week that will rock you all back on your heels.

> **MILDRED:** We appreciate what you are doing, Pastor, but I don't think you understand. We are still having our little battles and disagreements, but we aren't having catastrophes anymore.

> **COUNSELOR:** That seems hard to believe. Maybe it's just your own wishful thinking. Is what Mildred said about "difficulties" not turning into "catastrophes" your experience too, Sally? Henry?

When Sally and Henry affirmed that, in fact, their lives were not carefree or without occasional quarrels, but that the quality and the quantity of the fighting had changed from being unmanageable to manageable, the counselor asked each member of the family what he or she was doing differently. Each initially professed ignorance as to what he or she was doing differently, so the counselor made his inquiry more general, as to what seemed to be different living in the family. This drew the family members out a bit more, so they could share how they were each being more tolerant and less judgmental. The counselor used the technique of reflective listening to make sure that he understood what each of them was saying. In closing the meeting, the counselor continued the symptom prescription strategy:

> **COUNSELOR:** In talking with you more, I am impressed with how much effort each of you is putting into getting along better with one another, even to the point, in a few instances, of actually acting friendly

toward one another. But this still sounds too good to be true, at least for more than a while. I think that you're moving too fast and I would like to suggest to you that you slow down. The best way I can think of to do that is to have at least two intentional fights per person per week.

Again, the response was united: the family members wanted to fight less. The counselor compromised a bit by saying that he would accept one fight per person per week (compromising from six to three), but absolutely no less. The family left the session looking a bit disgruntled and rather irritated at the counselor.

At the next appointment, Henry began again as the family spokesman:

HENRY: Pastor, we appreciate all you have done for us, but this will be our last visit with you. We're not really fighting anymore and we just don't want the unpleasantness of even one more unnecessary fight.

Winding Up

COUNSELOR: Is that the way all of you feel? [All nod in the affirmative.] What's happened to make you all feel this way?

This question gave each family member an opportunity to recount the progress made: Sally was now being more cooperative at home, while her mother was making effective, but more reasonable and limited demands on her. The family was engaging in more activities designed to make more friends, since both Henry and Sally were new to the area and had few friends. Henry had been invited by Sally and Mildred (mother and daughter made the decision together) to live with them; he was in the process of making the plans and buying the materials to add a room to Mildred's home. All the family members insisted that they were more than ready to be nice to one another. They were also unified and insistent in their message that while they appreciated the attempts of their pastor, they refused to sacrifice their newfound relationships to his experimental fights.

COUNSELOR: Well, if you won't actually start a fight with one another, at least you could humor me along by telling me what you could do if you wanted to start a fight.

This question provided an opportunity to flush potential saboteurs from the bushes. The family members glanced around at each other until finally Henry nodded his head. Each, in turn, then went through all of the ways they knew to start and maintain a fight. After each confession, some paraphrasing of the general disclaimer, "Of course I wouldn't do this now," was added. Noting the family members' willingness to telegraph their secrets of provocation and subversion, the counselor was satisfied that each was now willing to take personal responsibility for creating and perpetuating the devastating intergenerational conflicts that had been chronic only a month before. Consequently, believing his obligations to the family to be met, the counselor felt he should move in the direction of termination by giving the family credit for what they had done, to anticipate some problems, and to end this final session on a note of useful, but restrained, optimism.

COUNSELOR: I must say that I am both surprised and impressed by what you all have done: surprised because you have done it so quickly, impressed because from what you tell me, all of you have given up some familiar, safe ways of relating to one another—namely quarreling—to move on as a family into being supportive friends. Being friends means being vulnerable, so I'm doubly impressed that you folks have gone as far as you have, as quickly as you have. I think you each deserve a pat on the back from me and from each other. Congratulations!

I must say, however, that the rapid progress you made needs to be viewed with caution. I know you would like me to be thinking more positively, but it's only realistic to mention that frequently after families have made a lot of progress, they slide back a bit. So you folks need to be aware of this probability and not be surprised or shocked when it happens.

But before we say good-bye to one another, there is one more item I feel we need to discuss—namely, the whole question of problems you may be having to face in the next year. What problems can each of you anticipate that will affect the whole family?

HENRY: There are lots of problems, but we can overcome them.

COUNSELOR: I appreciate your optimism, Henry, but I'm a great believer that "Forewarned is forearmed." If you can't think of any specific problems, I'm sure that I can.

HENRY: Well, I could get seriously ill.

COUNSELOR: That's certainly a possibility.

HENRY: And I could mess up the room I'm building and spend more money than I have.

COUNSELOR: Good, and *you* might not mess it up at all, but the weather might come in too soon and mess it up for you.

HENRY: Right, or I could fall off a ladder and mess myself up [laughing].

COUNSELOR: That's a good start, Henry. What about you, Sally?

SALLY: I could flunk out of school.

COUNSELOR: How would you do that?

SALLY: I could go back to cutting classes or smarting-off to the teachers.

COUNSELOR: What about the opposite? I can think of a problem you might have if you do too well in school!

SALLY: Yeah, I'd have to worry about what college to go to.

COUNSELOR: Can you think of some problems that situation might present to the family?

SALLY: If I went to college out of town, then I'd be breaking up the family just as it was getting back together.

COUNSELOR: Good. So if you were accepted to a big college, the family would have to figure out how to send you off to school without feeling as if the family was disintegrating. But I wonder if that's not a problem anyway. Won't you have to face a related situation when you graduate from high school at the end of this school year?

SALLY: I guess we will.

COUNSELOR: What about you, Mildred? Can you think of some problems that might happen in the next year?

MILDRED: I might get fired from my job.

COUNSELOR: Or the factory might burn down.

MILDRED: Don't even say that [laughing]!

COUNSELOR: What about closer to home? Sometimes when families with three generations stop having problems with the youngest generation they start having problems with the oldest generation. Can you see how that might happen in your family?

MILDRED: In some ways, it already has happened. I don't think Sally knows this, but in a lot of ways, it's harder for me to get along with Dad than with Sally. There are lots of things for Dad and me to argue about. Already we've had a "to-do" about what the new room should look like. And I have a feeling we have one brewing about how late I should stay out with the men I date.

COUNSELOR: So one of the issues that you can expect to come up during the next year is "How are an adult daughter and her adult father supposed to deal with each other?"

HENRY: We know it won't be easy, but we'll do it.

COUNSELOR: Well, I've enjoyed working with you folks, although I must admit it seems to me that you've done most of the work. If I can be of use to you after the dust settles in a few weeks or months, don't hesitate to call. In fact, why don't you corner me after church in a couple of months just to let me know how things are going.

16

Hypochondriasis

General Remarks

Preoccupation with Bodily Functions

The first reaction that many young people have when they begin to work with elders is that they seem to be preoccupied with talking about bodily functions, both of themselves and of others. While scientists may argue over whether or not the perception of one's own bodily functions becomes more acute with age, it is at least safe to say that as people age, they seem to become more aware of and concerned about their own bodies. This may not be pleasant, but it is understandable.

Consider this fact: From the death rate statistics it is clear that by the time an elder survives to 75 years of age, many of his or her peers are dead. Depending on demographic variables, the number of nonsurvivors may well outnumber the survivors! Of the acquaintances, friends, and family who did not survive, several, for example, will have died from intestinal disorders. Under such circumstances is it startling that a normal bowel movement frequently changes in value over the lifetime from a minor inconvenience to an event of natural wonder? The intestines, of course, represent but one organ system of many with which elders are rightfully concerned, given their experiences with the fragility of life and the proximity of death.

Just as elders are particularly pleased with signs of their good health, they are also frequently alarmed by signs of bad health. Again, with more experience as to the potential significance of ill health, the average elder is far more apt to be concerned over a minor physical symptom than the young adult—just as the young adult is far more apt to be concerned than the eight-year-old child.

Moreover, for most elders, physical pain and health disabilities are a part of old age. Most people by the time they are 65 are suffering from at least two chronic diseases. These diseases include, but are certainly not limited to, heart disease, emphysema, osteoporosis, kidney disease, diabetes, glaucoma, bursitis, and arthritis. If that were not enough, the two most frequent complaints of institutionalized elders involve their teeth and their feet. Almost all elders need reading glasses and most need bifocals. As with vision, almost all elders have some hearing impairment (usually a marked loss in the high-frequency range).

It would of course be wrong to claim that all elders are deaf, blind, and so frail that they have one foot in the grave, but it would not be unrealistic to say that almost all elders have more than one constant reminder that their bodies are not as functional as they once were. Thus, while old age is not a disease in and of itself, as some (Weisman, 1970) have remarked, it might as well be.

However, while there are thus very real reasons for an elder to be attentive to and concerned about the body and its functioning—and accordingly for counselors to expect an emphasis on this aspect of elders' lives—this still is only one side of the matter, and the other is at least equally important for counselor and client.

The issue is not just whether legitimate ailments exist. It is also a question of what quality of life can be expected, given the ailments. This is very largely a matter not simply of physical conditions and stimuli, but of their handling and interpretation—whether the best or the worst is made of them. This, in turn, depends very much on personal rather than physical circumstances. Elders' responses to health problems of all kinds will be greatly influenced by their social and emotional interactions with their friends, families, and health service providers.

Coping—for Better or Worse

The quality of life for elders with real physical problems may still be reasonably satisfactory if these problems are handled well by the elder and others who matter. Equally, however, if coping strategies are lacking or inappropriate and fail, then elders' physical problems, even relatively minor ones, may get the better of them.

Along these lines, human interaction and physical illness are apt to become intertwined in two main ways: *psychosomatic illness* and *hypochondriasis.* In the case of the former, environmental events are transformed via the nervous system into actual physical disease. For example, an elder may be in conflict with his son over some sort of matter; the conflict serves as an environmental stressor that acts through the nervous system on the cardiovascular system to cause high blood pressure. The high blood pressure (hypertension) is *real.* It can be objectively observed using the proper instruments and is clearly recognized to be dangerous to health. The conflict could have provoked other psychosomatic responses; for example, instead of high blood pressure, the elder (or his son) might have developed a stomach ulcer, colitis, or asthma. Any of these illnesses could be real in the sense that they would be observable using the proper diagnostic equipment and are potentially dangerous. In any event, *psychosomatic illness* should not be thought of as simply "being in the mind," since specific body tissues are demonstrably affected.

In counseling elders, the presence of serious psychosomatic health problems can add a great deal of urgency to counseling sessions. Psychosomatic knowledge, especially from an interactional viewpoint, is rather limited (Weakland, 1977), and in any case it is not the counselor's job to attack the physical problems directly. But it would be safe to say that when environmental stressors are reduced, the psychosomatic symptoms are also likely to be reduced, and that any family problem is a potential environmental stressor.

In the case of *hypochondriasis,* the elder may experience symptoms of one disease or another, but the physician cannot find the signs (objective measures) of any disease process corresponding to the patient's described symptoms. For example, an elder might come to the doctor's office with the subjective experience of debilitating stomach cramps; yet, after a full course of x-rays and laboratory work, the physician can find no objective sign that there is any disease process present. The symptoms might be said to be "in the patient's head," but the experience of the symptoms is real nonetheless.

Therefore, based on his objective data, the physician might tell the elder, "I can tell you with almost 100 percent certainty that these cramps are in your head." The elder could feel quite justified in replying, "Even if I agree with you, Doctor, that they are in my head, the problem is that my stomach still hurts." In other words, hypochondriacs are rarely consciously faking. In some ways, it is this fact that makes their problem so difficult; they are for some reason experiencing pain and suffering for which no cause appears to exist. Sometimes physicians may find some underlying cause for the physical difficulties being experienced, but then add, "The symptoms are disproportional to the problem." Either way, the feelings of the hypochondriac are invalidated.

For most hypochondriacs, then, the pattern is the same: no one credits them. Imagine the horror of believing that you are perhaps fatally ill and not being able to convince anyone of your sincerity and the reality of your symptoms. For hypochondriacs—as with everyone else—the less they are believed, the more desperately they try to convince everyone around them of the reality and seriousness of their problems. The harder they try to convince their relatives, friends, and physicians, the more put off and skeptical all these members of their extended kin network become. The skepticism of these significant others perpetuates the problem and simply leads to another escalation of the vicious circle of physically and emotionally painful experiences.

For family members too, the vicious circle is excruciating. They are afraid to ignore the pleas and complaints of their hypochondriacal elders for fear that "this time" the symptoms will prove to be "real" (objectively validated by a physician). Consequently, they attend to their elders out of duty and guilt, rather than out of real concern, much less out of pleasure at seeing and talking with them. Not unexpectedly, the families begin to resent the time they spend with their elders, since the quality of interaction is so disease-oriented, and tend to stay away from them except when drawn by guilt. The elders sense this poor quality of interaction, which increases their fears that they are moving closer to being abandoned to die in isolation. Predictably, in an effort to prove to their relatives the severity of their physical problems, these elders redouble their efforts, which may include feeling worse as well as saying more, to convince their extended kin network of the gravity of their illnesses until sufficient guilt has welled up in the family system to force a resumption of contact.

Therefore, while hypochondriasis leads to poor interpersonal relations between elders and their families, it usually serves to keep family members in contact with one another. It gets the elders some of what they want, but certainly at great expense in terms of their own suffering. Perhaps the greatest tragedy of all is that elders who rely on their hypochondria to gain for themselves some measure of attention preclude themselves from getting what they really want: love and esteem from those who are important to them.

Case Example

The following case was chosen for these reasons: First, it demonstrates how a simple request for "advice" can often represent a request for something more; second, while novel in some respects, the problem presented is fairly frequent among the population at large; and, third and most important, this case provides a good example of working with the entire family system in mind even though there is only one member present in the actual counseling session.

Approaching the Family System

The counselor was a community college faculty member who served as the instructor for several aging courses offered by the Department of Sociology. From time to time she also was asked for advice by both her students and her colleagues. In this instance, one of the junior members of the faculty drew her aside at the faculty lounge and said:

PETER: I am really having problems with my mother and I need some advice badly. Do you have a second?

COUNSELOR: I'd sure be willing to see if I could help, but I'll tell you one thing—I know I'll need more than a second to do it. How about taking our coffee back to my office where there is a little more peace and quiet?

The counselor takes seriously the request for assistance and tries to ensure that the two of them will have a time and place to discuss the matter. The counselor assumes responsibility for needing the time for herself ("I know I'll need more than a second") and suggests a more private spot. If Peter had not had time for a conversation at that time, the counselor would have suggested an appointment at a later time.

Determining the Problem

COUNSELOR: So what's going on between you and your mother?

The phrase "between you and your mother" implies an interactional component to the problem.

PETER: You wouldn't believe it. Well, I guess you would, but most people wouldn't. My mother lives in Vermillion, South Dakota. That's exactly 1,008 miles from here. To visit her it takes two airline transfers and a 67-mile drive in a rented car for a grand total of 9 hours and 17 minutes—at best. Under less than perfect circumstances—I once got snowed in for two days in Minneapolis when the airplane couldn't land in Sioux Falls—it has taken me almost three days.

You might ask, why am I such an expert on this particular itinerary? It's not a bad question, either. The answer—I am embarrassed to say this—is that I travel that long lonesome road to the heart of the Midwest at least six times a year to visit my poor dying mother. But, in fact, she is neither poor nor dying.

On the average of every other month, my mother calls me to tell me of her latest grave condition. Invariably she has been just admitted to the hospital. Why? For observation of course. She tells me that it's her heart—she takes nitroglycerin for angina—or her bowels—which always require either a laxative or an antacid—or whatever other organ system happens to be acting up at that moment. When I talk to her doctors—and she has lots of them—they always tell me the same thing: "Well, we can't be sure. After all, at your mother's age, there could be any number of problematic conditions which could prove to be potentially fatal. I don't really think she belongs in the hospital, but, frankly, I am not willing to dismiss her complaints and risk the chance that this time there really is something gravely wrong."

So what do you suppose my mother says to me at three o'clock in the morning, half a dozen times a year? She says, "Please come visit me, I may never see you again." My stomach groans for an antacid; I tell her I will think about it. I pace the floor and worry. I smoke too much. I think about the fact that she really does have a heart condition and really does have diabetes. She really is ill. But then I think about the fact that she has been calling me like this ever since I moved away from home eight years ago. She had a bad heart and diabetes then, too.

For the first four years it wasn't so bad. I was only living about 150 miles away, in Minnesota. It was just a short drive to see Mom. Even the first two years out here, it was rather expensive—it's not cheap to go back there, you know—but still tolerable. But now I'm married, we've got a kid on the way, and it's a real problem to get back there. I'm at the end of my rope.

COUNSELOR: I certainly can see why. Let me see if I got it all. Your mother has several chronic conditions, all of which are serious enough to merit reasonable concern. On a fairly regular basis, she summons you urgently to her bedside. This is a pattern that began about eight years ago, but because of changes in your geographical location as well as your responsibilities to your new family, you are feeling a need to change this old pattern.

As I am hearing it, you are caught because despite the history of false alarms, your mother might really be in as serious a condition as she claims. Should she die without you being there—or at least trying to get there—you are concerned that you would be eternally filled with guilt.

PETER: I think that's right. I'm less concerned with making my mother mad if she's really healthy than I am about having to deal with my guilt if I ignore her deathbed request to see me.

COUNSELOR: You mentioned that one of the ways that this problem is affecting you is that your stomach goes sour when she calls you. How else are you being affected?

The counselor is attempting to get Peter down to the specifics of how his problem with his mother is affecting him. The counselor is trying to move from the abstract notion of guilt to something concrete or measurable.

PETER: Let me tell you! I am being devastated economically. I can't concentrate on my work. My wife is ready to leave me. You wouldn't believe how mad she is at me for spending the money to go back there.

COUNSELOR: So aside from your own personal battle as to whether or not to go, you are also feeling caught between showing loyalty to your wife and loyalty to your mother?

The counselor's tone of voice indicates that she is simply checking out information rather than making an ironclad interpretation. Specifically, the counselor wants to know if the issue is simply money or really loyalty (which includes not only money, but time, effort, and many other specific factors).

PETER: I am loyal to my wife, but I'm loyal to my mother too. Of course, neither of them can understand that. I would much prefer to stay home and spend the money on my family. It is the fact that my mother could die that really gets me. My wife, Joan, just can't understand.

To be really honest, it's getting close to her saying, "It's her or me." I don't know what I'm going to do when that happens.

COUNSELOR: I get the impression, then, that Joan is pretty involved in this problem. It would be useful to me to have a chance to talk to her just to get her assessment of the situation.

The counselor takes the responsibility of wanting to see Peter's wife ("It would be useful to me . . .") when it becomes clear that the wife is very involved with the problematic situation.

PETER: No way. She'd murder me if she even knew I was talking to you about the problem.

COUNSELOR: What if I called her?

PETER: She'd murder me twice. I've got to ask you not to discuss this situation with anybody, especially my wife.

COUNSELOR: I understand. Under the circumstances, I'd probably feel the same way. But it sure does leave you in a lonely spot.

The counselor accepts Peter's wishes and empathically extends her understanding so that Peter will not feel he is being rejected for wishing to handle the situation himself. The counselor merely comments that the effects of Peter's approach have logical consequences: a sense of being alone.

Determining Attempted Solutions

COUNSELOR: Since this problem has been building up for some time, first between just you and your mother, but now between you, your mother, and your wife, I'm wondering what all of you have been trying to do about it?

Again, the interactional aspect of the problem (you, your mother, and your wife) is stressed.

PETER: It seems like I've tried everything.

COUNSELOR: Well, maybe you could begin with what you have done that has seemed to be particularly useful.

PETER: About the only thing that I have found that works is to just give up and go. After about three days, she finally gets off the topic of how sick she is and finally we get to talk about other matters.

COUNSELOR: I'm confused. It sounds to me as if continuing to meet her requests to go back to visit her hasn't stemmed the tide of requests. I'm not sure how that appears to you as dealing successfully with the problem.

Peter's contradictory statement is challenged gently by the counselor using a tone of voice and phrasing ("I'm confused") so that Peter will have an opportunity to realize what he has been doing has not been successful in solving the problem without feeling as if the counselor is showing how smart she is at his expense.

PETER: What I meant was that if I don't go back to see her, her telephone calls about her illness become so intense that I just can't stand it.

COUNSELOR: Then, what you are saying is that if you didn't go back, then she would keep up the pressure until . . .

PETER: I finally caved in!

COUNSELOR: So by solving the immediate problem of the pressure from your mother, you intensify the pressure from your wife.

PETER: Right.

COUNSELOR: Has anything seemed to be useful in dealing with your mother that doesn't increase the strain between you and your wife?

PETER: Nothing. Absolutely nothing.

COUNSELOR: What about attempts that you have made to solve the problem that haven't seemed to help?

PETER: Well, as you pointed out, the first thing that hasn't worked to improve the overall situation has been to give in to my mother.

But when I don't give in, then she tells me that I'm not being a good enough son—that she doesn't ask me for much but when she does, how hurt and rejected she feels when I don't respond. I have tried to logically explain to her that I can't afford to visit her and that her requests are tearing my home apart, but she just won't hear this.

COUNSELOR: Let me ask you to pause for a second, while I make sure that I'm getting what you said. If I'm inaccurate be sure to let me know, but I think what I'm hearing is that logically arguing with your mother doesn't seem to help. That is, for every point you make she makes another point until you end up feeling like a naughty little boy getting a scolding?

The counselor relabels Peter's description of how he logically explains his position to his mother as the process by which he creates an argument which he invariably loses, and requests his agreement.

PETER: [Nods]

COUNSELOR: What else have you tried beside acquiescing and arguing?

PETER: I've tried to involve my two older brothers. They both tell me the same thing when I ask them for advice: "Stop being a sucker." Actually, every time I call them to ask them to help me with Mom, I get depressed. Their refusal to get involved just puts more pressure on me to make up to my mother what she is not getting from them.

COUNSELOR: I'm not sure what you mean. Are you saying that they never see your mother at all or that they have some different kind of relationship with her?

The phrase "some different kind of relationship" implies that it is possible not to cater to every whim of Peter's mother while still maintaining some kind of relationship with her. The counselor is introducing this concept at this time since from what Peter has said thus far it is apparent that he sees himself faced with choosing between the relationship he currently has with his mother or of having no relationship with her whatever.

PETER: Oh, they see her all right. They both live in Sioux Falls—about 60 miles away—so they all get together about once a month for dinner and can spend Easter, Thanksgiving, and Christmas with her. But they just flatly refuse to go visit her every time she goes to the hospital. She doesn't even bother to call them anymore: she just calls me. That puts even more pressure on me, because if she really is sick, the only one to be there will be me.

COUNSELOR: How are they able to relate so differently with her? Just what do they do when she seems to be ill?

PETER: They just tell her how sorry they are that they won't be able to visit her and send her some flowers. That's it.

COUNSELOR: Doesn't your mother try to get them involved in explaining themselves as she does you?

The counselor attempts to differentiate the global concept of "arguing" (which involves at least two people) from an essential ingredient of any argument, "explaining oneself" unnecessarily (which one person can control).

PETER: Mother doesn't seem as demanding of them as she is of me. After all, I'm the baby of the family.

COUNSELOR: How does your position in the birth order seem to have made a difference?

"Baby of the family" is relabeled "position in the birth order" to clarify that there are no rules written in stone about how the "baby of the family" is supposed to behave.

PETER: Well, since the other two boys were older, by the time I got to junior high school, I was living at home alone. Mother and I had a lot more private time together than she had had with the older boys, so I guess we were a little closer. When Dad died, I was only 16, so again Mother and I had to lean on each other for support during a time of real stress for both of us.

COUNSELOR: What sort of relationships do your brothers have with your mother? It sounds as if they must be on fairly close terms if they get together over the major holidays.

The counselor pursues the line of questioning about the brothers since they seem to have resolved successfully how to deal with their mother's illnesses.

PETER: Oh, they have great relationships. They have all the fun and I do all the dirty work. I envy them.

COUNSELOR: Are you sure? From what you've told me it sounds as if you and your mother have a rather special relationship. It sounds to me as if every time she is feeling needy, she looks to you for help. In some ways, that makes you her most important child.
  Suppose that I worked a miracle somehow, so that your mother stopped calling you back to South Dakota, do you really think that you could give up being the most important child?

The counselor asks implicitly if Peter would be willing to relabel his position among his siblings from "the child who does all the dirty work" to "the child who has a special relationship with Mom." Such a relabeling would allow Peter to see that there are positive as well as negative aspects to being called in the middle of the night by his ailing mother.

PETER: Well, maybe I do appreciate the importance mother accords me, in a way. But at this point in my life, I'd gladly sacrifice that!

COUNSELOR: Perhaps you might need to give that idea more thought. Occupying a special position in a family, particularly when there are a couple of siblings with whom to compete, can sometimes be a pretty hard thing to give up. In any event, it's not something that most people can give up very quickly.

Permission and understanding (unconditional positive regard and empathy) are extended for Peter to be the way he is; and he is cautioned against hasty change.

I'm curious about one thing. Have you and your wife ever invited your mother out to spend any of the holidays with your family?

PETER: No. We've always felt overloaded by mother anyhow. If I'm seeing her six times a year as it is, why do I need to see her any more often? It's seeing her less often that I'm trying to work on.

COUNSELOR: What you say makes sense, but I am puzzled about one thing. If you and your mother do cease the interaction that is leading to your frequent visits to her bedside in the Midwest, when would you see your mother? What kind of contact would replace the contact you are having now?

PETER: I hadn't even thought of that problem.

COUNSELOR: I understand; after all, you have a lot of other things on your mind. I am wondering if you have any notion as to why I might have raised this question?

Peter is given an opportunity to observe what is happening between him and his mother rather than simply to sit passively by as the counselor expounds.

PETER: I think what you are getting at is that my mother and I are spending a lot of time together this way. If that situation changes while everything else stays the same, then we won't ever see each other.
I don't think that's a solution that either she or I would be happy with.

COUNSELOR: I don't think you should attempt right now to define the sort of relationship you would like to have with your mother to replace the one that you have currently. I think you need to have more time to think about it. After all, it's a big step, and at present it sounds as if you would rather have the relationship you have now than no relationship at all.

PETER: I guess that's right.

Determining Goals

COUNSELOR: I wonder if you could give me some notion as to what would be the smallest amount of change in the status quo that would give you a sense that you were making some progress in redefining your relationships with your mother and your wife.

PETER: Well, I'd know things were better if my mother stopped calling me every two months demanding I visit her at her deathbed.

COUNSELOR: You'd know you were making progress if you and your mother saw each other less than six times a year, or if you still saw each other six times a year but under different circumstances?

PETER: Both.

COUNSELOR: That's a lot to aim for. I would be more comfortable working toward either seeing her less or changing the quality of the interaction on the six visits you now have.

PETER: I'm not sure what you mean by that second one.

COUNSELOR: I'll try to be more clear. Rather than try to change both the frequency of your face-to-face visits and the reason for having the visits, I think it might be better to examine each issue separately. For example, you might want to set as a first goal simply going back to South Dakota less frequently, say, three times a year. Your mother would still call you, but in some way that we might work out together, you would be able to say "no"—successfully—at least half of the time.

Another approach would be to help you and your mother learn how to get together under different, more agreeable circumstances. For example, you might invite her to join you and your wife for Easter, Thanksgiving, and Christmas, which would only require you to visit her three additional times during the year. These meetings could be social visits instead of sick calls. Under these conditions, the quality of interaction between you, your mother, and your wife would be different, but the frequency of visits would remain the same.

PETER: You think you could get my mother to stop acting the way she is acting?

COUNSELOR: I wish I could make that kind of a guarantee! I'm afraid any change in the relationships between you, your mother, and your wife will have to come from you all, not from me, although I might have some suggestions that could help you toward making a useful change. Right now, I'm trying to approach the question of the number of visits versus the quality of the visits. Which would you rather work on first?

PETER: I'd rather work on the quality, but considering the economics of the situation . . . I don't know.

COUNSELOR: I don't know either. I'll even throw in a few more ideas to make the decision more complicated! In working on the quality of your relationship with your mother, you might or might not decrease the quantity of the visits. That is, you might find that if the two of you really had an opportunity to spend one good week together, that might be enough to make up for the six poor weeks you presently spend together. On the other hand, if you work toward reducing the number of visits, you might find that the quality of those visits which remain will have to be increased to compensate for the time lost.

The counselor attempts to validate Peter's feelings of confusion by pointing out to him that he is confused for good reason: there is no simple answer.

My experience is that the smaller the step, the better chance there is to begin some kind of lasting change. Why don't you give it some thought, and then we could get together later in the week—say after your ten o'clock class—to discuss some different approaches you might want to try.

Rather than leave the next appointment to Peter's initiative, the counselor offers to make herself available at a future time.

PETER: All right. Do you have any ideas of what I should do between now and then?

COUNSELOR: I'd like you not to do anything differently. You've already acknowledged the problem and done something about it by coming here. At this point, it's better to move slowly rather than too quickly. If your mother should call, go ahead and do the things you've already been doing, just to prove to yourself for one last time that they don't work. That is, go ahead and call her doctors to get their same quasi-reassurances; argue logically with your mother about why you can't come; experience fully how you allow your guilt strings to be pulled and how, simultaneously, you are experiencing a sense of importance and "specialness" with your mother. Then go ahead and fly back to see her. I would ask that while you are there you make no attempt to change the way the two of you normally interact. Having an opportunity to observe for yourself the way things actually are, rather than struggling with efforts to change, can often supply useful information.
I really do want to warn you about attempting to change this situation too rapidly. It's been going on for several years and it is just not realistic to expect changes overnight.

The message the counselor is trying to convey to Peter is, "You are all right the way you are. You will not be compromised in my eyes if you change your situation slowly. My support is not conditional upon your doing everything overnight.

PETER: Well, I don't know how long I can wait, but I'll try to be patient.

COUNSELOR: That's all right.

Comprehending the Family System

What is the extent of the family system?   The system includes mother, three sons, and at least one daughter-in-law. It should be expected that changes in the youngest son, Peter, will result in other changes within the system. Therefore, despite his brother's warnings that Peter is being a "sucker," it would not be surprising that should he cease to be a "sucker" his brothers would then express dissatisfaction. For example, if Peter should invite his mother out for Christmas (instead of flying to her sickbed in mid-December), the brothers might be quite put out that their traditional family Christmas was being spoiled.

Likewise, changes in Peter's relationship with his mother might increase the problems between him and his wife. For example, should the relationship with his mother improve to the point that he was no longer afraid to speak with her on the telephone, his wife might become even more threatened by her mother-in-law. Similarly, if Peter should stop going to South Dakota and the mother should begin to visit him, then open hostility between mother and daughter-in-law might break out. In the extreme, if Peter should resolve the difficulty with his mother, the daughter-in-law might well lose the excuse, "If only she were out of our lives, then we'd be happy." In fact, if the excuse of the mother-in-law is gone from their lives, the couple might have to deal with differences between them that now are obscured by this recurrent problem.

Where is the counselor in the family system? The counselor in this case is more of a confidante to Peter than a member of the family. Peter's insistence that his wife not be included is a good indication that he is feeling ganged up on and is unwilling to risk that his confidante will take the others' side as well. The counselor does not have to be handicapped by this position as long as she is able to comprehend the situation as a family systems problem—as opposed, say, to considering that the problem rests entirely with Peter and his weak ego. In keeping with the family systems approach, it will be important for the counselor to remember that solutions which are intolerable to the rest of the family are always unsatisfactory solutions.

What are the family rules? The most relevant family rule appears as: "Peter has a special relationship with Mother." Most likely it is this rule that is getting the brothers in the Midwest off the hook in relationship to their mother's hypochondriacal demands. Certainly it is this rule that is pressing Peter to accede to his mother's demands despite the negative cost/payoff ratio. This same rule is particularly difficult for Peter's wife since she seems to feel excluded from Peter and his mother's relationship. Since Peter is now married and about to have a child of his own, the rule needs revision to include the needs of his wife and his new family responsibilities.

Because the rule is "unwritten" (probably acknowledged only indirectly, in terms of Peter's being the "baby" of the family), such a revision will be difficult. Certainly any revision, or more realistically "renegotiation," of such a family rule will require that the rule be more explicit.

Is there an Identified Patient? The I.P. in this case is Peter's mother. She assumes the role of the I.P. by her constant display of physical symptoms, while Peter labels her as the I.P. because of the hypochondriacal aspects of her behavior. If she were not seen as the I.P., a crisis might arise in the special relationship between Peter and his mother since Peter's trips home would then accentuate the loyalty conflict between Peter and his mother and his wife even more. In this event, Peter's loyalty would probably go toward his wife, in which case Peter's mother would feel deserted. It is probably safe to assume that should she cease being the I.P., she would see less of Peter.

How is power exercised? Both Peter's mother and his wife exercise their power by appearing to be weak; both look to Peter to "provide" for them. Peter exercises his power by appearing to be strong. This system seems to have worked fairly effectively until both wife and mother demanded to be "taken care of" simultaneously. Now, however, Peter is feeling powerless to satisfy both his wife and his mother, while wife and mother are feeling powerless because they cannot get Peter to care for them in the way to which they have become accustomed.

Why has the problem not been solved? One of the reasons that the problem has not been solved is that at one level, people in the family system are having their needs partially met. Peter admits to enjoying his trips to visit his mother, after the first three or four days; his mother seems to enjoy having him back to visit; the brothers are free to enjoy their mother on a social basis and over all the major holidays, since they are assured that Peter is assuming major responsibility for their mother; and, finally, Peter's wife is at least somewhat reassured of her importance to Peter since he appears wracked with guilt over his neglect of her. As a consequence, the system is difficult to alter.

Another reason that the problem has not been solved is that this family system reflects the typical hypochondriacal vicious circle in which Peter's reluctance to fly to his mother's bedside serves as the stimulus for another round of escalatory behavior on the part of his mother. Their system is fueled by loneliness, guilt, and desperation. Ultimatums—or their implied threat—on the part of Peter's wife also serve to increase the desperation experienced by all members of the system. The more desperate each feels, the more tenaciously each clings to the habitual but dysfunctional responses perpetuating the problem.

Does the family still need a counselor? The vicious circle is continuing since no family member knows how to interrupt it. If left uninterrupted, it appears that Peter's wife will adopt the position that "loyalty to wife" and "loyalty to mother" are mutually exclusive emotional and physical behaviors. Such a position is clearly preposterous, but just as clearly it is rather prevalent in our society. The consequences of such a "me or her" ultimatum are potentially disastrous for everyone. Help from outside the family system may make a critical difference.

Mobilizing the Family System

Since Peter is a college instructor, it is fairly safe to conclude that his language is "logic." It is also clear that Peter values being a "loyal protector," although at present he is experiencing himself caught between his wife and his mother in that role. Therefore, Peter will probably be most open to changing his behavior—and thus the family system—when he is given a logical explanation for the counselor's experimental behavioral directives. The counselor will frame these experimental directives as changes in behavior designed to be more usefully protective of his wife and his mother. In other words, Peter needs the counselor to give him behavioral alternatives to the way he is presently unsuccessfully "taking care of" wife and mother.

Additionally, it is probably unrealistic to think that any solution will be viable that does not replace the amount of meaningful contact between Peter and his mother with an equal amount of meaningful contact, not necessarily an equal total time, which is less threatening to Peter's wife.

Therefore, the challenge to mobilizing this family system will be to allow Peter to change his behavior in a way that will signal to both wife and mother as well as to himself that he does not intend to abandon anyone.

The second session resumed in the counselor's office:

COUNSELOR: Let me see if I can recall where we left off. You were telling me of the conflict you are experiencing when you try to be simultaneously loyal to both your mother and your wife. What brings this problem into focus is your mother's physical symptoms, which she describes to you in such a way that you feel required to fly back to South Dakota to attend to her. The pattern of these visits, including your mother's inducements to come, don't appear to have changed very much over the last eight years, although your own response has changed rather drastically, particularly since your wife became pregnant. While you enjoy the special relationship you have with your mother, you would like to cut back on emergency visits without damaging the overall quality of your relationship with her. Is that close enough to how you were stating it?

The last visit is recapped and Peter is given an opportunity to comment on accuracy.

PETER: That's pretty close. Since we last talked, I spoke with my wife about some of the things we have been talking about—without telling her where the ideas came from! She said she would gladly trade my visits to South Dakota for one visit out here by my mother, maybe Thanksgiving through Christmas. What do you think of that!

COUNSELOR: I think it's terrific that you talked your dilemma over with your wife.

The counselor compliments Peter on the process of sharing his thoughts with his wife rather than just on the fact that he had a successful experience in getting her to agree with him.

I'm wondering how you are going to bring up the topic with your mother?

PETER: I already tried that. I called her after I talked with my wife. What I wanted to say was something like, "Mom, why don't you knock off all that sick crap and come out and visit us," but I knew she'd be hurt and offended and never come out. So I just told her that my wife and I wanted her to come out. Naturally, she declined due to anticipated ill health. You'd think after talking with you last week I would have been smarter. Anyway, after a few minutes of trying to convince her that her health would hold up while she was out here, I realized what I was doing and told her good-bye. Now I suppose she will have a special attack Christmas night just to prove to me how wrong I was.

COUNSELOR: It sounds as if you moved too fast too soon, but at least you gained some important information: your wife is willing to invite your mother out and, more important, seems willing to listen to your problems. You also learned that your mother isn't going to give up on her deathbed position easily and so will need some more help from you.

PETER: Swell! Just what I need, another telephone call from Mother.

COUNSELOR: I'm afraid I have to agree with you that the prospect isn't pleasant. I am concerned, though, that something be done, since as you pointed out last week, if the situation is left to itself, it probably won't be too long until your wife gives you the ultimatum to choose between her and your mother. Under those circumstances, I would be particularly concerned for your mother, since among the family members you seem to be her most valuable resource. I think it is important that the vicious circle perpetuated by your mother's worries about her health and her related telephone habits be broken. I have some ideas I'd like to test, but I am rather reluctant to bring them up because they would require you to change your behavior rather drastically, at least for a period of a month or so.

The counselor reminds Peter of his own observation that the vicious circle must be broken, reframes his mother's behavior as needing his help (implying he could protect her), and cautiously opens the topic of behavioral directives.

PETER: Tell me what they are anyway.

COUNSELOR: I'd like to, but I'm afraid this might be placing a rather large burden on your shoulders. After all, you will have to experiment a bit with your behavior to see how to break the vicious circle that is leading toward your mother losing you as a base of support. In a way, the weight and risk would all fall on you, even for an experimental period of a month. It seems to me to be a lot to ask.

By emphasizing the difficulty and gravity of the situation, the counselor communicates that her suggestions are not just "casual advice," nor easy to follow.

PETER: Honest, I'm ready to try anything for a month.

COUNSELOR: Well, all right. As I see it, it seems as if you and your wife are on the right track in wanting to exchange a reasonable visit over the holidays for the mediocre times you spend with your mother now. The problem is how to allow your mother to discover for herself that she is not too gravely ill to be able to enjoy relating to you in a slightly different way, without confronting her about her symptoms, which just makes her defend them all the more. When are you next expecting a telephone call from her?

PETER: Unless I stirred something up with my call, not for about a month.

COUNSELOR: Then let's talk about an experiment to try when it comes. As I recall, you usually check with her doctors, who are always noncommittal. [Peter nods.] Next time, I'd like you to call your oldest brother to check the situation out with him. That way, he'll know to call you if a genuine state of emergency exists or comes about.

Then, as I understand it, you normally call your mother back after you have talked to her doctors to try to convince her that her condition isn't as serious as she has led you to believe? [Peter again nods in affirmation.] Then she takes your argument as a sign that you aren't taking her condition seriously, so she escalates the intensity of her demands. You argue back for a while until half-heartedly you acquiesce? [more nodding].

The main experiment I would like you to try involves the telephone call you ordinarily make to your mother after you have talked to her doctors. This time, rather than attempt to explain to her that her condition isn't serious, I would like you to say something like this:

"Mother, I just can't bring myself to even call your doctors. I know your age and your conditions, and despite the fact that I've tried to minimize them in the past I just can't fool myself anymore. I know that you would like me to come back to visit. I would like to. In fact, Joan and I were just talking about how far away South Dakota is and how much we would enjoy seeing you more often. But, frankly, right now I'm afraid to come back to visit you because I'm afraid of what I'll find."

PETER: In other words, instead of trying to argue with her, agree with her.

COUNSELOR: Right, instead of making her tell you how sick she is, tell her how sick you fear she might be.
   In some ways, speaking to the other side of her feelings may seem extreme. But if you give it a bit of deeper thought you will see that, for the first time, your mother may finally feel as if someone in her family understands how ill she feels. For some elders, just the sense of being understood by their relatives is enough to allow them to look for another way of expressing their needs.

PETER: What about the part of being "afraid of what I might find"?

COUNSELOR: What can you make of that?

PETER: Beats me. It seems a bit like I'm overdoing just "understanding" her.

COUNSELOR: You're right. In saying that you would like to visit her but are afraid of what you might find, you're giving her the message, "I want to see you under different circumstances." And by using your wife's name in a positive way—that is, telling how much the two of you miss her—you are also giving her the message that both you and Joan are available under different circumstances.

PETER: Do you really think this will work?

COUNSELOR: It's a difficult, longstanding system. I'm not at all certain that any approach will work, especially at the first trial. I guess I'm more concerned about learning what your mother will do than I am about some instant cure. To me, what is most important is to learn enough about your mother from how she reacts to changes in your behavior to be able at some later time to make some meaningful change in your relationship, before your wife puts the ultimatum to you.
   Again, it's asking you to make all the initial changes in your behavior. I'm wondering if you really want to save your mother from the consequences of that ultimatum that much? After all, she is only one person in this family system.

PETER: I really do. I told you, I'll try anything once.

COUNSELOR: While you're trying anything, I would like you to collect one more bit of information for me. This time, instead of arguing with her if she accuses you of being a bad son, I'd like you to agree with her.

PETER: I'm not sure I know what you mean.

COUNSELOR: Can you give me a statement that she might put to you when she is really desperate to get you to come back?

PETER: That's easy enough: "Do you value me so little that you're not willing to inconvenience yourself for a few days to see me for the last time?"

I might add that my normal response would be something such as, "Mother, I do love you. You know that. It's just that this isn't the last time we'll ever see each other. And Joan and I just don't have the money. How many times do I have to tell you that?"

Naturally, she would reply, "I never thought I would see the day that you, of all people, would tell me money was more important than seeing your dying mother." Then she starts to cry.

COUNSELOR: That really is pressure.

PETER: You'd better believe it.

COUNSELOR: I'd like to try this approach—again, just as an information-gathering experiment for the next time she calls. I would like you to say, whenever she explicitly states, or simply implies, that you are not living up to what you should be: "Mother, I feel terrible. I wish I could be the son you would like me to be."

PETER: That's exactly the way I do feel.

COUNSELOR: I understand that; that's why you get so caught up in the arguments. But what's important for your mother to grasp is that just because you can't be the son she would like you to be, that doesn't necessarily mean you have to go back to visit her six times a year.

PETER: What should I say after that?

COUNSELOR: I'd prefer that you didn't say anything. Let your mother break the silence. If she doesn't break the silence, just go ahead and hold the telephone. See what happens. After all, this is an experiment, not a cure.

PETER: Well, it sounds worth a try. After all, what I've been trying certainly hasn't been that successful.

COUNSELOR: Good. Let's practice with some role-playing until you have the main points down.

After about 30 minutes of role-playing and rehearsing, Peter was sent off to await his mother's next call. Just before he left the room, the counselor gave one warning:

COUNSELOR: Peter, one last thing. You know, what we've been talking about, even on a one-shot experimental basis, represents a whole lot of change, with you taking all the risks. If for some reason, at the last minute, you would rather retreat to the familiar by calling the doctor, getting into an argument, and then eventually going back to South Dakota, it would be okay with me. I guess what I'm saying is that if the anxiety builds up too much, it's all right with me if you take care of yourself by doing the familiar.

A month passed, and Peter again approached the counselor in the coffee line. Again, the counselor made an appointment to see him where they could exchange more than just a few words.

PETER: It's scary. It worked!

COUNSELOR: Slow down. What was scary? What worked?

PETER: The advice you gave me. I told my mother the things we practiced and it stopped her cold. She didn't know what to say. She was too bewildered to even cry.

COUNSELOR: What did you do differently?

PETER: The main thing was that I didn't argue. I just told her "I wish I could be more the son you wanted" and didn't say any more. Normally, whenever there is silence on the telephone, I rush in to fill it up. Not this time. Finally she said she had to take her sleeping medicine and hung up. It was amazing.

The next night she called up to tell me she had taken a turn for the worse. I told her I wasn't surprised and that it is probably better that I hadn't gone back because I doubted that I could have stood to see her take a turn for the worse in front of me. She didn't know what to say.

So I apologized to her again for not being the son she wished I was, and said good night.

COUNSELOR: What happened then?

PETER: I got a conference call from my brothers! It was great! I don't know how much it cost them, but it must have been plenty. They were really steamed at me. There they were, the two of them on the line at once giving me hell about the way I was treating Mother. Talk about turning the tables!

So I figured if it was working with Mother, it might work with them: I told them I was sorry I couldn't be as good a brother as they wanted me to be. They were floored. They didn't know what to say— and they have always known what to say to their little brother.

Finally, I told them that I had invited mother out from Thanksgiving to Christmas but that I was afraid I might have to take back my invitation because Mother's health might be so bad that she wouldn't be able to make the trip. Naturally, as soon as they finished our conversation they called Mother to tell her.

COUNSELOR: Did your mother call again?

PETER: I'm coming to that. I didn't hear from anybody for a week. Then I got a call from Mother saying that she was feeling a bit better and that her doctors had alarmed her unnecessarily. I told her how pleased I was to hear it. I told her Joan would be relieved too, since now it meant that Mother could take us up on our invitation to visit from Thanksgiving to Christmas to see her new grandchild. I added on my own that it was important Mother be well when she was visiting us, since with the baby we couldn't take care of her very well if she got sick. She said she'd need some time to check with her doctors about her condition for travel and then began to tell me about the value of vitamin C in the prevention of influenza!

COUNSELOR: How is Joan feeling about all of this?

PETER: Well, she still doesn't know that I came to see you, and I'd like to keep it that way. Otherwise, things are okay between us. She still seems angry and moody at times—which I had attributed to her being put out over my mother—so I'm a little surprised about that.

Winding Up

COUNSELOR: I'm not surprised. Not infrequently, when a couple is dealing with a difficult situation, they both tend to put small annoyances on the "back burner" until the major difficulty is resolved. As a consequence, the level of harmony often dips after a crisis is cooled. It sounds as if you haven't experienced that dip yet, so you should be on the lookout for it. It may be that, in your case, with the baby on the way, you will have a double post partum depression.

PETER: Oh, swell. I can hardly wait.

COUNSELOR: I know that when things are going well, it's not pleasant to contemplate how they might get worse. Still, I'm wondering if that might not be a good idea, particularly in this case when the change to the positive came about so quickly.

PETER: What do you mean, "How things could get worse?"

COUNSELOR: Well, you know what you did to bring about the change that has transpired at this point. Suppose that you wanted to "undo" all the good you have just done. What would you do?

PETER: But I wouldn't want to.

COUNSELOR: Humor me, then.

PETER: Okay. I guess I would call up my mother and apologize for what I did. I'd invite her to call me the next time anything went wrong with her health and promise her I'd fly back immediately. Then I'd call my brothers and tell them I was sorry for getting them involved and having to serve as go-between between mother's doctors and me. I'd promise to be a good little brother and faithfully do all the taking care of mother when she is ill.

COUNSELOR: What could you do to sour things with your wife?

PETER: That's easy. I'd just explain to her for the 3,000th time that she was putting me in a bind between her and my mother and ask her to stop. Oh, I've got another one. When my mother comes out to visit, I could warn my wife to take extra care with my mother since her health is so fragile.

COUNSELOR: It sounds like you've got the idea.

PETER: Oh yes. I don't expect the time between Thanksgiving and Christmas to be a picnic, but I am hopeful that it will be better than what it has been.

The counselor spent a few more minutes anticipating problems that might occur during the mother's visit. The counselor also warned Peter that, because this change had come about so quickly, he shouldn't be surprised if his mother reverted back to her old way of asking for attention between now and the holiday season. She also left open the possibility of talking with Peter again should the situation change. In that regard, the counselor emphasized that in dealing with elders, the situation can frequently change without getting better or worse, and that it would be important for Peter to remember that fact, if and when the situation with his mother did change.

17

Alternative Living Arrangements

General Remarks

Very frequently, consideration of the question "What are we going to do about Mother (or Father)?" involves the search for alternative living arrangements. Correspondingly, a common error that counselors should avoid when dealing with questions relating to alternative housing is the trap of taking for granted that alternative living arrangements are actually necessary. In other words: who says the elder needs to move, and why?

When Elders Request Information
about Alternative Living Arrangements

When elders raise the issue of alternative housing, they are frequently seeking more than just information regarding what is available. It is important for a counselor to be able to provide this information, and it should be remembered that what is available depends greatly on the geographical area in which the elder wishes to dwell. We therefore encourage you to become informed on the various possibilities for alternative living arrangements in your local area. We discourage you, however, from premature involvement in discussing these alternatives with any inquisitive elder, until you know the answer to at least two questions: First, *why is the elder presently concerned about alternative housing?* Are there any events, especially within the family, that have precipitated this interest? Second, *what are the elder's expectations for alternative housing?* What needs would be met in new living arrangements that cannot be met under present living arrangements?

If the counselor has the feeling that the elder is under some external pressures to move, usually from the extended kin network, then it is a helpful step to explore those pressures with the elder until they are clear and explicit. Is the elder moving to meet his or her needs, or to meet some presumed needs of the family system? As counselor, your responsibility is not to decide for the elders with whom you work where they should live; instead, your responsibility is to help them cautiously and explicitly explore their motivations for changing their present living conditions and their expectations of the results of such change.

When Family Members Request Information about Alternative Living Arrangements

When requests about alternative living arrangements for elders come from family members, you can be certain that family system motivations will be complex. How is it that the family member who calls on you feels responsible to gather the information about alternative housing? What pressure is this person experiencing? From whom? Who has decided something has to be done? Why? Whenever someone besides the elder is seeking information, the counselor must be very alert to the probability that major changes are taking place in the family system which may not be dealt with usefully by simply supplying an interested relative with a list of alternative housing possibilities in the community.

The Stereotypical "Alternative Living Arrangements Crisis"

Because the "crisis" described below is so common, it is useful to include a brief description of it for informational purposes. As with all stereotypes, the situation describes no one situation, but bears considerable resemblance to many.

The family consists of a recently widowed, elder mother and her three middle-aged children. All of the children are married and living in different parts of the country. The oldest and youngest of these siblings are male, while the middle sibling is female. The crisis begins when the oldest brother begins to receive regular telephone calls from his mother's neighbor. The neighbor complains that his mother is behaving "peculiarly"—staying in all day behind drawn blinds, being a pest over the telephone, and gardening late at night. The neighbor advises, "Something has to be done."

The brother responds to this pressure and his conscience by calling his brother and sister to advise them, "Something has to be done about Mother. She can't go on living alone." Rather than ask their mother what she would prefer for them to do, the three siblings, acting in what they consider to be the best of faith, decide to check the situation out for themselves. They find their widowed mother to be clear in conversation and well-oriented in thought, but her behavior concerns them. She seems lonely, isolated, and "depressed." They are worried over her midnight gardening. When they visit the neighbor, they are again advised: "Something has to be done."

Instead of asking their mother if she needs or wants something to be done, they present her with a fiat: "Mother, you can't go on living like this. We won't allow it." The mother is overwhelmed. Her arguments are ignored, or worse still, dismissed as nonsensical prattle. None of the children seem to notice that she is still able to do her own shopping and cooking. Instead, they are shocked that she is still driving and express concern that she might forget to turn off the stove, and thereby "set the house on fire."

The children return to their homes and families, but remain in increasingly closer contact, closer contact than they have experienced in the last several years. The alternatives they choose between are "putting Mother in a 'home'" or "having Mother live with one of us."

Again, without asking their mother how she would like to spend the rest of her life, the children continue to agitate one another. Finally, the sister and her husband volunteer to have Mother live with them. The brothers offer financial support. Mother is presented with a *fait accompli* and dares not resist the orders of her three children, who seem so united and so determined.

She is moved 500 miles to her daughter's home, away from her friends and her familiar surroundings. Her home is sold and her daughter named her conservator. She becomes increasingly depressed, as does her daughter, who is unable to cheer up her mother. The more the daughter discounts her mother by telling her, "Things aren't so bad, you shouldn't feel so down," the worse Mother becomes. The worse the mother becomes, the more desperate the daughter becomes.

Because she is in new surroundings, the mother's sensory deficits become more pronounced since she is unable to compensate for them by familiarity with her home of 20 years. Her sight is poor, so she collides with furniture in unexpected places. The kitchen is new, so she fails to return cooking utensils and ingredients to their proper spots. Her daughter is the only person she knows in town, so she leans heavily upon her for emotional support. The daughter, unaccustomed to these circumstances, begins to panic. She feels overwhelmed and cornered. At this point, the family is most likely to appear in your office.

The mother will appear depressed and deteriorating, while the daughter will be emphasizing, and most likely exaggerating, her mother's "depression" and "deterioration," so she can move her mother out of her home without having to feel so guilty. The son-in-law will refuse to come to sessions because he is very resentful toward both his wife and his mother-in-law and is afraid his true feelings will become too explicit. The probability of the counselor being maxi- · mally useful to a family in this condition obviously is not very high. The family's energy has been spent applying an inappropriate solution to a minor problem or non-problem until a real problem has come to exist.

A much happier outcome could have been expected had the family approached the counselor after the neighbor's initial telephone call. At such a time, the counselor could have helped explore the pressures and expectations that all of the family members (including the mother) were feeling. The neighbor's opinions could have been examined and their accuracy evaluated. The pace could have been slowed so that alternatives beyond "putting Mother in a home" or "living with one of the children" could have been considered. Much of this work could have been accomplished over the telephone or through direct work with any one of the children and the mother.

The Values Attached
to "Something Has to Be Done"

There is no question that there are times with elders, as with anyone, when "something has to be done." The difficulty is that no clear set of objective criteria exist for making the discrimination of those times manifest. When do you want "something done" about you? Are you willing to let your family system allow you to act eccentric (midnight gardening)? To wander? Possibly to be run over by a car? These are questions of values, not absolutes. Consequently, you can be of maximum use to clients by helping them to deal with the question of "something has to be done" within a framework of explicating their own personal values. Your responsibility is to help your clients to become free from viewing the world in absolute "rights" and "wrongs" so they can usefully make judgments and compromises which respect, not only their own value systems, but those of other family members as well.

Case Example[1]

This example was chosen for many reasons: First, it is a good example of how large families can work together to solve their own problems when large agencies, such as teaching hospitals, get out of the way. Second, it demonstrates how a counselor's guidance can be useful to middle-aged children seeking how best to "do their duty" toward their parents. Third, the case example shows the importance for successful problem resolution of asking and answering difficult questions. Fourth, it demonstrates how a realistically "ideal" solution is just a solution that "everyone can live with"—as opposed to "be enthusiastic about." And, finally, this case illustrates that even good "solutions" are not permanent in this world, as the I. P. elder in this case died from a recurrence of his cancer some three months after the conclusion of the sessions described below.

Approaching the Family System

The counselor was a nurse interested in working with older people and their families. After a few weeks of low-key promotion within the large hospital in which he worked, the counselor got a call from a medical social worker on a psychiatric self-care ward who had a case for him. According to the social worker, an 83-year-old man had been brought in by his family to the emergency room suffering from a "seizure." The elder denied that he had had a seizure—that day or any other. The family insisted, so the medical staff took the family's word and put him through two weeks of observation and tests. All they found was a clear-thinking, delightful 83-year-old farmer with an abdominal cancer (in remission). Not a seizure in sight. When the medical ward tried to release him, the family, represented by his oldest daughter, refused to take him. Since the oldest daughter threatened a lawsuit if they released him, and since he had limited money, the medical ward transferred him to a self-care psychiatric

---

[1]Material from this case was also presented by the authors, in more summary form, in Chapter 20 of I. Burnside, ed., *Working with the Elderly: Group Process and Techniques* (N. Scituate, Mass.: Duxbury Press, 1978).

ward for more observation. Again, he was observed to be intelligent, witty, and perfectly delightful. Still no seizures to be seen. In fact, all the old man wanted was bus fare back to his farm in Wisconsin.

The medical social worker was at the end of his rope. The family insisted the man was sick. The oldest daughter was tormenting the hospital administrator by writing letters to her Congressional Representative, Senator, and lawyer. The staff on the psychiatric ward had become quite attached to the old man and were supporting him in his claim that his family was just trying to "dump" him in the hospital where he would be safe so the family would not feel guilty. The old man had told the staff that his children had "kidnapped" him to bring him out from Wisconsin to the state of Washington; now that they had him, they would not let go. The psychiatric and medical staff consensus was that the old man was sane, that his oldest daughter was very disturbed, and that the hospital should do all it could to get the old man bus fare back to his farm in Wisconsin.

It was obvious to the counselor that the hospital staff had become surrogate family members, locked into a classic "Us" (the people who are logical and sensitive) versus "Them" (the people who are disturbed and unfeeling) struggle. The battle was escalating and everyone (staff and family) was in turmoil.

At this point it was clear to the counselor that the children (daughter, 55 years old; son, 50; son, 48; daughter, 45) were being led by Daughter-55. Consequently, she became the first contact. The counselor called her up to validate her feelings about the "appalling treatment" she was getting from the hospital.

COUNSELOR: I don't blame you at all for writing your Congressman. In fact, all things considered, I'm surprised you didn't do it sooner. Your family's wishes just don't seem to have been taken into account at all. Sometimes it seems like the families of patients around here are treated as if they don't even have feelings. I'd really like to meet with the whole family to see if I could be helpful to you in straightening out this whole mess that the hospital seems to have made. I'd even be willing to come in nights to do it.

The counselor is attempting to use what he knows of the family's language (anger at the hospital) to validate the feelings of the daughter and establish his credibility with the family.

In this case, as in every other, a counselor does not have to resort to telling lies to validate the feelings of his clients. It cannot be stressed enough that in every case a counselor can understand (validate) how a client feels without expressing approval or disapproval of what the client is doing. The concepts of understanding (empathy) and approval (judgment) are independent of one another. Never confuse being honest with being unable to control an impulse to blurt out a value judgment. Conversely, never consider yourself dishonest because you can control your impulses enough to have empathy for your clients even when their behavior is not congruent with your own values and beliefs. To deny a family or its individual members the sense of being understood because their actions do not meet with your approval is nothing short of empathic malpractice.

Being willing to meet after hours not only set the counselor apart from the rest of the staff but also made any potential "I can't possibly leave work" excuse invalid. Since Daughter-55 was the family spokesperson to the hospital, the counselor left her in that role by asking her to arrange for a meeting time with the rest of the family. She did; the appointment was set for all four children with their spouses, in addition to the mother and father.

When the family arrived at the appointed hour, they were greeted formally, offered coffee and doughnuts, and then led into the conference room. It was a large group. Spouses were included because of the obvious consequences any placement would make on both members of each couple.

Determining the Problem

> **COUNSELOR:** Well, now that we're all assembled, I wonder what sense each of you makes as to why you are here.
>
> **SON-50:** I don't make any sense of it at all. Everyone knows that the lives of all of us, Mommy's and Daddy's included, are in the hands of the Lord. This should be the work of Jesus Christ Almighty. We need less talk and more praying.

Rather than argue the merits of fundamental Christianity, the counselor met the family where they were. If religion was part of this family's language—as apparently it was because Son-50's declaration was met with nodding heads and sighs of "Amen" from other family members—then that fact should be used to the family's advantage. In this case, the counselor was a rather inactive Episcopalian, but decided his religious values should not be forced on this family.

> **COUNSELOR:** Would you be willing to at least consider that God could work through our meeting here tonight?

Even if Son-50 had had his doubts as to whether or not God might actually do it, he had to admit that he would be willing to at least consider the possibility. After all, only unreasonable people are unwilling to at least consider possibilities. When the family nodded assent, the counselor asked Son-50 to lead an invocation so that the meeting might be more productive. Extending the opportunity for Son-50 to lead an invocation communicated to Son-50 that the counselor needed his help if the counselor was going to be useful. Such a message, even though offered symbolically, was sufficiently reassuring to Son-50 that he changed his position from feeling unnecessary, defensive, and oppositional to necessary, useful, and supportive.

After the invocation, as with many large, anxious groups, everyone began to spill out thoughts and ideas at one time. The counselor moved to slow down the pace to allow individuals to speak without being interrupted:

> **COUNSELOR:**   I know that all of you are used to hearing each other's voices, but it's very difficult for me to make sense out of what one of you is saying when others are talking. I guess I'll have to ask your patience, and ask you to speak one at a time.

> *Here the counselor is able to make the interruptions his problem, not the family's. Imagine how much easier such a statement is to hear and respond to than, "It's rude to interrupt your brother," or "The reason you have such big problems is that you people never listen to what the others say."*

As the family story emerged, it seemed that about a year before, the mother, age 75, had contacted the children in Washington to ask if she could move out to join them. She was suffering from a combination of congestive heart failure, arthritis, obesity, and lethargy which left her confined to a wheelchair. The children agreed and placed her in a nursing home central to all. A few months after she moved off the farm, the father had three episodes of public drunkenness and had to be driven back from town to his farm by the sheriff (who fortunately lived on the adjoining farm). Daughter-55 had received three calls from the sheriff expressing his concern. As a result of these calls, Daughter-55 and her husband drove back to Wisconsin "to bring Daddy back for an *indefinite visit.*" A point of family conflict was that the children and their spouses all agreed that Daddy knew the visit was *permanent,* while Daddy insisted that he understood he was only coming for a *temporary* visit. When pressed on the point, Mother was able to display an affinity for the abstruse that could only have developed from a lifetime of practice. Since the mother was housed in a convalescent hospital, the father had been circulating from child to child until his "seizure." As the meeting progressed, the father steadfastly refused to admit ever having been troubled by "spells" or "seizures" of any sort.

Getting down to specific problems that affected each family member personally, the family was quite cooperative: Daughter-55 said "this whole thing" was hurting her work; her husband said it was "deteriorating" their relationship. Son-50 was losing sleep; his wife felt he was taking out his frustration on the kids, which left her feeling quite unsettled. Son-48 complained that his whole life was disrupted by the telephone, which seemed to ring with a new family crisis hourly. Daughter-45 complained bitterly that this crisis just reemphasized her traditional role of being the family baby; she was fighting mad at all her brothers and her sister for not taking her seriously. Daughter-45's husband said that he was working late at the office because he did not like to come home from work with her feeling the way she was feeling. The mother said she felt very distressed that the whole family was torn apart and thought it might be her fault for coming out in the first place. The father felt very hurt because he believed the kids had lost respect for him.

Determining Attempted Solutions

When the counselor turned to discuss attempted solutions with the family, he was overwhelmed. It seemed that everyone had tried everything. There were, however, some common themes that ran through all the attempted solutions. First, every attempted solution had been "talked to death" in attempts to get everyone to agree happily on a common course. Since ten adults seldom, if ever, contentedly and happily agree on anything, the several attempted solutions, based upon careful, logical consideration but judged on the basis of everyone contentedly and happily agreeing, inevitably ended in family quarrels in which everyone felt counted out and misunderstood.

Second, the more extreme solutions—such as inviting the father out for an *indefinite* visit with the intent of making the visit *permanent*—were invariably arrived at unilaterally, when the family was exhausted from talking and quarreling. Not surprisingly, these attempted solutions ended in pronounced failure when the rest of the family noticed and disapproved of what had happened.

Third, almost all the attempted solutions had an element of intrigue, or at least indirectness. This indirectness was excused and explained by family members as a method of "protecting feelings."

Therefore, when the father was brought to the hospital emergency room, it was unclear if the "seizures" some family members had observed were real or simply a face-saving tactic to make the father's institutionalization more palatable to the father and the rest of the family.

In sum, the picture emerged of a family system in which there was considerable emphasis on talk about things that were not really important, with little direct discussion among family members of what each needed and wanted from the others. There was so much posturing—taking proper stances—that nobody knew where anybody else really stood. As a consequence, any actions family members took toward solving their problems were destined to be ill-adapted because they were based on inaccurate information.

Determining Goals

COUNSELOR: Suppose we were living in the best of all possible worlds; given the realities of your father's and mother's physical conditions, how would you like things to work out? Tell me what would be best for you, not necessarily best for the whole family. Remember, just because you say what you want that doesn't necessarily mean that's what you're going to get. But if nobody knows what you want, your chances of getting it are certainly greatly reduced.

DAUGHTER-55: Well, I'd like Daddy to live with one of the kids, but I don't think that's practical.

COUNSELOR: Fortunately, at this point, it doesn't have to be practical. By the way, do you have any preference of which of the kids you would prefer your father and mother to live with?

DAUGHTER-55: Do you want me to be perfectly honest?

COUNSELOR: I hope you will be; I don't see how else we can ever hope to come up with a real solution.

DAUGHTER-55: Okay, then: Daddy, this is really hard for me to say because I really love you and Mommy, but I wouldn't care which of the kids you lived with as long as it isn't me.

The guillotine had dropped. The horrible secret (that everybody already knew) was out. All eyes focused on Daddy. The old man looked Daughter-55 squarely in the eye:

DADDY: I understand, honey. I love you and your family too, but I don't want to live with you either. That's what I've been trying to tell you ever since I came to Washington.

Everyone was relieved. As two of the other children and their spouses had an opportunity to say what they wanted, they made statements similar to the oldest daughter's. To each of these children the father reaffirmed his love and stated flatly that he was not interested in living with them either. Only Son-48 and his wife said that they wanted both the father and mother to live with them. At this point, the other three children jumped in to proclaim that Son-48 and his wife "couldn't handle it."

Given their opportunity to speak, the mother said she would like to live with Son-48 as soon as her medical condition allowed; the father said he would like to move back to the farm in Wisconsin. He did not say that he would be unwilling to live with Son-48.

The session had already lasted for an hour and a half, so an agreement was made to reconvene in a week to give everyone a chance to consider what had been discussed.

> **COUNSELOR:** I think it's important not to make any decisions during the next week on what to do, but to go slow and just sort of think things over. Things have been moving pretty fast up till now and I think we need to slow the pace of decision making down.

The counselor asked Son-50 to lead a benediction to conclude the session.

Comprehending the Family System

What is the extent of the family system? This family system counts as significant members at least the sheriff-neighbor in Wisonsin, the four children and their spouses, the mother, the father, and the staffs of both the medical and psychiatric wards in which the father resided. The number of people involved is staggering, not only to the counselor, but to all members of the family system. Imagine the frustration of trying to please that many people simultaneously.

Where is the counselor in the family system? Aware of how previous hospital staff members had been drawn into the family system by taking sides with the father, the counselor is taking special care to recognize and validate the feelings of all members of the family, not just the father. By way of technique, he has not leaned in obvious sympathy nor in differential allocation of time toward the elder. Instead, the counselor has attempted to make the family system a more "manageable" size by becoming the personalization of the hospital staff, in a more professional, neutral stance. Such a posture allows the family the opportunity to regain responsibility in a personal way for their family problems.

What are the family rules? One family rule most certainly is, "This family is religious." Another rule appears to be, "No matter how much we quarrel, we stick together." A third important rule seems to be, "You don't say or do anything to hurt family members' feelings *unless you have to.*"

Taken together, these rules explain a great deal of how it is that the family members have difficulty confronting one another openly (which *might* lead to hurt feelings) while at the same time continuing to confront each other obliquely (which *is* leading to hurt feelings). It is very likely that the children's feelings of responsibility for their father come from the very religious training he gave them. This is a family that believes very strongly in "rights" and "wrongs," yet cannot agree on what is "right" and what is "wrong."

Is there an Identified Patient? There are actually two I.P.'s. First, the father has been labeled the I.P. by the children. Since in the past he has been a very powerful figure in the family, the I.P. label gives the rest of the family, particularly Daughter-55, some maneuvering room toward wresting away his leadership. Believing herself to be doing the "right" thing, Daughter-55 would be justified in taking over the role of family head only if Daddy was actually failing. Since she personally presided over his "kidnapping," she has a particularly high stake in preserving the notion that her extreme actions were justified; after all, the family rule reads, "You don't say or do anything to hurt family members' feelings *unless you have to.*" Consequently, any solution the counselor suggests will have to take into account Daughter-55's special needs to justify her behavior.

The second I.P. is Daughter-55. She has been labeled by the hospital administrator and the staff on the two wards as "troubled." Just as Daughter-55 has used the I.P. label on her father, so has the hospital staff and administration used the label on her so they can avoid having to deal with some of the serious family issues she has raised. Hopefully, the counselor can prevent this labeling from doing additional damage by treating Daughter-55 with the respect to which every human being is entitled.

How is power exercised? At this point, the father is expressing his power by threatening to go back to Wisconsin—thus breaking up the family. The children are expressing their power by labeling their father as the Identified Patient. The mother expresses her power through being "helpless." The hospital staff are expressing their power by threatening to cooperate with the father—thus threatening to cooperate in breaking up the family.

Why has the problem not been solved? This case is a good example of the solution becoming the problem. It is fairly obvious that this present crisis would not have occurred had the father and mother remained in Wisconsin. Rather than putting all their energies into bringing their parents out to Washington, the children could have put their energies into building a stronger base of psychosocial support for their parents in the Midwest. In their attempt to be "good, responsible" children, they attempted to replace the entire psychosocial significance of a home place with themselves, a task at which they were singularly unsuccessful. Alternatively, the parents could have asked directly for the help they needed from their children rather than coming on as "helpless" in the case of the mother and "naive" in the case of the father.

In any event, the situation now exists wherein the children, particularly Daughter-55, are increasingly adamant that their father is terribly ill, while the father and the hospital staff are being equally adamant that there is nothing at all the matter with him. The children's position toward their father's health has become so preposterous as to be laughable, as they describe his physical condition in such exaggerated terms that even a lay person can see how they have distorted the picture. After all, their father has a twinkle in his eye, a spring in his step, and a delightful sense of insightful humor. On the other hand, the hospital staff has taken the obverse position to the same extreme ends. They minimize the significance of his cancer; his limited strength (he can only walk with a "spring in his step" for about 10 yards; after that he slows down, and 100 yards is his limit without a walker or a wheelchair); and his very limited socioeconomic resources. The staff presents the equally preposterous position that even after 80 years of life to accumulate material and social strengths, it falls perfectly within the bounds of reality for a man to claim he could live in peace alone with God and Nature on his farm, when he lacks even the physical ability to get to the bus station, and the economic ability to pay the bus fare to get to his hometown.

Neither father (and hospital staff) nor family (led so crusadingly by Daughter-55) seems able to back off. The space between being "terribly ill" and "perfectly healthy and competent" seems not to exist in the minds of staff, father, or family.

Does the family still need a counselor? Because the staff–family interaction would probably not abate in the counselor's absence, the counselor's role in helping the family solve its problems remains important.

Mobilizing the Family System

From the tones of voice and expressions of concern as well as the fact that everyone made time to meet, it was obvious that the family was close. The fact that the father said he wanted to go back to Wisconsin but had not really moved to do so also suggested that at some level he was willing to compromise. It was also clear that all the children would have liked to see the parents living in one of their (the children's) homes. Only Son-48 offered this—with the concurrence of his wife. Since the father declined to say he *would not* live with Son-48, the counselor concluded that residence with Son-48 would be a solution the father and the family could live with.

A compromise decision that everyone can live with is not nearly so desirable as one in which every member of the family is able to get exactly what he or she wants; however, the "something you can live with" solution is far more likely to be achievable in the real world.

In terms of strategy, it seemed that the father's power was most fragile. If he moved back to Wisconsin—his bluff having been called —the possibility existed that the family would be so angry with him that if he needed their help at a subsequent time, they might either fail to respond or would bring him back to Washington only on the terms of "unconditional surrender." Therefore, the counselor wanted to help the father settle into local living circumstances while the elder still had some negotiating power left. Since, first, one child had volunteered his home; second, the others said that they would like to see him living with one of them; and, third, the father had not ruled out that possibility, the best solution seemed to be to lead the family to "try out" placing the parents in Son-48's home.

There was a real obstacle to this course, however, which was displayed when Son-48 first mentioned that his home was available. At that time, the other children jumped in to say he "couldn't handle it." What they really meant, of course, is that under the same circumstances, they could not handle it! In some ways, it was as if they were saying, "If you take Daddy and Mommy, it means I could have taken them. Since I won't take them, that makes me feel like a bad child. I don't like feeling like a bad child. Therefore, it's very important to my sense of self-esteem that you don't take Daddy and Mommy." Consequently, the role of the counselor was to allow the father and mother to move in with the child that wanted them in a way such that each of the remaining children could still preserve their sense of feeling like a "good child."

Daughter-55 seemed to be the key in family decision making. It was imperative that she continue to feel that she was moving the family, but her energy had to be put to use in a more positive way. It was also apparent in regard to Daughter-55 that this entire family incident was taking its toll on her. She was feeling cornered and tired —which explained her threatening gestures toward her parents and the hospital staff. The more cornered and tired she felt, the harder she pushed for the "final solution." The "final solution" in this case was institutionalization of both parents. The counselor needed to help create enough space for her to get out of the corner, while still allowing her to feel like a significant—as opposed to rebuffed—member of the family.

At the next session, the counselor began by restating how he remembered the last meeting:

> **COUNSELOR:**   I am feeling the need to recall how things seemed to be shaping up at the end of last week's meeting. Be sure to correct me if I misstate something you were saying or feeling. As I recall, all of the children agreed that you'd like to see your folks living together with one of you, but only Ed and Julie [Son-48 and his wife] felt that they would really be comfortable with Mr. and Mrs. Smith [the parents] moving in with them. It seemed to me that all of you love your mother and father very much, as you, Mr. Smith, seem to care very much for your children. But all of you recognized what people all over the world know: you can love someone without being able to live with them. I also had the impression that you, Mr. Smith [looking at him], would prefer to move back to Wisonsin to be on the farm, but that moving in with Ed and Julie was a solution that you would at least be willing to try out. [Mr. Smith nodded his head in grudging affirmation.] It seems to me that one of the places where you all are trapped is that this is a close, loving family that doesn't want to see some of its members take on more responsibility than you think they might be able to handle. I am wondering, what might the rest of the family be able to do to make your parents moving in with Ed and Julie more possible? If it turns out the rest of the family can help sufficiently, then we have a situation everybody can live with. If, on the other hand, after giving it a try, we fail, then we're just back to where we are right now.

The rest of the hour was spent in straightforward negotiation. The counselor continued to urge each person to speak honestly and to offer only what he or she was sure could be delivered comfortably, whether the offer for support was economic (money, furniture, food, etc.) or social (providing rides, visits, etc.) in nature. After about an hour, tentative plans for mutual support and a schedule for when the move would take place were agreed upon. At that point, the counselor asked each person directly: "Is this a decision that *you can live with?*" Each family member affirmed that it was.

At the end of the session, the counselor asked Daughter-55 to see that all the economic odds and ends be finalized. The session was concluded on a warning:

> **COUNSELOR:** We seem to have made some progress here tonight. But remember, there are no easy solutions. This one is no exception. You can probably expect that the next week will be a stormy one in both the family and your own homes. You will probably have some second thoughts about what you have volunteered to do and may decide to change your minds. That's to be expected. I'd really like all of you to think about what you've agreed upon tonight, to decide if you really do have enough energy to see this thing through for three months. I'd also like you to anticipate both in the privacy of your own minds and with one another any problems that might come up.

Winding Up

The last meeting was taken up discussing what might go wrong. Son-48 anticipated the problem of "Daddy's spells." Now that the threat of being institutionalized for life was lifted, the father confessed that from time to time—every three or four months—he did, in fact, have blackouts. The counselor agreed to see that the information was provided to the hospital staff so that if the father had another "spell," the hospital staff would be supportive instead of antagonistic to the family. This offers a good example of how anticipating problems, even though painful, may be essential to making new solutions effective.

The father's admission that he did have blackouts is also significant because it demonstrates that the one-sided picture of "the family as perpetrators" drawn by the hospital staff was erroneous; the father was, in fact, having seizures that the medical and psychiatric teams simply missed.

In this third and final session, Daughter-55 and her husband failed to appear. In her absence, the father reassumed his position as family head and led the rest of the family in confiding to the counselor that Daughter-55 and her husband had been having severe marital difficulties which involved a "drinking problem." The children admitted that while "what to do with Mommy and Daddy" had been pressing on their minds, they were equally worried about Daughter-55. The family made an impromptu decision that Son-50, who at one time had had to deal with his own drinking, and the father should call on Daughter-55 to share the family's concern and offer support to her. Since the family chose not to ask the counselor for his help with Daughter-55, the counselor did not volunteer it. This family had been solving its own problems rather successfully until they found themselves stuck with this one particular situation. Now that their collective energies were freed up, there was no reason to suspect they would not return to their previous pattern of competently dealing with life's impositions and difficulties.

The meeting was closed on a prayer. The counselor stepped aside to let the family leave to savor their success and contemplate future challenges.

18

Independence and Loneliness

General Remarks

Independence and loneliness are really obverse sides of the same coin. Elders who achieve independence, by their definition, do not want or need to depend on anyone. This "I am a rock" existence avoids the experience of interdependence, which for most people means, positively, a sense of connectedness and relatedness with other human beings. Consequently, the elders who achieve the mythical state of independence must pay the high price of loneliness. In any event, the issue is really moot: "true independence" at any age is a myth, as is complete isolation. We all are interdependent with one another to a large extent, whether we like it or not.

The Myth of "Independence"

For example, an elder who is able to drive to the supermarket is far from being "truly independent," even in regard to the acquisition of her food. Without even thinking about it she not only depends on those who run the market, the processors and distributors who get the food there, and the farmers who grow it, but on the major oil corporations who produce the fuel she needs for her automobile, and they for their machinery and trucks. Beyond even all that, again without conscious recognition, she is dependent on governmental stability to permit the orderly exchange of goods from country to country, state to state, county to county, and city to city. For better or worse, we are all interdependent. Yet often "independence" becomes *the problem*. Because of the cultural myths that surround independence, even as a counselor it is often easy to forget that independence is more a state of mind than a fact of being; and the same, perhaps more subtly, is also true of "loneliness." Usually issues of "independence" are really issues of control—"Dare I let another person influence my feelings and actions?"—or of personal worth—"Can I really be a worthwhile person even if I can't do everything for myself?"

When Personal Worth, Personal Preference, and Loneliness Become Confused

In the United States, the major political programs concerned with the aging have been oriented toward providing elders the maximum opportunity for independent living on the one hand, and creating and funding programs of socialization and activity to minimize the possibility of being lonely on the other. Certainly, as an applied gerontologist, you are quite aware of the plethora of programs to keep elders in their own homes (independent living) or at their senior centers (socialization and activity to avoid loneliness). Many elders are able to benefit substantially from these programs, and hence will not be your clients. Elders and their families who are dealing successfully with "independence" will be aware, consciously or otherwise, that interdependence is simply a fact of life and does not decrease personal worth. Similarly, those who are dealing successfully with loneliness are those who have come to grips with the reality that we are all both interrelated and alone; that utopian formulas that promise "loneliness can always be conquered" or "busy hands are happy hands" are unrealistic; yet, for them, organized or self-directed activity helps.

Many elders, unfortunately, increasingly conceive of loneliness as the "essential human condition," yet think it can and should be radically "cured." Consequently, they do not find it a condition easily assuaged by chatting with "friendly visitors," playing card games at the senior center, helping retarded children as Foster Grandparents, or educating coal miners through VISTA. When counseling these elders, you should not be surprised when the most creative of your suggestions on how to stay busy to avoid loneliness will be dismal failures.

Actually, when loneliness is presented by elder or family as *the problem*, feelings of personal worth and personal preference are probably at issue.

Case Example

This case example was chosen for these reasons: First, the problematic situation described usually presents benignly, but has the potential to intensify into a family crisis in which the elder is institutionalized. Second, this case example highlights how the conflict of personal values regarding what constitutes "loneliness" is often more the problem than the problem of loneliness. And, third, the case demonstrates that the needs of the family may be met without the counselor having to use any specific techniques to mobilize the family system; the family members mobilize themselves after having the opportunity to convene and openly discuss their feelings.

Approaching the Family System

The counselor, an undergraduate social work student doing a half-day per week field placement at a senior center, was approached by a woman in her late 40s:

MRS. SMITH: How do you do. I am Mrs. Smith. I am having a problem with my mother that I hope you can help me solve.

COUNSELOR: I'll try to be as useful as I can, but I'm afraid I'm not always a help—my name is Phil Jones and I am a social work student at the university. What seems to be the problem?

MRS. SMITH: It's my mother. She seems to be getting worse and worse. All she ever does is sit inside her home and never come out. I am really worried for her. I just hope there is something that you can do to get her involved in some new activities. I'm sorry I'm so nervous, but I am a widow with two grown children who live out of state, so that mother is all that I have. I just don't know what I'm going to do if she keeps "giving up."

COUNSELOR: Let me see if I have heard you accurately. It sounds to me as if you feel rather close to your mother since she is all the family —at least locally—that you have. You are concerned for your mother since it seems to you that she is withdrawing from the world around her by staying in her home; what's worse, there doesn't seem to be much that you are able to do about it.

MRS. SMITH: Is there anything you think you could do about it?

COUNSELOR: I know you'd like to hear something encouraging from me, but at this point I really just don't have enough information to say anything. Before I commit myself to making any optimistic or pessimistic statements, I wonder if it would be possible for the three of us to get together so I can get some more information?

MRS. SMITH: Well, I hadn't planned on meeting with you and Mother together. I was rather hoping you might be able to say something directly to her to motivate her to be more active.

COUNSELOR: I appreciate your confidence in me, but at least for the first visit, it would be very helpful for me to have you both here.

MRS. SMITH: Well . . . if that's what you think best. I know Mother. She'd do almost anything to get me off her back.

In this exchange the counselor got enough information to know that a family interaction was involved, so he made the next appointment for both mother and daughter. By keeping the first appointment short, he avoided establishing an alliance with Mrs. Smith, which might later prove a detriment to establishing a trusting relationship with the mother.

The daughter gave a valuable clue about family system interaction which the counselor will be certain to consider throughout the next session. Specifically, the clue was that Mrs. Smith wanted the counselor to "motivate" her mother. Usually when clients want counselors to "motivate," they really want counselors to "manipulate." A client who has expectations of a counselor to help in the "motivation" of another family member is really asking for help in a struggle for control. The daughter acknowledges that her mother perceives her as being "on her back," suggesting that the struggle between mother and daughter might be quite intense.

Determining the Problem

COUNSELOR: Mrs. Bass, I would like to hear your understanding of why your daughter asked you to come down here today.

MRS. BASS: I will be happy to tell you, young man. My daughter is worried that I don't get out enough, so she is constantly trying to drag me all over creation in the hopes that I will suddenly become inspired to become a socialite. Well, I'll tell you right now that I am not interested in becoming a socialite. I am 84 years old. I have arthritis in every joint from my eyebrows down. It hurts to sit, it is torture to walk, and only a sadist would make me get into and out of an automobile. The alternative to my pain is to take the medication that a fine young doctor down at the clinic prescribed for me. Unfortunately, his "pain pills" make me sick, dizzy, and constipated. At my age, I cannot afford any of those side effects, so I have learned to endure my pain.

Endure, that is, until my daughter begins her relentless invasion of my privacy and forces me out of my home at least once a day. Young man, I have outlived all but one of my close friends and both of my husbands. Consequently, there are few places I want to go. When I walk

I must lean heavily on a cane and feel as if I am creating a public spectacle. It hurts.

Am I so old and evil that I can't enjoy my last few years sitting peacefully by my window, reading my books, looking through my photographs, and watching my television? Am I not entitled to peace?

MRS. SMITH: Oh, Mother! You know that isn't true. You're only telling half the story. You make me so mad I could cry. [As if to prove the point, Mrs. Smith begins to sob.]

COUNSELOR: Mrs. Smith, you obviously feel misunderstood. But before you clear up how you see the situation, would you bear with me so I can make sure that I fully grasp what your mother has told me? Mrs. Bass, correct me if I am inaccurate. What I think you are saying is that it seems to you that the reason your daughter wanted you to come down here today was that she wants you to be more active and she is hoping that in some way this meeting, or those that follow, might make you more active.

MRS. BASS: Yes, that's close enough.

COUNSELOR: I'm curious; Mrs. Smith, is that why, in your mind, you asked your mother down here today?

MRS. SMITH: That's just part of it. I also wanted my mother to be more active so she would be happier. What she didn't tell you about is how she sits by the window all day long crying and miserable.

MRS. BASS: That's not true.

COUNSELOR: Please, wait for me. The two of you are going way too fast for me. You're going to have to be patient with me because I can't think as fast as the two of you can talk. To make sure that I have heard you both accurately, let me review: I think I just asked Mrs. Smith if Mrs. Bass was accurate in her assessment of why you wanted her to attend. Your response, at least as I understood it, was that you did hope this session would serve to motivate Mrs. Bass to be more active in the future, but that your concern for her activity was based more on your desire to see her happy than to force her to become a "socialite" against her will.

MRS. SMITH: Yes.

COUNSELOR [turning to Mrs. Bass]: I also thought I heard you say, Mrs. Bass, that you are not eager to be more active because activity causes problems with your painful arthritis. I also got the impression that your inactivity seems to worry your daughter more than you. That is, I believe I understood you to say that staying home and reminiscing about the past, or doing some reading or watching television, was meeting your needs for activity.

MRS. BASS: [Nods her head affirmatively.]

COUNSELOR: Then as I hear it, you both are agreeing that there is a problem. It's just that from your point of view, Mrs. Bass, the problem stems from your daughter's overeagerness to keep you active in ways that she defines as "active," while for you, Mrs. Smith, the problem seems to be more related to your perceptions that your mother's present activities are not sufficient to make her happy, despite her claims to the contrary. Would you tell me some of the behaviors you observe in your mother that suggest to you that she isn't happy?

The counselor reframes the problem from being Mrs. Bass' loneliness and unhappiness to a problem of differing opinions between mother and daughter. Additionally, the counselor attempts to get Mrs. Smith to specify the behaviors of her mother that suggest she is unhappy.

MRS. SMITH: Well, I didn't want to get into this with Mother here, but as long as you asked, about half the time when I go to visit Mother, her eyes are red and swollen and she has such a long face. When I see her like that, I know she's miserable and lonely. All I want to do is to cheer her up. Is that so awful? I would want to be cheered up too if I were in her position. Another thing she does that worries me when we just stay at her home is she starts to talk about the past: old stories about Daddy, or her childhood, or one event or another out of half a century ago. Occasionally, during these stories, she'll get a distant look in her eye and begin to cry. I just know that sort of thing isn't good for her.

COUNSELOR: Mrs. Smith, I want to check something out with you. From the urgent tone of your voice and the strained look on your face, it seems that you are feeling as if *you* are responsible for your mother's happiness. Is that right?

MRS. SMITH: Aren't all children responsible for their parents?

COUNSELOR: I don't know. In my experience it varies from family to family. Could you ask your mother if she expects you to take responsibility for her happiness?

The counselor moves off the position of judge and into the position of facilitator by helping Mrs. Smith to personalize her question and direct it to her mother:

MRS. SMITH: [turning toward her mother]: Mother, do you expect me to be responsible for your happiness?

MRS. BASS: Of course not! That's what I've been trying to tell you. I want to be responsible for my own happiness. How could you possibly know what makes me happy?

COUNSELOR: Would you tell your daughter specifically what does make you happy?

MRS. BASS: First, thinking and talking about the past make me happy. Sometimes, I suppose, it makes me cry, but just as often from a peculiar kind of joyful nostalgia as sorrow. The fact is, whether you can accept it or not, most of my life is behind me. So I take much of my enjoyment from the past. I so enjoy thinking about and talking about the past that I wish that you would do it more with me. When I start talking about this or that that happened 40 years ago and you shush me up, I feel terrible.

COUNSELOR: How does it feel to feel that kind of "terrible"?

MRS. BASS   [looking at her daughter]: I feel like you're not interested in me anymore.

COUNSELOR: Mrs. Smith, did you know that when you discouraged your mother from talking about the past she felt terrible and thought you weren't interested in her anymore?

MRS. SMITH: No, I'm very surprised. Mother, how could you possibly think that?

COUNSELOR: So it sounds as if that wasn't the way you wanted your mother to feel, but that was the way she was feeling. Isn't it amazing how often the message one person sends is different from the one the other receives. Mrs. Bass, what else makes you happy or brings you pleasure?

MRS. BASS: A lot of things. I enjoy talking on the telephone with my grandchildren and my other daughter in Detroit. I enjoy seeing them.

I'm almost afraid to admit this, but as long as we're being honest, I do, from time to time, enjoy dining out with my daughter: preferably where there are no stairs and where we can go early in the evening before the dinnertime rush.

MRS. SMITH: I am amazed.

MRS. BASS: Another thing I do enjoy is watching television. I only wish I could afford a color set. But I know, dear [looking at Mrs. Smith], you think that would lead to my ultimate degeneration.

Determining Attempted Solutions

COUNSELOR: I wonder if we might back up a bit from what makes you [looking at Mrs. Bass] happy, and explore a little the other side of the coin—namely, what you, Mrs. Smith, have been trying to make your mother feel better.

MRS. SMITH: I've tried a little of everything to get her to become more active. I've begged her. I've bribed her. I've gotten angry with her. Once I actually physically dragged her out to the car to go to a play with me. Nothing works. It is always a battle. Lately, I have been trying every day to get her to go out, but only succeeding about three times a week.

COUNSELOR: How do you feel when you are unsuccessful?

MRS. SMITH: I feel totally defeated. I just want to give up.

COUNSELOR: Did you know that's how your daughter feels when she can't get you to share any of her activities with her?

MRS. BASS: No. I always thought she was just mad at me because she couldn't get her way.

COUNSELOR: Mrs. Smith, you mentioned earlier that you have tried to keep your mother's mind off of the past to help her to be more in the present or future.

MRS. SMITH: Oh yes. I've tried that. I always go to Mother's house with a smile on my face and in an optimistic mood. It hasn't always been easy either. I don't know if I told you at our last visit, but my husband passed away nine months ago last Tuesday. His death was very sudden and came to me as quite a shock. But I've tried not to let it get me down. I've remained active and it has been my salvation ... [a minute of silence].

COUNSELOR: Would you be willing at least to consider that being active might not be your mother's salvation? [Another minute of silence.]

MRS. SMITH: I guess so. After all, we are different people.

MRS. BASS: Well, I'm glad to hear you finally admit it. As long as you've brought up the topic of Bob's untimely passing, there are some things I want to say. Frankly, young man [looking at the counselor], I haven't been particularly cooperative with my daughter and her frenetic social schedule. I've probably made it more difficult for her than I needed to. She and Bob led a very active social life and I have felt thrust into his role in the last nine months. I have made it difficult for my daughter because I was afraid that if I showed the least bit of enthusiasm, she would literally consume me with activities.

COUNSELOR: Then it sounds to me as if the way you have been dealing with your daughter's demands has been to automatically say "no" to everything, even to some of the things you would actually like to do.

Determining Goals

COUNSELOR: At this point, I am wondering how things might change between the two of you so that you would each have a sense that you are making progress.

MRS. SMITH: Well, I would like to be able to invite Mother to go out with me without feeling as if I have to beg her to come along.

COUNSELOR: You would like her to say "yes" right away?

MRS. SMITH: Uhh, I guess so. But that would be too good to be true.

COUNSELOR: I think I have to agree with you. It is very unlikely that any two people would always be wanting to do the same thing at the same time. I'm wondering what would be the smallest number of times a month, if you and your mother could reach agreement to do something together, that would leave you feeling satisfied that things are getting better.

MRS. SMITH: I would say twice a month.

COUNSELOR: Fine. Mrs. Bass, how would you know that things were getting better?

MRS. BASS: I would know things were better if my daughter only asked me to go out once a week, and respected my wishes if I said "No."

COUNSELOR: How would you know if she was respecting your wishes? Specifically, how would she act after you said "No"?

MRS. BASS: She would just say, "I just wanted you to know you were invited," and leave it at that. She wouldn't criticize me for staying in my home.

COUNSELOR: So you would know that things were better if your daughter limited her invitations to you to once a week, and if you declined her invitation she would show respect for your decision by not being argumentative or critical.

MRS. BASS: Yes.

COUNSELOR: I have one question for you, Mrs. Bass. When you say that you would like your daughter to limit her invitations to once a week, are you saying that you would actually be eager to go out once a week if you felt accepting one invitation wouldn't lead to many more?

MRS. BASS: Do you want me to be honest?

COUNSELOR: Only if you feel comfortable enough.

MRS. BASS: Well, at the beginning, I was more concerned about talking in front of my daughter, but I might as well be honest. I would enjoy going out about once a week, but no more. I won't promise I'll always say yes; after all, she might want to do something I'm not at all interested in doing. But in general, I would look forward to going out once a week.

COUNSELOR: How do you feel when you hear your mother saying that?

MRS. SMITH: Surprised, certainly.

COUNSELOR: I have another appointment coming up, but before we part, I'm wondering how each of you is feeling right now.

MRS. SMITH: I'm feeling amazed and much much better.

MRS. BASS: I'm feeling suspicious that nothing that was said today is going to make any difference.

COUNSELOR: I think you have a good point, Mrs. Bass. You have good grounds for skepticism. After all, people usually have very good reasons for acting exactly the way they are acting, and change isn't easy. I myself was not expecting that today's session would result in some kind of permanent change, only that some kind of new light might be shed on a serious problem that has been bothering both of you. On that limited basis, I'm wondering if our meeting today was useful. Did you gain any new information?

MRS. BASS: I'm not sure that I did, but I think my daughter did.

COUNSELOR: Well, I'd like to ask you both, do you think it would be worth coming back next week for another visit?

MRS. SMITH: It would be for me.

MRS. BASS: Well, I don't know what good it would do, but if Joan thinks that it will be useful to her, then I'll come back one more time.

COUNSELOR: Then we'll set the appointment for the same time and place next week. I would like to make one final request, though, before you go. Coming here has been a rather big step for both of you. I think it would be most useful if between now and next week you didn't attempt to make any changes in your behavior. Just observe what's happening instead of trying to change it.

Comprehending the Family System

What is the extent of the family system? The family system is composed of Mrs. Bass, Mrs. Smith, and the deceased Mr. Smith. That is, even though the family has been reduced in size, the influence of the recently deceased husband is very important. This point was emphasized when Mrs. Bass said that she was reluctant to talk about him. People and topics that "cannot" be discussed are often covering *issues* that "cannot" be discussed. Their avoidance obscures the path to problem determination and problem resolution.

The small size of the living family suggests the importance of maintaining a mutually supportive relationship between mother and daughter. The fact that they must rely so heavily on one another for support might also suggest that they are in danger of overloading one another in their needs for intimacy. This case may be particularly true for the daughter, who, since her husband's death, is looking more and more to her mother for social and emotional fellowship, but is overwhelming her mother's resources to meet these needs.

Where is the counselor in the family system? Probably too close to the daughter for comfort. The counselor could acknowledge this situation in the next session by saying something such as, "Mrs. Bass, I'm aware that your daughter and I are both a good deal younger than you, and I'm wondering if you are feeling ganged up against."

What are the family rules? It would probably be a good guess that there are at least two applicable family rules affecting the present problematic situation: First, "Family members are responsible for one another"; and, second, "Real weakness should not be acknowledged publicly." Evidence for the first rule comes from the fact that the daughter is feeling obligated to worry—through thought and deed—about her mother, while her mother is willing in thought but unwilling in deed to *absolutely* lay down the law that "It is Mrs. Bass' responsibility to take care of Mrs. Bass."

In terms of disclosing "real weakness," the counselor has the impression that the death of Mr. Smith has not been fully explored between mother and daughter, since it is a topic that is labeled "sensitive." Again avoiding "real weakness," both mother and daughter seem willing to deal with the problems of the mother's advancing age mostly in terms of *activities*. The daughter expresses concern over the fact that her mother might be crying about "something," yet, by pushing activities, seems intent on denying that those feelings about "something" might be significant. The mother seems to have no readily available outlet to express her own concerns about her aging and infirmities, or anyone with whom to discuss and review her life.

Is there an Identified Patient? The mother was initially labeled by the daughter as the Identified Patient. Interestingly, by the end of the first session, the daughter was willing to back off from "Mother has *the problem*" and was willing to admit that she and her mother shared a problem in terms of their deteriorating relationship. The fact that the daughter said she felt better after the session might suggest she was feeling the most powerless and hopeless in the beginning. Given the fact of her recent widowhood, these feelings are quite understandable.

How is power exercised? Mrs. Bass exerts her power by saying "No." That is, when her daughter finds her crying, Mrs. Bass says, "No, there is nothing wrong." When the daughter invites her out, her mother says, "No, I don't want to go." In some ways, always saying "No" is the same power tactic as always saying "Yes": if your behavior is invariable, nobody really knows where you stand, so nobody can intentionally get in the way of what you want—but equally, they cannot help you get it. Mrs. Smith exerts her power by always saying "Yes," and by allying herself with the inherent socioeconomic power of the middle generation: she drives the car, buys the restaurant dinners—and contacts the social worker when things are not going her way!

Why has the problem not been solved? This question can be answered at several levels. At the first level the problem has not been solved because it is a power struggle without end: the more insistent the daughter becomes, the more determined the mother becomes. Instead of backing off, the daughter tries harder by being more insistent her mother say "Yes," resulting in her mother being more determined to say "No." At every confrontation, the daughter feels increasingly powerless and ineffective, so she tries even harder. The circle remains vicious and unbroken. The daughter has convinced herself that should she back off her mother would become a hermit; the mother has convinced herself that were she to say "Yes," her daughter would become even more voracious in her social demands, leaving the mother without her last remaining power—the choice to say "No."

At a deeper level, there exists the possibility that the daughter has been worrying about her mother to avoid dealing with the realities of her own widowhood. That is, it is far less depressing for the daughter to be worrying about her mother's activities than it is for the daughter to come to grips with the rather severe social, economic, and emotional adjustments that accompany losing a spouse. It is not unrealistic to suspect that when the daughter stops worrying about her mother she may experience many of the feelings of isolation and loneliness that she now solely attributes to her mother.

Finally, if the daughter is using her own "hyperactivity" as a defense mechanism to postpone dealing with some of the unpleasant realities in her life, her mother's refusal to join her frenzied life style might be quite threatening: "If being active won't make you happy, then it may not make me happy either. I can't bear to examine that thought, so it is important that you agree with me by being as active as I am."

It should be added that dealing with many of life's difficulties (a job that needs to be quit, a spouse that needs to be divorced, a serious illness that needs to be attended, to name but a few) can be postponed by hyperactivity in all walks of life (the frenzied business person, the frenzied housewife, the frenzied mother, the frenzied father, again, to name but a few). Thus, many middle-aged children find themselves openly resenting—although politely labeling their resentment as worry—the less intense and more sedate activities of their elders.

Does the family still need a counselor? At this point the answer is a guarded "Perhaps." On the one hand, mother and daughter are willing to make another appointment and no changes in the presenting problem have yet taken place. On the other hand, communication between the two has been greatly enhanced; there is a good possibility that, acting on newly acquired information from the counseling session, mother and daughter will work out their own solutions to their problems.

Mobilizing the family system.   Since whether or not the family needs to continue counseling remains a viable question, it is premature to determine a specific plan to mobilize the family energy. Since the last meeting, mother and daughter have had a week to interact on the basis of new information. The counselor needs to gather more information on how they made out on their own before even considering specific interventions.

> **COUNSELOR:**   It's nice to see you both again. I'm wondering how things have been for you both this last week.
>
> **MRS. SMITH:**   I'm afraid I didn't follow your directions. I don't know if you remember, but at the end of our meeting last week, you told us not to do anything differently—that we had done enough changing just coming to see you. I tried, but every time I thought of inviting mother to go out with me, I just started to think of the hassle it would create, so I didn't do it.
>
> **MRS. BASS:**   She's right! She didn't even call for the first two days after we saw you. I was concerned something might have happened to her, so I called her. Imagine that!
>
> **COUNSELOR:**   What was that like for you, Mrs. Smith, to have your mother pursuing you for a change?
>
> **MRS. SMITH:**   It was wonderful. I felt like I had a mother again. She even invited me over for dinner.

After a few minutes of discussion, it was apparent that Mrs. Smith and Mrs. Bass had broken the vicious circle of their behavior. The original problem clearly was solved. Equally clear, from certain remarks made by the daughter, was that the issues of her widowhood were only beginning to surface. Rather than taking on the topic of widowhood without specific invitation, the counselor decided to terminate even these informal counseling sessions, but to leave the door open for future meetings, should the need arise.

Winding Up

> **COUNSELOR:**   Well, I certainly am pleased to hear that the pressure seems to be off this week. I'm wondering what you both did to make that happen.
>
> **MRS. SMITH:**   For me, it was a matter of realizing that I couldn't impose my values on Mother. I realized last week that even though I may feel responsible in some ways for Mother's happiness, I just can't control what she does. So I made up my mind I'd stop trying so hard

to change her and try harder to enjoy doing what she likes to do—which is mostly sitting around the house watching television or talking about old times. To my surprise, although I'm almost embarrassed to admit it, when I stopped changing the subject every time she brought up the past, I found myself enjoying our time together and I even learned a lot.

COUNSELOR: What a pleasant surprise. Mrs. Bass, what about you? What did you do differently this week?

MRS. BASS: I didn't do anything differently. I will say, though, that when my daughter didn't call for two days, it was very pleasant to hear her voice over the telephone. I'm sure that she could tell I was glad to hear from her and I'm sure that made some kind of difference.

MRS. SMITH: It certainly did. I can't even begin to tell you how nice it was to hear you happy to talk to me.

COUNSELOR: I hate to change the subject to bring up something unpleasant, but can either of you see how the changes you've made in your relationship might create problems in the future, which might be important to anticipate?

MRS. SMITH: For the first time in months, our lives are looking better. I don't want to have to talk about how they are going to turn bad again.

COUNSELOR: I certainly can't blame you for feeling that way. But sometimes, particularly when people have experienced a rapid change for the better, it's useful to anticipate problems so that when they occur they don't seem to appear out of nowhere. Can either of you anticipate any?

MRS. SMITH: Well, I suppose I'll eventually get tired of watching television with Mother.

COUNSELOR: That's a good one. I think it would be fair to expect that as the two of you no longer disagree so insistently on how to be active, you will probably both experience more minor disagreements on a wide variety of topics, certainly television among them. I'm curious, though; do you think it might be possible for you, Mrs. Smith, to dislike television yourself but not feel you have to criticize your mother for enjoying it?

MRS. SMITH: That doesn't sound too difficult to me.

COUNSELOR: I'm wondering what other problems might come up [a minute of silence]. I can understand how the two of you would be reluctant to discuss future problems. But let me see if I can't think of some. For example, Mrs. Bass, I know that you have some physical problems that at some future date might force you to restrict your out-of-home activity even more. I can foresee a great deal of difficulty when and if that should happen, if at that time your daughter is unwilling to accept your decision on how active you want to be.

I also can foresee a problem developing for you, Mrs. Smith. Over the past few months, you have spent a great deal of energy trying to solve the problem of your mother's loneliness and seeming unhappiness. Now that the problem has been at least partially solved, that energy will be freed up. In my experience, energy can go into making your life's experiences either more positive or more negative. So in the next few weeks and months I would expect you to find this recently released energy beginning to find a path. Since you are a recent widow, I think this problem may be even more accentuated because, as a single person, you have so many potential paths along which your energy might flow.

For example, traveling down a positive path, you might find your interests and energies leading you toward finding a satisfying job, making new relationships, going back to school, or becoming actively involved in some kind of volunteer work that makes use of your intellectual skills. On the other hand, you might find the path leading in a negative direction, such as finding yourself intruding into the lives of your adult children, becoming preoccupied with some small physical complaint, or resuming the unsatisfactory involvement in your mother's life that brought you here initially. For example, instead of her activities, you might find yourself becoming overconcerned with her finances, or for that matter the condition of her roof or the door of her garage.

I'm aware I've been doing a lot of talking. Am I making any sense with this talk of positive and negative flows of spare energy?

After a short discussion in which both mother and daughter acknowledged the reality of possible difficulties such as the counselor had suggested, but did not pursue this matter any further, the counselor concluded the meeting in the following way:

COUNSELOR: I'd just like to say I've enjoyed talking with you both. I'm delighted that you've had a good week and have a sense of how to keep future weeks just as good. I feel I ought to warn you, though, that good weeks are usually followed by not-so-good or even downright bad weeks. If you find yourselves slipping back a bit next week, or the week after, or any of the weeks after that, you might remember that such a bit of a slip backwards is perfectly normal and to be expected. If at some later time you'd like to come in again, I'd be happy to see you. Incidentally, you don't have to come in only when life is going poorly. I enjoy hearing how things are going well too.

19

Grave Disabilities, Death, and Grief

Everyone's life is filled with events that can be classified as "life's difficulties." Ordinarily, such difficulties are impositions on the reasonably smooth course of daily existence that are temporary or compensable. That is, these events are not only possible to survive, they are possible to overcome or transcend, and some measure of gain in growth, understanding, or strength may even be attained in the process. After all, it is only realistic to recognize that meeting and dealing with difficulties and challenges is one essential part of life and growth. This class of events includes breaking a leg, suffering a large loss in the stock market, being hospitalized for pneumonia, or even being born with some physical handicap.

But there are also in every life, from time to time, life difficulties of more major proportions. These would include such events as a gravely debilitating illness (a severe paralysis, crippling arthritis, or chronic brain syndrome), one's own impending death, or the death of a loved one. Clearly, such major life difficulties occur in increasing number with increasing age. Equally plainly, they powerfully affect not only the specific person suffering the major difficulty but also the members of that person's family.

This chapter is concerned with being useful, to whatever extent is possible, to clients who are facing these very unpleasant and inherently painful situations.

At first glance, it would seem that such events and situations are unlike all lesser life difficulties, that they cannot be overcome, compensated, or transcended and can only be endured, so that discussion of them is pointless. We do not see it this way. How can any fixed line be drawn between serious but approachable problems and problems so grave that nothing can possibly be useful to those who suffer from them? From another angle, this comes down to what we have said before: Whatever the specific problem is, how it is handled also makes a difference. Perhaps things can be made better even in extreme situations; at least we may try to minimize their being made even worse. If our general approach to helping people deal with problems associated with aging has some validity, it should not be abandoned in extreme situations, when any help is most important. Even when unpleasant things must be endured—a matter that may be part of coping with both lesser and greater problems in life—there may at least be worse and relatively better ways of enduring, and we must consider how we as counselors may be useful to those who must do the enduring.

To say this is not quite to echo those writing today who claim that progressive and irreversible diseases associated with old age, including the final process called "dying," provide an opportunity for "growth." It is not that we see this as an impossibility; there is presumably always a possibility of growth, in some sense, inherent in coming to terms with a life difficulty, even the most severe and final. But we do not wish to minimize the reality and seriousness of such difficulties either; neither denial nor magnification of difficult realities is helpful to people.

This chapter will be brief, not because there is so little to say about the end of life, but because there is so much. Within the last ten years, death and dying have gone from being rather taboo subjects to being major topics in gerontology. We cannot review or summarize this considerable literature, though we encourage students to gain some acquaintance with it. Even this literature represents only a limited perspective on the subject, reflecting a Western culture, scientific–professional outlook. All other times and places necessarily have grappled with the problems of death and dying. Their practical, social, and religious responses have been very diverse. Some knowledge of these varied stances can be quite valuable, if only to indicate that for this ultimate question especially, there is no final definition of right and wrong, better and worse.

Accordingly, each of you should use your own reading, and your own always growing personal and professional experience, to move toward an approach to death and dying consonant with your own observations, beliefs, and values. Here we will limit ourselves to discussing how our approach might be applied in three main areas: counseling with the gravely disabled, with the dying client, and with upset and grieving families. We recognize that in these circumstances especially, where the stakes are highest all around—for clients, for families, and for counselors—our position is only a beginning, and only one among many. Yet we hope that the limited discussion we offer will be of some use, and we suggest that in extreme situations even a little improvement can mean a lot.

Being Useful to the Gravely Disabled

Because of modern medicine, there has arisen in the last 50 years a group of elders able to survive for years despite the fact that they suffer from progressive, gravely disabling illnesses. These illnesses include (but are certainly not limited to) cerebral vascular accidents (strokes), slowly progressing forms of cancer, emphysema, arthritis, Parkinson's disease, and other degenerative diseases of the nervous system that result in impaired physical or psychological functioning. In the not too distant past, such diseases led rather rapidly to the point where the afflicted individuals were confined to bed or a chair. The consequent inactivity rendered the patients particularly liable to infections, especially pneumonia. Pneumonia led in turn to death within a few days. With modern medical techniques and antibiotics, death by pneumonia no longer comes to visit as "the old man's friend." We are referring here, not to the special, and relatively rare, heroics of modern medicine that keep people alive on a machine indefinitely, but simply the use of commonly available drugs, diagnostic equipment, and medical/nursing procedures that represent current standards of good practice. Because of these advances, many more elders than ever before may be faced with months or years of confinement—probably in a convalescent hospital—with no realistic hope of recovery. Correspondingly, more families than ever before may be faced with a long period of waiting for the inevitable end, largely separated while still attached.

Yet while this situation is more common than ever before, it is not really new in kind. In fact the main difficulties involved, while they may exist over a longer period and to a higher degree, are quite familiar human problems.

For the disabled elder, the most likely problems are feelings of isolation, helplessness, and hopelessness. These often, understandably, lead to apathy or depression. What is potentially useful for a counselor to do in such a situation is rather simple to state: be patiently available and accepting of the realities of the client's situation and feelings. To act in these ways when a client is in such unfortunate circumstances, however, can be very difficult. It calls for all the humanity and all the professional responsibility that a counselor can summon. Instead of being evidently but patiently available, it almost always will be easier to avoid the gravely disabled client—"good reasons" for doing so will always be easy to find—or to go to the other extreme and busily press attentions on the client whether they are welcome or not.

Similarly, it is not easy to accept the difficult realities of a gravely disabled elder's circumstances, even though this limited sharing of the situation may be the most you have to offer your client. On the one hand, it is always a temptation to "cheer up" a client in serious distress; that is, in some form or another to say, "It's not as bad as it seems." But any such message, despite its good intent, is most likely to make the client feel that even the counselor does not understand, and therefore to feel even more alone and hopeless.

An extreme but not uncommon example may serve to put this in sharp focus. What if a disabled elder, already a long resident in a nursing home, says to you seriously, "I wish I were dead"? It is hard not to respond with some variant of "While there's life there's hope." But it is much more likely to be useful—even if the usefulness is necessarily limited to conveying understanding and the human support this supplies—if you can say, "I can certainly understand your feeling that way. I'd probably feel about the same in your circumstances." And it might help a bit more if you could also say, "I really don't know how you have been able to carry on this long; lots of people would have given up completely before now." While overtly this may appear a discouraging message, at a deeper level it offers the client credit for the reality of endurance, instead of the blame for thoughts about death that is implicit in any form of "You shouldn't think like that."

On the other hand, though probably this is less usual, it is also possible to make too much of a client's disabilities by becoming overconcerned about apparent behavioral difficulties or deficits that are not really so important in themselves, or by neglecting the influence external life circumstances may be having on the client's feelings and behavior. A common enough example of the first case exists when an elder has a moment or moments of confusion or amnesia and gets lost in the middle of a conversation. This can be quite disconcerting to a counselor—and probably even more so to family members—but is it really so important, compared to the other problems involved in grave disability? In any event, there is one thing we can be sure of: the situation can be made much worse by handling it badly, which is easy to do. If a counselor simply ignores the lapse, this is apt to be a transparent "overlooking" that will convey the message that the slip is too bad to talk about. Yet it is equally unhelpful to express great concern, which is apt to convey, "My God, you seem senile as well as disabled; pull yourself together." This may lead to greater effort but also greater confusion, which for anyone is a common result of trying too hard. In such a situation, it would be more useful to the elder to say, "You know, a minute ago it seemed like you lost your place in what we were talking about—anyway, I got a bit lost. It's not all that important, but is that worrisome for you?"

The prime example of the second case occurs when a gravely disabled elder appears depressed, and people react to this as if it were a sign of a serious mental problem—"depression"—added onto the problems of disability. It is more useful for the counselor to recognize and acknowledge that the life circumstances of a disabled elder client, especially if institutionalized, may realistically be depressing in themselves. Such recognition may make them easier to bear and reduce their effects; neglecting this fact only leads to further invidious labeling of the client and to more anxiety in others concerned.

As to the family of such a disabled client, perhaps the most important thing a counselor can do is to recognize that they are liable to react in ways similar to those just described, only more so; they are more closely involved with the disabled elder and are probably under added pressures of grief or guilt ("If only we had done differently, when there was still time to make a difference"). To help them take useful attitudes toward their loved one, avoid the extremes of denial or overreaction.

Impending Death

Not just dying clients but all of us are in a state of impending death: It is certain that we will all die sometime, and no one can be sure it will not be tomorrow. It can be helpful to recognize this fact as long as we also realize that its significance depends on one's view of it. There is no final view even of this most final matter. Many religious views have interpreted death as positive, the start of a better existence. Existential philosophers have seen death, and especially the knowledge that one must die, as the burden of mankind. It is equally possible to see this knowledge as giving special meaning and purpose to human existence. In any case, two points are of prime importance to any counselor who works with dying clients. First, while we all equally will die, views of dying do vary. Second, it is necessary first to learn the client's view of dying and to accept this as a reality. Argument is worse than useless, but acceptance may open the way to make the inevitable a bit easier.

In general, in dealing with dying clients it is important to be gently available, to be quiet, and to be compassionately realistic. Being gently available means not pushing yourself on clients; it also means being perceptive and open to the possibility that a client may wish to talk of impending death even if this is not the first subject mentioned. Elders who suddenly seem interested in disposing of their property are frequently giving such a message. Other indications might be arranging for the welfare of pets, seeking alternative living arrangements, or giving up valued hobbies or activities. To be aware means to be willing to seek the hidden agenda in a way that will help the client allow it to come out.

Being quiet does not mean stony silence, but keeping enough grip on your own anxiety or concern about death so that you can be patiently quiet and receptive with a dying client, not nervously busy. This in itself is calming and reassuring. Quiet listening also gives your client the maximum opportunity to say what is most on his or her mind. Then you can respond with an appropriate kind of compassionate realism—which means refraining from being unrealistically optimistic without being pessimistically confrontive.

Recent studies of dying, especially those of Kubler-Ross (1969), indicate that people facing their own imminent death typically pass through a series of stages. It is not certain whether these stages are fixed and immutable. They could be artifacts of our times and our culture; they could depend at least in part on typical reactions of closely involved others to the dying person. In a practical sense, however, this does not matter. A counselor dealing with the dying is apt to encounter such typical reaction-to-dying patterns, so it is relevant to note them and suggest how they may best be met if and when they are encountered.

First, there is the stage of *denial*. Such denial may be expressed covertly by avoidance of physical examinations or not talking about evident signs of ill health; it may be explicit ("I'm all right; the doctors don't know what they are talking about") or it may be expressed indirectly in action—driving dangerously, smoking heavily. In addition to being aware of such signs, a counselor may have information from a doctor, a priest, a friend, or a family member that a client is dying. A counselor should not ignore such information; he should take steps to see and be gently available to the client. But the counselor should avoid confrontation and argument as worse than futile. If, for example, a client does not pay attention to first warning signs or warning words, insisting on them will probably only harden his position of denial. It is hard to say, "Well, those chest pains you're having could be only indigestion," but this stance is more likely to get an elder to the doctor than saying, "Those pains might be very serious; you'd be foolish to go on neglecting them." In all probability, your client knows that already, and your insisting on it only increases his fear and resistance. In a more extreme case, the family of an 80-year-old man you know from your work at the senior center may tell you that he has had recent exploratory surgery that showed he had terminal cancer. When you next see him, it might be most appropriate to say, "Your family told me of your surgery, and I was concerned," and then be silent until he speaks. You have made yourself gently available. The elder may take up your lead; if so, fine. You may find he says little or nothing. If so, accept this, at least for the time being; trying harder will only change availability to abrasiveness. Or the elder may even reassure you of his good health and begin to discuss his plans for the long-term future. Until it is time for you to leave, perhaps with, "I hope we will be able to get together again," you may listen with attention. But it is not up to you to confront him with the reality of his illness, nor to support enthusiastically his unrealistic plans for the future.

The next stage of dying, when it can no longer be denied, is *anger*. In those close to death, it is likely to take the form, "Why me and not you?" Those more remote from death, yet perhaps uneasy about it, may feel and react, "If it happened to you, you must have deserved it somehow." Not only the dying but those concerned with the dying person may be angry. There seem to be two main bases for such anger by relatives or hospital staff. Probably the main one is a reaction to a form of ultimate helplessness: "We have done our utmost for you, and your dying shows it was inadequate." The other is a reaction to loss, to the prospect of being left alone, abandoned, after long and close involvement with the dying person. It is always hard to accept anger rather than become angry in return, and hard to accept that life and death, including one's own, are unpredictable and chancy. Yet perhaps the only reasonable answer to, "Why me and not you?" expressed or implicit, is "I don't know how these things happen."

Anger may be an especially difficult stage for counselors wishing seriously to be useful to their clients. Elders' anger may be venomous, widespread (aimed at everyone and everything), and apparently quite unjustified and unfair. Yet it is of no use to defend the objects of their anger to dying elders or to try to mollify them in any way. Such acts by a counselor can only be seen by the elder as invalidating, at a time when validation is most essential. Dying elders are literally fighting mad for their lives. They are not asking you to stop their anger but to hear it, to validate their feelings and existence.

The only useful course is to accept such anger, to acknowledge its reality and significance, even if not agreeing with its particulars. This can be especially difficult when you as a counselor find yourself, despite your efforts to be useful, the object of a dying elder's anger. Still it is important to avoid defending yourself or fighting back. Instead, you might say, "I'm sorry I made you angry. That's not what I intended, but I guess I just don't know how to help you feel any better." If you are ordered to leave, do so. Let the elder have at least that power and control over his life. But be ready to return another time to see whether things have changed and you are welcome then.

The third stage is *bargaining*. For both the about-to-die and the many-years-yet, bargaining takes many forms. The most obvious form is religious: making a deal with God. Other forms of bargaining include holding a fervent belief in exercise, nutrition, or other means to the fountain of youth. We all seek it in some way, though at bottom we all know this is illusory. The more a counselor can recognize both of these sides of hope, the more he or she can accept a client's hopeful or anxious bargaining for just what it is.

That is, again it is best to be *compassionately realistic*. When people are bargaining, they are usually feeling hopeful. This is easier to face than anger, and it may be accepted and shared to a reasonable degree. If a client is only a little hopeful ("What have I got to lose by trying this new diet?") you can agree rather fully ("Certainly anything that might help is worth a trial"). If the client is more unrealistically hopeful ("I know this nutritional program will cure my cancer"), you can also hope it will be useful—again, there is no value in arguing—but your hope should be tempered with caution. To join with hope in any way that would raise it unrealistically only sets up your client for a worse letdown into the next stage.

This fourth stage of dying is a very common experience of mankind, often appearing long before dying is imminent. This is *depression*. In the young, this may involve the question "Why go on?" In elders, the matter is more likely to be one of "I won't ever have any further chance to go on, to change anything." Basically, this is realistic—although there is always, until the very end, a possibility of changing, not the events of one's life, but one's interpretation of these, and therefore their meaning. If this is to happen at all, though, it must come about through meeting the reality of one's approaching end, in which depression is expectable. Often, the depression of the dying is so profound that the non-dying, also feeling helpless in the face of the situation, avoid them in self-defense. A counselor should remain available; then at least the client is not both depressed and abandoned. Depression is contagious; you may as a counselor feel about as hopeless as your dying client. This too, though difficult, is understandable and in a sense even appropriate. If your own depression is evident, your client may feel less alone in his sadness. Certainly this is better than trying to lift your depression. At best it is useless to try to convey "Things will be better tomorrow" or "If you only take a more positive attitude . . ."; more probably, things will be made worse. If you do try to be too positive, the client is likely to feel, with some reason, that you are there but you are not with his reality, *right now*.

The fifth and final stage is *acceptance*—having a sense of one's life and its significance, feeling at peace with the world and even with death as a part of it. This may often not be achieved—certainly it should not be *expected* of clients—but it is the end toward which all said here has been directed. Certainly, when it is reached this stage is no problem in itself, but there are possible problems associated with it in which a counselor may still be useful. For the client, this usually becomes a time for finishing old business. Because of their own matter-of-fact attitudes toward what needs to be done, dying individuals are frequently frustrated when well-meaning friends and relatives refuse to deal matter-of-factly with them about the reality of their impending death—not taking them seriously in their requests to finish their life's business, from practical matters to saying final good-byes. As a counselor, you can both help with practical matters that need completion, and help convene family and friends for last good-byes. Also, perhaps, you can help them toward saying these good-byes, so that artificial optimism about the nearness of the end does not prevent people from taking this last opportunity to say what life together has meant and how they will miss each other.

Being Useful to Families of the Dying

This matter has already been touched on explicitly at several points in this chapter. Furthermore, when the primary client is a dying person the position of the counselor is more parallel to that of the family than in any other counseling situation, and so almost all that has been stated for the counselor has relevance for the family members also, though their situation, with its much closer involvement, is more difficult.

To whatever extent family members also can be gently available and compassionately realistic toward their dying relative, the better for both the dying person and themselves. But this may often be a difficult task for them, and one in which they could use a counselor's help. If you are asked for advice on how to deal with their dying elder by concerned family members, you can share with them what you know. It is particularly useful to convey the significance and importance of not invalidating their dying elders through continued cheerfulness or unrealistic optimism, for families who can understand such matters.

You may often meet families, however, who do not appear able, or ready, to understand this; then remember that understanding cannot be forced. Like their dying member, families also often go through stages of grief similar to the stages of dying. If families are overwhelmed by denial, anger, or depression, they most need not your advice but your acceptance, shown through quiet availability and compassionate realism.

To be accepting, however, does not mean to abandon your own perceptivity. For example, families may deal with their overwhelming feelings about an impending death (or similarly with grief over a recent death) by developing an unrealistic concern about a healthy family member—a substitute focus of anxiety, in effect. Thus, a family might come to counseling showing great concern that "Grandmother has been very forgetful since Grandfather became ill," when the real issue is that everyone is denying that Grandfather is about to die. Rather than face their own grief—something that is difficult but ultimately helpful—the family members join in worrying about Grandmother, who may be holding up much better than the rest of them. Accordingly, with families that include an "ailing" elder and an emphasized other problem of whatever sort, counselors should always be alert to the possibility of serious physical illness.

Work with the families of the dying, as with the dying themselves, is not a matter of simple interventions to make bad situations good. Yet as a counselor you can still help people avoid making a painful and difficult situation even worse, and at least sometimes to reach acceptance of the difficult realities together. These goals, while limited, are still worth your best efforts.

20

Cautions and Exhortations

Cautions

The ideas and techniques presented in this book are powerful. This does not mean, however, that they will be useful to everyone at all times. Cases differ, and so do counselors. No approach will always succeed, and none fits all possible users. Therefore, what has been presented here should be considered as simply offering new options when working with elders and their families facing problematic situations.

A story about a young man and his father comes to mind in this connection. The young man had just graduated from Harvard University. He returned to his hometown and, while considering his future, took a job in a gas station. When his father drove into the gas station and saw his son working in soiled clothes under the hood of a car, he became livid with rage. "You think I scrimped and saved all those years to send you to Harvard so you could come home to work in a gas station?" the father screamed incredulously. "I thought," his son remarked, "that you sent me to Harvard to increase my options on what I might do with my life, not reduce them."

Obviously, opinions vary, even as to options. The techniques described in this book are intended to increase your options, not reduce them. If you are satisfied with how useful you are currently being with the elders you serve, then it would be pointless to change your style simply to prove to yourself that these methods can be useful as well. Even if you are unsatisfied, but would find it unpalatable to feel uncertain or to seek help while you give these techniques a trial, certainly you are not obligated to try them. Moreover, just because some of the techniques in this book might prove useful to you and the elders you serve, that does not mean that you must accept and apply all of the techniques presented. Taking "some" does not imply you must take "all." Similarly, in working with the elders and families you serve, you may find it possible to make the commitment in terms of time and energy to develop a counseling relationship, even informally, in some situations, but not all. It is far better to limit your efforts and be useful to a few clients than to overextend and be no use to many. It is also important to keep in mind that even when you do set such realistic limits and try your best, you will not always be successful, no matter what your approach is. To put it plainly, even in being helpful, "You can't win them all." Expecting to only increases failure.

At the beginning, we warned that the intent of this book is not to make you a psychotherapist, but instead to provide you with some practical tools drawn from the experience of psychotherapists and counselors to make your work with elders more effective, that is, more useful to your clients. Accordingly, be careful to limit your work to areas in which you are competent and be willing to seek help immediately when you find your clients failing to make progress or getting worse; but also remember, as the examples demonstrate, that severe problems often derive from correctable misunderstandings and errors.

Exhortations

Just because the techniques in this book are powerful and need to be respected and handled responsibly, that does not mean they need to be feared. It is important to remember that all relationships between you and the elders you serve are powerful, whether you acknowledge that power or not. There is no way to interact with people without affecting them, for better or for worse. It is our hope, then, that you will find the approach we have described applicable and helpful in your day-to-day interactions as an applied gerontologist.

Learning any new skill takes practice. We urge you to avoid the trap of setting your sights too high too soon. Allow yourself to exercise the prerogative of going slowly. If you find yourself pressing and becoming discouraged, ease up for a while. Learning how to be useful to other people is an endless process, not an end point. We encourage you to move at a pace and with an individual style that maximizes your satisfaction in learning and improving as you participate in that necessarily gradual process.

Appendix A
Further Reading in Mental Health and Aging

Berezin, M. A., & Cath, S. H., (Eds.). *Geriatric psychiatry: grief, loss, and emotional disorders in the aging process*. New York: International Universities Press, 1965.

Brody, E. M. *Long-term care of older people*. New York: Human Sciences Press, 1977.

Burnside, I. M. (Ed.). *Psychosocial nursing care of the aged*. New York: McGraw-Hill, 1973.

Burnside, I. M. (Ed.). *Working with the elderly: Group process and techniques*. N. Scituate, Mass.: Duxbury, 1978.

Busse, E. W., & Pfeiffer, E., (Eds.). *Mental illness in later life*. Washington, D.C.: American Psychiatric Association, 1973.

Butler, R. N., & Lewis, M. I. *Aging and mental health* (2nd ed.). St. Louis: Mosby, 1977.

Butler, R. N., & Lewis, M. I. *Sex after sixty, a guide for men and women for their later years*. New York: Harper & Row, 1976.

Eisdorfer, C., & Lawton, M. P. *The psychology of adult development and aging*. Washington, D.C.: American Psychological Association, 1973.

Howells, J. G. (Ed.). *Modern perspectives in the psychiatry of old age*. New York: Brunner/Mazel, 1975.

Kastenbaum, R., & Aisenberg, R. *The psychology of death* (concise ed.). New York: Springer, 1976.

Levin, S. & Kahana, R., (Eds.). *Psychodynamic studies on aging*. New York: New York International Press, 1967.

Lowenthal, M. F. *Lives in distress*. New York: Basic Books, 1964.

Post, F. *The clinical psychiatry of late life*. London: Pergamon Press, 1965.

Schulz, R. *The psychology of death, dying, and bereavement*. Reading, Mass: Addison-Wesley, 1978.

Schwartz, A. N., & Mensh, I. N., (Eds.). *Professional obligations and approaches to the aged*. Springfield, Ill.: Charles C Thomas, 1974.

Simon, A., Lowenthal, M. F., & Epstein, L. *Crisis and intervention*. San Francisco: Jossey-Bass, 1970.

Wasser, E. *Creative approaches with the aging*. New York: Family Service Association of America, 1966.

Whitehead, J. M. *Psychiatric disorders in old age: A handbook for the clinical team*. New York: Springer, 1974.

Verwoerdt, A. *Clinical Geropsychiatry*. Baltimore: Williams & Wilkins, 1976.

Appendix B
Further Reading in Family Counseling and Family Therapy

Block, D. A. (Ed.). *Techniques of family psychotherapy: A primer.* New York: Grune & Stratton, 1973.

Boszormenyi-Nagy, I., & Spark, G. M. *Invisible loyalties: Reciprocity in intergenerational family therapy.* New York: Harper & Row, 1973.

Ferber, A., Mendelsohn, M., & Napier, A. (Eds.). *The book of family therapy.* New York: Science House, 1972.

Glick, I., & Haley, J. *Family therapy and research: An annotated bibliography of articles and books published 1950–1970.* New York: Grune & Stratton, 1971.

Guerin, P. J., Jr. (Ed.). *Family therapy: Theory and practice.* New York: Gardner Press, 1976.

Haley, J. *Strategies of psychotherapy.* New York: Grune & Stratton, 1963.

Haley, J., & Hoffman, L. *Techniques of family therapy.* New York: Basic Books, 1967.

Haley, J. *Changing families.* New York: Grune & Stratton, 1971.

Haley, J. *Uncommon therapy.* New York: Norton, 1973.

Haley, J. *Problem-solving therapy.* San Francisco: Jossey-Bass, 1976.

Howells, J. G. (Ed.). *Theory and practice of family psychiatry.* London: Oliver & Boyd, 1968.

Jackson, D. D. (Ed.). *Communication, family and marriage.* Palo Alto: Science & Behavior Books, 1968.

Jackson, D. D. (Ed.). *Therapy, communication and change.* Palo Alto: Science & Behavior Books, 1968.

Kiesler, D. J., Bernstein, A. J., & Anchin, J. C. *Interpersonal communication: Relationship and the behavior therapies.* New York: Psychological Dimensions, 1977.

Minuchin, S. *Families and family therapy.* Cambridge, Mass.: Harvard University Press, 1974.

Rabkin, R. *Strategic psychotherapy: Brief and symptomatic treatment.* New York: Basic Books, 1977.

Satir, V. *Conjoint family therapy.* Palo Alto: Science & Behavior Books, 1967.

Satir, V. *Peoplemaking.* Palo Alto: Science & Behavior Books, 1972.

Walrond-Skinner, J. *Family therapy: The treatment of natural systems.* Boston: Routledge Kegan & Paul, 1976.

Watzlawick, P. *An anthology of human communication* (tape commentary and script). Palo Alto: Science & Behavior Books, 1964.
Watzlawick, P., Beavin, J. H., & Jackson, D. D. *Pragmatics of human communication.* New York: Norton, 1967.
Watzlawick, P., Weakland, J. H., & Fisch, R. *Change: Principles of problem formation and problem resolution.* New York: Norton, 1974.
Watzlawick, P., & Weakland, J. (Eds.). *The interactional view.* New York: Norton, 1977.

References

Ackerman, N. W. *Treating the troubled family.* New York: Basic Books, 1966.
Auerswald, E. H. Interdisciplinary vs. ecological approach. *Family Process,* 1968, *7,* 202–215.
Bateson, G., Jackson, D., Haley, J., & Weakland, J. Toward a theory of schizophrenia. *Behavioral Science,* 1956, *1,* 251–264.
Beels, C. C. & Ferber, A. *Family therapy: A view* (mimeo). Bronx, N.Y.: Family Studies Section, Department of Psychiatry, Albert Einstein College of Medicine, (no date).
Bell, J. E. *Family group therapy* (Public Health Monograph No. 64). Washington: U.S. Government Printing Office, 1961.
Berezin, M. A. The psychiatrist and the geriatric patient. Partial grief in family members and others who care for the elderly patient. *Journal of Geriatric Psychiatry,* 1970, *3,* 53–64.
Bowen, M. The use of family theory in clinical practice. *Comprehensive Psychiatry,* 1966, *7,* 345–374.
Bowen, M. Theory in the practice of psychotherapy. In P. J. Guerin, Jr. (Ed.), *Family therapy: Theory and practice.* New York: Gardner Press, 1976, 42–90.
Bowen, M., Aysinger, R. H., & Basamania, B. The role of the father in families with a schizophrenic patient. *American Journal of Psychiatry,* 1959, *115,* 1017–1020.
Brody, E. H. Aging and family personality: A developmental view. *Family Process,* 1974, *13,* 23–38.
Brody, E. H. The aging family. *Gerontologist,* 1966, *6,* 201–206.
Brody, E. H., & Spark, G. M. Institutionalization of the elderly: A family crisis. *Family Process,* 1966, *5,* 76–90.
Cath, S. H. The geriatric patient and his family. The institutionalization of

a parent—a nadir of life. *Journal of Geriatric Psychiatry*, 1972, *5*, 25–46.

Davies, N. H., & Hansen, E. Family focus: A transitional cottage in an acute-care hospital. *Family Process*, 1974, *13*, 481–488.

Fleck, S., Freedman, D. X., Cornelison, A. R., Lidz, T., & Terry, A. *The intrafamilial environment of the schizophrenic patient: V. The understanding of symptomatology through the study of family interaction.* Paper presented at American Psychiatric Association meeting, May 15, 1957.

Gottesman, L. E., Quarterman, C. E., & Cohn, G. M. Psychosocial treatment of the aged. In C. Eisdorfer & M. P. Lawton (Eds.), *Psychology of adult development and aging.* Washington, D.C.: American Psychological Association, 1973.

Guerin, P. J., Jr. Family therapy: The first twenty-five years. In P. J. Guerin, Jr. (Ed.), *Family therapy: Theory and practice.* New York: Gardner Press, 1976, 2–22.

Gurian, B. S. Psychogeriatrics and family medicine. *Gerontologist*, 1975, *15*, 308–310.

Haley, Jay. *Strategies of psychotherapy.* New York: Grune & Stratton, 1963.

Haley, Jay (Ed.). *Advanced techniques of hypnosis and therapy: Selected papers of Milton H. Erickson, M.D.* New York: Grune & Stratton, 1967.

Haley, Jay. *Uncommon therapy: The psychiatric techniques of Milton H. Erickson, M.D.* New York: W. W. Norton, 1973.

Haley, Jay. *Problem-solving therapy.* San Francisco: Jossey-Bass, 1976.

Haley, Jay & Hoffman, L. *Techniques of family therapy.* New York: Basic Books, 1967.

Jackson, D. D. The question of family homeostasis. *The Psychiatric Quarterly Supplement*, 1957, *31*, Part 1: 79–90.

Jackson, D. D., & Weakland, J. H. Conjoint family therapy: Some considerations on theory, technique and results. *Psychiatry*, 1961, *24*, (Supplement to No. 2), 30–45.

Kahana, R. J. & Levin, S. Aging and the conflict of generations. *Journal of Geriatric Psychiatry*, 1971, *4*, 115–135.

Kubler-Ross, E. *On death and dying.* New York: Macmillan, 1969.

Lidz, T., Cornelison, A. R., Fleck, S., & Terry, D. The intrafamilial environment of schizophrenic patients: II. Marital schism and marital skew. *American Journal of Psychiatry*, 1957, *114*: 241–248.

Lidz, T., Cornelison, A. R., Terry, D., & Fleck, S. The intrafamilial environment of the schizophrenic patient: VI. The transmission of irrationality. *A.M.A. Archives of Neurology and Psychiatry*, 1958, *79*, 305–316.

Madanes, C., & Haley, J. Dimensions of family therapy. *Journal of Nervous and Mental Disease*, 1977, *165*, 88–98.

Machen, Arthur. *The terror.* New York: W. W. Norton, 1966.

Maruyama, M. The second cybernetics: Deviation-amplifying mutual causative processes. *American Scientist*, 1963, *51*, 164–179.

Miller, M. B., Bernstein, H., & Sharkey, H. Family extrusion of the aged patient: Family homeostasis and sexual conflict. *Gerontologist,* 1975, *15,* 291–296.

Miller, M. B. & Harris, A. P. The chronically ill aged: Paradoxical patient-family behavior. *Journal of the American Geriatric Society,* 1967, *15,* 480–495.

Minuchin, S. *Families and family therapy.* Cambridge: Harvard University Press, 1974.

Minuchin, S., Montalvo, B., Guerney, B., Rosman, B., & Shumer, F. *Families of the slums: An exploration of their structure and treatment.* New York: Basic Books, 1967.

Peck, B. B. Physical medicine and family dynamics: The dialectics of rehabilitation. *Family Process,* 1974, *13,* 469–480.

Peterson, J. A. Marital and family therapy involving the aged. *Gerontologist,* 1973, *13,* 27–31.

Peterson, J. A. Therapeutic interventions in marital and family problems of aging persons. In A. Schwartz & J. Mensh (Eds.), *Professional obligations and approaches to the aged.* Springfield, Ill.: Charles C. Thomas, 1974, 220–241.

Rogers, C. R. The necessary and sufficient conditions of therapeutic personality change. *Journal of Consulting Psychology,* 1957, *21,* 95–103.

Satir, V. *Conjoint family therapy: A guide to theory and technique.* Palo Alto: Science and Behavior Books, 1964.

Savitsky, E., & Sharkey, L. The geriatric patient and his family. Study of family interaction in the aged. *Journal of Geriatric Psychiatry,* 1972, *5,* (1), 3–24.

Scheflen, A. E. *Stream and structure of communicational behavior* (Behavior Science Monograph No. 1). Philadelphia: Eastern Pennsylvania Psychiatric Institute, 1965.

Shanas, E., & Streib, G. F. (Eds.). *Social structure and the family: Generational relations.* Englewood Cliffs, New Jersey: Prentice-Hall, 1965.

Soloman, M. A. A developmental conceptual premise for family therapy. *Family Process,* 1973, *12,* 179–188.

Speck, R. V., & Attneave, C. L. Social network intervention. In Jay Haley (Ed.), *Changing families: A family therapy reader.* New York: Grune & Stratton, 1971, 312–332.

Spark, G. M., & Brody, E. M. The aged are family members. *Family Process,* 1970, *9,* 195–210.

Sussman, M., & Burchinal, L. Kin family network. Unheralded structure in current conceptualizations of family functioning. *Marriage and Family Living,* 1962, *24,* 231–240.

Watzlawick, P., Beavin, J. H., & Jackson, D. D. *Pragmatics of human communication.* New York: Norton, 1967.

Watzlawick, P., Weakland, J. H., & Fisch, R. *Change: Principles of problem formation and problem resolution.* New York: W. W. Norton, 1974.

Weakland, J. H. "Family somatics"—A neglected edge. *Family Process,* 1977, *16,* 263–272.

Weakland, J. H., Fisch, R., Watzlawick, P., & Bodin, A. M. Brief therapy: Focused problem resolution. *Family Process,* 1974, *13,* 141–168.

Weisman, A. D. The psychiatrist and the geriatric patient. Partial grief in family members and others who care for the elderly patient. Discussion. *Journal of Geriatric Psychiatry,* 1970, *3,* 65–69.

Wender, P. H. Vicious and virtuous circles: The role of deviation amplifying feedback in the origin and perpetuation of behavior. *Psychiatry,* 1968, *31,* 317–324.

Whitaker, C. The hindrance of theory in clinical work. In P. J. Guerin, Jr. (Ed.), *Family therapy: Theory and practice.* New York: Gardner Press, 1976, 154–164.

Wynne, L. C., Ryckoff, I. M., Day, J., & Hirsch, S. I. Pseudomutuality in the family relations of schizophrenics. *Psychiatry,* 1958, *21,* 205–220.

Index